FIX-IT!
Grammar and Editing
Made Easy with Classics

Pamela White

Second Edition © January 2009
Institute for Excellence in Writing, Inc.

Acknowledgments

Fix-It! began as a collaboration with my dear friend and fellow teacher Vicki Graham, to whom I am particularly indebted for her inspiration, aid, and humorous contributions to "The King and the Discommodious Pea." I am also most grateful to my IEW students and their parents, whose lively discussions and penetrating grammatical questions have fine-tuned these stories.

I welcome questions and comments. You can reach me at pamela@excellenceinwriting.com.

Fix-It! Grammar and Editing Made Easy with Classics
Second Edition

Copyright © 2007 Pamela White
ISBN-10: 0-9779860-6-3
ISBN-13: 978-0-9779860-6-4

Available with *Fix-It!* are files of the student sentences in an e-book, which you must download from www.excellenceinwriting.com/FIX-E
If you do not have an account yet, simply create one.

Institute for Excellence in Writing
8799 N. 387 Road
Locust Grove, OK 74352
800.856.5815

illiriamy
buchanan

Accessing Your Downloads

The purchase of this book entitles its owner to one free downloadable copy of the *Fix-It! Student Pages* (five separate files). To download your complimentary e-books, please follow the directions below:

1. Go to our website, www.excellenceinwriting.com
2. Log in to your online customer account. If you do not have an account, you will need to create one.
3. After you are logged in, go to this web page: www.excellenceinwriting.com/FIX-E
4. Click on the red download arrow.
5. You will be taken to your File Downloads page. Click on the file name and the e-book will download onto your computer.

Please note: The student materials contained in the accompanying e-books may be freely printed and copied by a teacher or mentor for use in a classroom or with any group of students. The teacher's book may not be copied. Thank you.

If you have any difficulty receiving this download after going through the steps above, please call (800) 856-5815.

Institute for Excellence in Writing, LLC
8799 N. 387 Road
Locust Grove, OK 74352

Contents

Introduction

Fix-It! offers a delightful and effective way to teach grammar through editing and to reinforce understanding of Excellence in Writing style. Students hunt for and correct errors in Fix-It sentences that cumulatively tell a story. Daily editing trains students to locate errors in their own writing and can help with achievement tests, which ask students to identify errors in sentences. Targeting different age groups through high school, the five Fix-It stories incorporate multiple levels of difficulty. Easily adapted to the home or the classroom, *Fix-It!* reinforces what you teach your students through their writing.

The Stories and Recommended Levels

The recommended levels are suggestions only. You could teach a later level to more advanced students, while students whose grammar understanding is weak might need to start with an easier story. The first three include optional, built-in advanced concepts, indicated by an exclamation [!], which can offer challenge and instruction to more advanced students.

Tom Sawyer: Adapted from Mark Twain's *Adventures of Tom Sawyer*, this abridged and paraphrased version covers the major events of the original story and is divided into chapters with specific objectives. Includes advanced [!] concepts. Recommended for grades 3–6.

Frog Prince, or Just Desserts: A humorous remake of the classic fairy tale about a princess who is forced to keep her promise to a frog who befriended her. Includes advanced [!] concepts. Recommended for grades 4–8.

The Little Mermaid: Hans Christian Andersen's beloved tale, abridged and edited for modern grammar but faithful to the original. Readers may be surprised to find little similarity to the Disney movie. Includes advanced [!] concepts. Recommended for grades 6–9.

The King and the Discommodious Pea: A humorous remake of "The Princess and the Pea," about a king's search for a suitable wife. Recommended for grades 7–10.

Sir Gawain and the Green Knight: An abridged translation of the medieval adventure tale about a knight of the Round Table whose courage and honor are put to the test in unexpected ways. Recommended for grades 9–12.

Recommended Materials

- Dictionary
- The Institute for Excellence in Writing's *Teaching Writing: Structure and Style* or *Student Writing Intensive*, by Andrew Pudewa. You do not have to use IEW's writing system to teach these stories, but *Fix-It!* complements IEW's approach.

Teaching Procedure

Each story consists of 132 Fix-It passages with embedded errors and challenging vocabulary. Designed to teach for thirty-three weeks with four each week, the Fix-Its can be presented to students on a blackboard or an overhead in a classroom or worked on paper with individual students.

Four days each week, have students copy and correct **one** Fix-It passage from the story. Students should do the following with each Fix-It:

- Find the bolded vocabulary word. Look it up in a dictionary, then write the definition that *best* fits that context. (It is easiest if the student writes out the story on a right hand page, completing the vocabulary definitions on a left hand page.)

- Copy the passage, correcting all errors. **Write on every other line** to allow room for additional, teacher-directed corrections.

- Copy the passages as a continuous story, indenting when appropriate to begin a new paragraph. (See Appendix for rules about starting paragraphs.)

- Underline all dress-ups. Optional. (See Appendix for an explanation of IEW's dress-ups.)

- Mark sentence openers with numbers in brackets. Optional. (See Appendix for an explanation of IEW's sentence openers. I do not mark all #1 sentences, but continue if your students need the added practice.)

To the right of each Fix-It, you will find brief explanations of errors in that passage, with the exception of obvious or frequent errors, such as periods at the ends of sentences. The Appendix contains additional information about grammar and punctuation covered in the stories.

Please take the time to preview the answers and rules before discussing the sentences with your students. In class or at home, discuss the Fix-Its after students have rewritten them. **Cover as many or as few skills as you deem appropriate.** These following steps work well:

- Begin by reading the selection aloud, which can help students untangle the punctuation. Check that they understand the storyline.

- Ask for a definition of the bolded vocabulary word in the context of that passage. Note that the definitions provided to the right of each Fix-It fit that context only.

- When applicable, discuss the reasons for starting new paragraphs.

- Elicit from students their suggestions for grammar corrections, using the Fix-Its as a springboard to introduce or review punctuation and grammar skills you wish your students to learn. You will find on page A-16 in the Appendix a helpful explanation of abbreviations used in the teacher's comments and on page A-19 an index to grammatical terms discussed in the Appendix.

- You can also ask students to locate dress-ups and identify sentence openers (see Appendix).

Included in the first three stories are optional advanced concepts, indicated by an exclamation [!], which make the story adaptable to stronger students when teaching to a mixed group.

Few students will find all errors. Encourage them to know this is expected. The sentences are designed to be challenging, which allows you to teach new concepts on the spot and reinforce them in later Fix-Its. Some students may benefit by knowing the total number of errors to fix.

If you are teaching "Tom Sawyer," note that each chapter has unique instructions, which follow these basic introductory guidelines but with variations. The other stories replicate the student's task in editing his or her own writing, where neither the number nor the nature of errors is known in advance.

Handwrite or Type?

Ideally, students should copy the sentences by hand, which forces their brains to slow down and process every word and mark of punctuation. If handwriting presents unusual challenges, however, you may wish to allow your student to edit the sentences directly on the computer.

Student Sentences Available on E-book

Available with *Fix-It* are files of the student sentences on e-book, which you must download from www.excellenceinwriting.com/FIX-E. We request that fellow teachers purchase their own copy of the book, but you may print multiple copies of the Fix-It sentences for your own students.

Print sentences for one week at a time for your students. Classroom teachers may wish to print these on overhead transparencies to discuss more easily in class rather than writing them out on a dry erase board or blackboard.

Should I Also Teach a Formal Grammar Program?

In the elementary years I recommend using some formal grammar instruction in conjunction with *Fix-It!*, although do not overwhelm students with a time-consuming program. They will learn more grammar from these stories and from grappling with it in their writing than they will from traditional exercises because this method is more enjoyable, it is rooted in writing itself, and the embedded repetition instills the concepts.

Elementary students should learn parts of speech and basic mechanics of writing, such as capitalization, agreement, apostrophes, end-of-sentence punctuation, quotation marks, and indentation for new paragraphs. By the time they are in seventh or eighth grade, they should ideally be able to isolate dependent clauses, independent clauses, and phrases in their sentences. It helps to introduce elementary-age students to punctuation rules, especially the easier rules, such as commas with dates, but do not expect them to master punctuation. The frequent repetition of rules that students hear with the Fix-It stories gradually and painlessly trains them to be grammar savvy!

For seventh through twelfth graders, if you wish to reinforce concepts with a formal program that teaches punctuation rules, it can be helpful, but conventional exercises in punctuation may be counterproductive. In my experience, they rarely translate to student writing and often render students grammar-phobic. Instead, teach concepts *through* student writing, reinforced by teaching the rules in the Fix-Its. Students enjoy the stories and find it challenging to see how many errors they can locate, which makes them more receptive to instruction about grammar than with traditional approaches.

Reinforcing Punctuation through Writing: Grammar Corrections

Using the Institute for Excellence in Writing's system of teaching style is a painless and effective method of teaching many grammar concepts for all ages (see Appendix under Dress-ups and Sentence Openers for details).

By the time students are in high school, I find traditional grammar exercises ineffective. Instead, I teach rules through Fix-Its and reinforce them by holding my students accountable for their own mistakes in writing. Generally, high school students make the same punctuation errors in their writing over and over again. One student may struggle with comma splices and run-ons, while another student omits the comma before coordinating conjunctions that connect main clauses. Focus on teaching students mastery over the problems they have individually, and you will help them conquer the majority of their errors.

To hold students accountable for their own errors, I require them to write **Grammar Corrections.** On every paper turned in, I mark two sentences for correction by putting brackets around them and writing "GC" in the margin, choosing sentences with serious punctuation errors or with errors that student needs to overcome. Students must do three things with each sentence:

- Cut and paste or copy the incorrect sentence onto a new sheet of paper
- Rewrite the sentence, correcting all errors
- Write out the rules that explain the punctuation errors

The bulk of their grade for Grammar Corrections comes from accurately explaining to me the rule that applies to *their* sentence. They must use a grammar handbook, such as *The Blue Book of Grammar and Punctuation* by Jane Straus, to find the rules or deduce why a comma they had used should *not* be in the sentence.

Sample Grammar Corrections from High School Papers

Original: The carps come from an habitat were it is very hot in the summer and frightfully cold in the winter, they also have spread more than any other fish. For these fish have traveled the rivers of Central Asia to the streams of Europe.   sp; CS   frag

Correction: The carps come from <u>a</u> habitat <u>where</u> it is very hot in the summer and frightfully cold in the <u>winter.</u> <u>They</u> also have spread more than any other <u>fish, for</u> they have traveled the rivers of Central Asia to the streams of Europe.

Rule: Comma splice because the sentence joins 2 main clauses with only a comma and it needs more.

Note: I require rules for punctuation errors only. Errors like fragments, spelling, and agreement must be corrected but no need for an explanation.

Original: Because they have such amazing adaptability they could be called super adaptors.   punc

Correction: Because they have such amazing <u>adaptability, they</u> could be called super adaptors.

Rule: Comma after #5 Sentence Opener, or introductory adverb clause.

8

Tom Sawyer

Introduction

An abridged and paraphrased version of Mark Twain's classic novel, "Tom Sawyer" covers the major events of the original story. Intended for elementary students, this is the easiest of the Fix-It stories. The chapters in this story focus on specific rules while continuing concepts taught earlier. Each chapter is further subdivided into weekly units, with four Fix-Its per week, allowing for a total of thirty-three weeks of instruction.

The first chapter involves simple concepts. Advanced students might skip over the Fix-It practice of Chapter 1 but just read the story. Chapter 7 covers commas, which are challenging, although I do not require students to deal with advanced comma rules here. Do not expect elementary students to master all rules, especially comma rules. "Tom Sawyer" will get them started. Through frequent exposure, concepts will gradually sink in.

In the notes beside some of the Fix-Its, exclamations in brackets [!] will alert you to a new concept you may wish to introduce to your students, depending on their ability. Students are not expected to locate errors involving these concepts, but you may wish to teach the rules. Some of these concepts recur in a later chapter as part of the instruction there. In the Appendix you will find a fuller discussion of the dress-ups and sentence openers as well as most grammar issues.

King's English or Southern Dialect? "Tom Sawyer" has presented its own challenges because of the rich dialect Twain sprinkles abundantly through his novel. The characters Huck Finn and Tom Sawyer speak in a local dialect and often use slang. While attempting to preserve the flavor of Twain's local color, I am mindful of the many infractions of grammar. Except in the final chapter where I address agreement errors, however, I have left untouched faulty agreement, slang, and similar errors *in the dialogue*. This does not seem to confuse students, probably because most do not speak as Huck does, but you may find it helpful to discuss with them Twain's choice to imitate real speech patterns and my choice to leave them alone. I confess that I cringe when reading my own emendation of the following passage near the end of the last chapter, wanting to apologize to Twain for converting Huck's speech to King's English:

> Original: "I've tried it," said Huck, "and it don't work. Them fancy clothes smothers me."
> "Correction": "I've tried it," said Huck, "and it doesn't work. Those fancy clothes smother me."

My hope is that students will want to read the original story as they correct these Fix-Its, which is told far better than this simple abridgment.

Because the Fix-It stories are usually taught over the course of a school year, students may sometimes have trouble following the storyline. When you introduce them to the Fix-It exercises, you may wish to tell them a little about the story and author. As you discuss the sentences each week, I recommend you check students' reading comprehension first, discussing the events leading up to and including that week's reading.

Background to Mark Twain (1835–1910) and *Adventures of Tom Sawyer*

An American author best known for his humor and satire, Mark Twain peopled his fiction with characters who live beside and on the Mississippi River. As a young man, Twain studied for the prestigious position of steamboat pilot and navigated the often treacherous waters of the Mississippi as a captain, which provided rich fodder for his imagination. He described *Adventures of Tom Sawyer* as his "boys' book," and he followed it with the deeper and more satiric *Adventures of Huckleberry Finn*. Both novels evoke the world of the Mississippi River with its vernacular idiom and river customs. *Tom Sawyer* chronicles the boyish adventures of a mischievous youth living in Missouri before the Civil War. St. Petersburg, a fictional port town, is based on Hannibal, Missouri, where Twain spent much of his childhood.

Chapter 1: Subjects, Verbs, Indentation, and Sentence Opener #1

Instructions for students:
- Define bolded words, writing only the definition that fits the context of that sentence.
- Underline all subjects.
- Double-underline all verbs and verb phrases.
- Indent to start new paragraphs.
- Correct faulty homophones (words that have the same sound but different spelling and meaning).
- Starting Week 2, identify Sentence Opener (SO) #1, Subject Opener, putting numbers in brackets before sentences.

Fix-Its and Corrections	*Grammar, Skills, and Vocabulary*

Week 1

Tom's **perplexed** Aunt Polly punched under the bed with the broom.	**Perplexed:** bewildered; puzzled Indent ¶ (new topic) <u>Subject</u>: single underline <u>Verb</u>: double underline
Tom's perplexed <u>Aunt Polly</u> <u>punched</u> under the bed with the broom.	[!] Sentence Opener #1 (subject)
She **resurrected** a cat—but not a boy—from under the bed.	**Resurrected:** brought back to life, notice, or use Same ¶, no indent. <u>Subject</u> and <u>Verb</u>
<u>She</u> <u>resurrected</u> a cat—but not a boy—from under the bed.	[!] Sentence Opener #1 (subject)
Secretly in the closet Tom **gobbled** up a sticky jam sandwich.	**Gobbled:** ate hastily or quickly Indent ¶ (new topic) <u>Subject</u> <u>Verb</u>
Secretly in the closet <u>Tom</u> <u>gobbled</u> up a sticky jam sandwich.	[!] Sentence Opener #3 (-ly adverb)
He **burst** out of the closet, but not fast enough.	**Burst:** issued forth suddenly and forcibly Same ¶, no indent. <u>Subject</u> and <u>Verb</u>
<u>He</u> <u>burst</u> out of the closet, but not fast enough.	[!] Sentence Opener #1 (subject)

Week 2

Aunt Polly seized her **mischievous** nephew by his collar.	**Mischievous:** causing annoyance or trouble Indent ¶ (new topic) <u>Subject</u> and <u>Verb</u>
[1] <u>Aunt Polly</u> <u>seized</u> her mischievous nephew by his collar.	Sentence Opener (SO) #1, marked with brackets
"I might 'a' guessed your **foolery**, Tom!"	**Foolery:** foolish action or conduct Same ¶, no indent. <u>Subject</u> and <u>Verb</u>. SO #1
[1] "<u>I</u> <u>might 'a' guessed</u> your foolery, Tom!"	[!] Commas around nouns of direct address (Tom)
In a **shrill** tone Tom yelled, "My! Look behind you, Aunt Polly!"	**Shrill:** high-pitched and piercing in sound Indent ¶ (new speaker) <u>Subject</u> and <u>Verbs</u> ("you" implied subject of "look")
In a shrill tone <u>Tom</u> <u>yelled</u>, "My! <u>Look</u> behind you, Aunt Polly!"	[!] Commas around nouns of direct address (Aunt P.) [!] Sentence Opener #2 (prepositional phrase)

Aunt Polly **reeled** around, and Tom fled.

[1] <u>Aunt Polly</u> <u>reeled</u> around, and <u>Tom</u> <u>fled</u>.

Reeled: whirled or turned around quickly
Same ¶, no indent.   <u>Subject</u> and <u>Verb</u>
SO #1
[!] Compound sentence: MC, cc MC

Week 3

"That Tom will **play hooky** from school today," she thought too herself.

    [1] "That <u>Tom</u> <u>will play hooky</u> from school today," <u>she thought</u> to herself.

Play hooky: be absent from school with no excuse
Indent ¶ (new speaker)
<u>Subjects</u> and <u>Verbs</u>
Homophone: to/two/too
SO #1

During supper Aunt Polly questioned Tom in a **roundabout** way.

    During supper <u>Aunt Polly</u> <u>questioned</u> Tom in a roundabout way.

Roundabout: indirect
Indent ¶ (time has passed; new scene)
<u>Subject</u> and <u>Verb</u>
[!] Sentence Opener #2 (prepositional)

"The heat must 'a' been **overpowering** in school today, hmm, Tom? Maybe you wanted a swim?"

[1] "The <u>heat</u> <u>must 'a' been</u> overpowering in school today, hmm, Tom? Maybe <u>you</u> <u>wanted</u> a swim?"

Overpowering: very strong; overwhelming
Same ¶, no indent
<u>Subjects</u> and <u>Verbs</u> ("overpowering"=predicate adj.)
SO #1
[!] Comma: NDA (noun of direct address—Tom)

Suddenly **wary**, Tom replied coolly, "No'm, but we dunked our heads under the pump, Auntie."

    Suddenly wary, <u>Tom</u> <u>replied</u> coolly, "No'm, but <u>we</u> <u>dunked</u> our heads under the pump, Auntie."

Wary: watchful; alert; on one's guard
Indent ¶ (new speaker)
<u>Subjects</u> and <u>Verbs</u>
[!] Comma: NDA (Auntie)
[!] Sentence Opener #3 (-ly adverb)

Week 4

Vexed, Aunt Polly tried a different line of questioning. "Well, then, you busted the stitches on your collar, hmm?"

    Vexed, <u>Aunt Polly</u> <u>tried</u> a different line of questioning. "Well, then, <u>you</u> <u>busted</u> the stitches on your collar, hmm?"

Vexed: irritated or annoyed
Indent ¶ (new speaker)
<u>Subjects</u> and <u>Verbs</u>
[!] Sentence Opener #7 (advanced: -ed opener)

Phew! Tom was safe. His shirt collar was sewn **securely**.

    Phew! [1] <u>Tom</u> <u>was</u> safe. [1] His shirt <u>collar</u> <u>was sewn</u> securely.

Securely: firmly; not in danger of coming loose
Indent ¶ (new topic)
<u>Subjects</u> and <u>Verbs</u>.   SO #1
[!] Exclamations can follow introductory interjections

Then Tom's cousin Sidney **chimed** in. "Well, now, if I didn't think you sewed his collar with white thread, but it's black.

    Then Tom's cousin <u>Sidney</u> <u>chimed</u> in. "Well, now, if <u>I</u> <u>didn't think</u> <u>you</u> <u>sewed</u> his collar with white thread, but <u>it's</u> black."

Chimed: spoke in singsong
Indent ¶ (new speaker)
<u>Subjects</u> and <u>Verbs</u>
[!] It's = it is

"Why, I did sew it with white! Tom!" In a flash Tom was out

the kitchen door **muttering** two himself, "I wish to geeminy she'd stick too one or t'other!"

"Why, I <u>did sew</u> it with white! Tom!"
In a flash <u>Tom</u> <u>was</u> out the kitchen door muttering to himself, "<u>I</u> <u>wish</u> to geeminy <u>she</u>'d stick to one or t'other!"

Muttering: speaking indistinctly and complainingly

Indent ¶ (new speakers)
<u>Subjects</u> and <u>Verbs</u>
Homophones: to/two/too
[!] Sentence Openers: T (transition), #2

Chapter 2: Quality Adjectives, "ly" Adverbs, and Sentence Opener #3

Instructions for students:
- Define bolded words with the definition that fits the context.
- Indent to start new paragraphs.
- Dress-ups: underline quality adjectives and strong -ly adverbs, but do not underline -ly sentence openers.
- Sentence Openers (SO): identify [1] subject and [3] -ly adverb, putting numbers in brackets before sentences.
- Correct faulty homophones.

Fix-Its and Corrections	*Grammar, Skills, and Vocabulary*
Week 5	
On this bright Saturday morning Tom felt **prodigiously afflicted** because Aunt Polly had sternly ordered him too whitewash the fence.	**Prodigiously afflicted:** greatly or hugely tormented Indent ¶ (new topic) Dress-ups: underline quality adjective & -ly adverbs Homophone: to/two/too
On this <u>bright</u> Saturday morning Tom felt <u>prodigiously</u> afflicted because Aunt Polly had <u>sternly</u> ordered him to whitewash the fence.	[!] Sentence Opener (SO) #2 (prepositional phrase) [!] Dress-up: because clause

Presently Ben Rogers **ambled** buy. He taunted Tom. "Poor chap, two bad you cain't come a-swimmin' with me on such a hot day since you gotta work."	**Ambled:** strolled at a slow, easy pace
	Discuss quality vs. weak adjectives (*poor, bad, hot*)
	   Mark only strong dress-ups
	Sentence Openers (SO): #3, #1, marked with brackets
	   Note: Don't underline -ly adverbs used as openers

[3] Presently Ben Rogers ambled by. [1] He taunted Tom. "Poor chap, too bad you cain't come a'swimmin' with me on such a hot day since you gotta work."	Homophones: buy/by; to/two/too [!] Dress-up: adverb clause ("since …")
"Why, ain't a boy in a hundred gets too whitewash an **illustrious** fence like this one," Tom proudly announced two Ben.	**Illustrious:** highly distinguished; famous Indent ¶ (new speaker) Dress-ups: quality adjective; -ly adverb [!] SO "T" (interjection) Homophones: to/two/too
"Why, ain't a boy in a hundred gets to whitewash an <u>illustrious</u> fence like this one," Tom <u>proudly</u> announced to Ben.	
Enthusiastically Ben offered too **barter** his shiny red apple in exchange four a turn two whitewash.	**Barter:** to trade or exchange goods or services Indent ¶ (new topic) Dress-ups: quality adjective SO #3
[3] Enthusiastically Ben offered to barter his <u>shiny</u> red apple in exchange for a turn to whitewash.	Homophones: to/two/too (twice); four/for
Week 6	
Unexpectedly Johnny Miller then came along and willingly traded his dead rat four the **opportunity** too whitewash.	**Opportunity:** chance or favorable circumstance Dress-ups: -ly adverb SO #3 Homophones: four/for; to/two/too
[3] Unexpectedly Johnny Miller then came along and <u>willingly</u> traded his dead rat for the opportunity to whitewash.	[!] No comma before *and* to join 2 compound verbs ("came … and … traded")

Approximately to hours later Tom was a **prosperous** man with three pennies, a rusty key, a tin soldier, a shriveled garter snake's head, a brass doorknocker, and a little brown bottle of wart medicine.

[3] Approximately two hours later Tom was a <u>prosperous</u> man with three pennies, a <u>rusty</u> key, a tin soldier, a <u>shriveled</u> garter snake's head, a <u>brass</u> doorknocker, and a little brown bottle of wart medicine.

Prosperous: well-to-do
Dress-ups: quality adjectives
SO #3
Homophones: to/two/too
[!] Commas with 3 or more items in a series

The distinguished fence now had three coats of fresh whitewash, so Tom **intrepidly** reported two Aunt Polly that the fence was finished.

[1] The <u>distinguished</u> fence now had three coats of fresh whitewash, so Tom <u>intrepidly</u> reported to Aunt Polly that the fence was finished.

Intrepidly: boldly; without fear
Indent ¶ (new scene)
Dress-ups: quality adjective; -ly adverb
SO #1
Homophones: to/two/too
[!] Compound sentence: MC, cc (so) MC

Sadly Aunt Polly **gazed** at Tom and complained, "You know it breaks my poor heart when you lie too me, Tom."

[3] Sadly Aunt Polly gazed at Tom and complained, "You know it breaks my poor heart when you lie to me, Tom."

Gazed: looked steadily and intently
SO #3
Homophones: to/two/too
[!] Dress-up: adverb clause ("when …")
[!] No comma before *and* to join 2 compound verbs
[!] Comma: NDA (Tom)

Week 7

"I surely ain't a-lyin' two you, Auntie, because I worked a mighty piece too make you're fence real **respectable**."

[1] "I <u>surely</u> ain't a-lyin' to you, Auntie, because I worked a <u>mighty</u> piece to make your fence real <u>respectable</u>."

Respectable: suitable to be seen; worthy
Indent ¶ (new speaker).   SO #1
Dress-ups: -ly adverb; quality adjectives
Homophones: to/two/too; your/you're
[!] Dress-up: because clause
[!] Comma: NDA (Auntie)

Aunt Polly placed **slight** trust in his word and went out too observe four herself. She would have been content two find twenty per cent of Tom's statement true.

[1] Aunt Polly placed <u>slight</u> trust in his word and went out to observe for herself. [1] She would have been content to find twenty per cent of Tom's statement true.

Slight: of little degree
Indent ¶ (new scene)
Dress-ups: quality adjective
SO #1
Homophones: to/two/too; four/for
[!] No comma before *and* to join 2 compound verbs

When she found the entire fence elaborately coated, her astonishment was almost **unspeakable**. "Well, I never! Theirs no getting around it—you *can* work when you've a mind too, Tom."

When she found the <u>entire</u> fence <u>elaborately</u> coated, her astonishment was almost <u>unspeakable</u>. "Well, I never! There's no getting around it—you *can* work when you've a mind to, Tom."

Unspeakable: beyond description; not to be spoken
Dress-ups: quality adjectives; -ly adverb
Homophones: theirs/there's; to/two/too
[!] Sentence Opener #5 (adverb clause + comma)
[!] Comma: NDA (Tom)

Swiftly Tom sneaked a fresh doughnut into his pocket while Aunt Polly reached into the barrel two select a **choice** apple four his reward.

[3] Swiftly Tom sneaked a fresh doughnut into his pocket while Aunt Polly reached into the barrel to select a <u>choice</u> apple for his reward.

Choice: of fine quality; worthy of being chosen
Indent ¶ (new topic)
Dress-ups: quality adjective
SO #3
Homophones: to/two/too; four/for
[!] Dress-up: adverb clause ("while …")

Chapter 3: Prepositional Sentence Openers and Strong Verbs

Instructions for students:
- Define bolded words with the definition that fits the context.
- Indent to start new paragraphs.
- Dress-ups: underline quality adjectives, -ly adverbs, and strong verbs.
- Correct faulty homophones.
- Sentence Openers (SO): mark [1] subject, [2] preposition, and [3] -ly adverb.

Fix-Its and Corrections	*Grammar, Skills, and Vocabulary*

Week 8

Before school on Monday, Tom stopped too **dillydally** with Huckleberry Finn. [2] Before school on Monday, Tom stopped to dillydally with Huckleberry Finn.	**Dillydally:** waste time; loiter Indent ¶ (new topic) SO #2 (prepositional sentence opener) Homophone: to/two/too
In St. Petersburg, Missouri, most of the older boys envied Huck Finn because he **habitually** lived buy himself and came and went as he pleased. [2] In St. Petersburg, Missouri, most of the older boys <u>envied</u> Huck Finn because he <u>habitually</u> lived by himself and came and went as he pleased.	**Habitually:** by habit; commonly used or followed Dress-ups: strong verb; -ly adverb SO #2 Homophones: buy/by [!] Dress-up: because clause [!] Commas between city and state, and after state
"In this hear sack I got me a dead cat to cure warts with," **boasted** Huck proudly. [2] "In this here sack I got me a dead cat to cure warts with," <u>boasted</u> Huck <u>proudly</u>.	**Boasted:** bragged; spoke with too much pride Indent ¶ (speaker) Dress-ups: strong verb; -ly adverb SO #2 Homophones: hear/here [!] Comma: direct quotation with verb of speaking
"At about midnight," he continued **confidingly**, "you take you're cat to the graveyard when somebody wicked has just been buried. *[quotation continues]* [2] "At about midnight," he <u>continued</u> <u>confidingly</u>, "you take your cat to the graveyard when somebody wicked has just been buried. *[quotation continues]*	**Confidingly:** trustingly (as in telling secrets) Dress-ups: strong verb; -ly adverb SO #2 Homophone: you're/your [!] Discuss quotation marks with interrupted speech [!] Dress-up: adverb clause ("when…") [!] No close quotation marks: quotation continues

Week 9

When some devils come to take that feller away, you **heave** your cat after 'em and say, 'Devil follow corpse, cat follow devil, warts follow cat, *I'm* done with you!'" When some devils come to take that feller away, you <u>heave</u> your cat after 'em and say, 'Devil follow corpse, cat follow devil, warts follow cat, *I'm* done with you!'"	**Heave:** lift or throw with effort or force Dress-ups: strong verb [!] Continue quotation where the last sentence left off [!] Sentence Opener #5 (adverb clause + comma) [!] Comma: direct quotation with verb of speaking [!] Single quotation marks for quotations within quotations [!] <u>Italics for emphasis (use sparingly)</u>

In an instant Tom **entreated**, "If your gonna' go to the old cemetery tonight, can I come, Huck?"

      [2] In an instant Tom <u>entreated</u>, "If you're gonna' go to the old cemetery tonight, can I come, Huck?"

Entreated: asked earnestly; begged; implored
Indent ¶ (new speaker)
Dress-ups: strong verb.   SO #2
Homophone: you're/your
[!] Comma: NDA (Huck)

With a handshake Huck agreed to bring Tom along, and they separated. There friendly **chat** made Tom late four school.

      [2] With a handshake Huck agreed to bring Tom along, and they separated. [1] Their friendly chat made Tom late for school.

Chat: casual conversation
Indent ¶ (new topic)
SO #2, #1
Homophone: there/their/they're; for/four
[!] Compound sentence: MC, cc MC
[!] *friendly* = imposter -ly (adjective, not adverb)

In **haste** Tom took his seat, and immediately the schoolmaster demanded too know why Tom was tardy again.

[2] In haste Tom took his seat, and <u>immediately</u> the schoolmaster <u>demanded</u> to know why Tom was tardy again.

Haste: swift, speedy action
Dress-ups: -ly adverb; strong verb
SO #2
Homophone: to/two/too
[!] Compound sentence: MC, cc MC

Week 10

Across the room Tom noticed the only **vacant** seat—next two a girl with long yellow braids.

[2] Across the room Tom noticed the only <u>vacant</u> seat—next to a girl with long yellow braids.

Vacant: not in use
Dress-ups: quality adjective. SO #2
Homophone: to/two/too
[!] Use em-dashes to draw attention

Without **wavering** Tom blurted out, "I stopped too talk with Huckleberry Finn."

[2] Without wavering Tom <u>blurted</u> out, "I stopped to talk with Huckleberry Finn."

Wavering: hesitating; feeling or showing doubt
Dress-ups: strong verb. SO #2
Homophone: to/two/too
[!] Comma: direct quotation with verb of speaking

From the schoolmaster came an **appalling** punishment. "Thomas Sawyer, go and sit with the girls!"

      [2] From the schoolmaster came an <u>appalling</u> punishment. "Thomas Sawyer, go and sit with the girls!"

Appalling: frightful; causing dismay or horror
Indent ¶ (new speaker)
Dress-ups: quality adjective
SO #2
[!] Set off NDAs with commas (Thomas Sawyer)

In a **jiffy** Tom obeyed, four in truth he liked Becky Thatcher. She was the loveliest girl in St. Petersburg, Missouri.

[2] In a jiffy Tom <u>obeyed</u>, for in truth he liked Becky Thatcher. [1] She was the <u>loveliest</u> girl in St. Petersburg, Missouri.

Jiffy: very short time
Dress-ups: strong verb; quality adjective
SO #2, #1
Homophones: four/for
[!] Commas between city and state

Chapter 4: Capitalization and Adverb Clauses

Instructions for students:
- Define bolded words with the definition that fits the context.
- Indent to start new paragraphs.
- Check for proper capitalization and correct as needed (lc = lowercase).
- Dress-ups: underline quality adjectives, -ly adverbs, and strong verbs.
- Dress-ups: underline subordinating conjunctions that begin adverb clauses (but do not underline SO conjunctions).
- Sentence Openers: mark [1] subject, [2] preposition, [3] -ly adverb, and [5] adverb clause.
- Correct faulty homophones.

Fix-Its and Corrections

Grammar, Skills, and Vocabulary

Week 11

at midnight huckleberry finn **caterwauled** under tom's window while everyone was asleep.

[2] At midnight Huckleberry Finn caterwauled under Tom's window while everyone was asleep.

Caterwauled: cried or screeched like a cat
Indent ¶ (new topic)
Capitalize first word of every sentence
Capitalize proper nouns
Dress-ups: strong verb; adverb clause ("while...")

---

after tom climbed out, the boys **stealthily** headed for the old st. petersburg cemetery to cure they're warts with the dead cat.

[5] After Tom climbed out, the boys stealthily headed for the old St. Petersburg cemetery to cure their warts with the dead cat.

Stealthily: secretly and with quiet and caution
Capitalize proper nouns, first word of sentences
Dress-ups: -ly adverb. SO #5 (adverb clause)
Homophones: there/their/they're
[!] Use commas after #5 Sentence Openers

---

when the moon went behind the clouds, tom and huck felt **jittery**. they stopped behind three grate elms that grew near a fresh grave.

[5] When the moon went behind the clouds, Tom and Huck felt jittery. [1] They stopped behind three great elms that grew near a fresh grave.

Jittery: extremely tense and nervous; jumpy
Capitalize proper nouns, first word of sentences
Homophones: grate/great
SO #5 (adverb clause + comma), #1
[!] Use commas after #5 Sentence Openers

Because they heard someone approaching, the boys grew silent. muff potter, injun joe, and young doc robinson **tramped** right up to the grave with a lantern, shovels, and a wheelbarrow.

[5] Because they heard someone approaching, the boys grew silent. [1] Muff Potter, Injun Joe, and young Doc Robinson tramped right up to the grave with a lantern, shovels, and a wheelbarrow.

Tramped: walked with firm, heavy steps
Indent ¶ (new topic)
Capitalize proper nouns, first word of sentences
Capitalize titles used with names (Doc Robinson)
Dress-ups: strong verb
SO #5, #1 (Discuss when it *is* okay to begin a sentence with *because*)
[!] Use commas after #5 Sentence Openers
[!] Commas with 3 or more items in a series

Week 12

that **distressing** tuesday night tom and huck watched helplessly while injun joe and muff potter dug up and pried open a coffin.

[2] That <u>distressing</u> Tuesday night Tom and Huck watched <u>helplessly</u> <u>while</u> Injun Joe and Muff Potter dug up and <u>pried</u> open a coffin.

Distressing: causing anxiety or suffering
Capitalize proper nouns, first word of sentences
Capitalize names of the week
[!] SO #2, disguised (*During* that distressing night)
Dress-ups: quality adjective; -ly adverb; adverb clause ("while…"); strong verb

---

The men rudely dumped a corpse with a **pallid** face into the wheelbarrow, covered it with a blanket, and bound it in place with a rope.

[1] The men <u>rudely</u> <u>dumped</u> a corpse with a <u>pallid</u> face into the wheelbarrow, covered it with a blanket, and <u>bound</u> it in place with a rope.

Pallid: pale; faint in color
Capitalize first word of sentences
Dress-ups: -ly adverb; strong verbs; quality adjective
[!] Commas with 3 or more items in a series

---

insolently injun joe held out his hand for more money, but doc robinson struck him. "you ruffians have been paid plenty already."

[3] Insolently Injun Joe held out his hand for more money, but Doc Robinson <u>struck</u> him. [1] "You ruffians have been paid plenty already."

Insolently: rudely; disrespectfully
Indent ¶ (new topic)
Capitalize proper nouns, first word of sentences
Capitalize titles used with names
Capitalize 1st word of a quoted sentence ("You")
Dress-ups: strong verb
[!] Compound sentence: MC, cc MC

---

muff potter dropped his knife. In the pale moonlight he began to **scuffle** with the Doctor, protesting, "don't be hittin' my partner!"

[1] Muff Potter dropped his knife. [2] In the <u>pale</u> moonlight he began to <u>scuffle</u> with the doctor, protesting, "Don't be hittin' my partner!"

Scuffle: fight in a rough, confused manner
Indent ¶ (new speaker)
Capitalize 1st word of a quoted sentence
Capitalize proper nouns
Use lowercase (lc) for titles when they act as a description without a name ("the doctor")
Dress-ups: quality adjective; strong verb

Week 13

injun joe grabbed muff potter's knife. Just as the Doctor knocked potter out cold, the **vile** thief stabbed doc robinson in the chest.

[1] Injun Joe <u>grabbed</u> Muff Potter's knife. [5] Just as the doctor knocked Potter out cold, the <u>vile</u> thief <u>stabbed</u> Doc Robinson in the chest.

Vile: evil; morally degraded
Capitalize proper nouns
Use lc for titles without a name ("the doctor")
Dress-ups: strong verbs; quality adjective
[!] Use commas after #5 Sentence Openers

---

when muff potter came to, injun joe **slyly** lied to him. "you done murdered the Doc," he sneered, "But I won't let on it was you, muff."

[5] When Muff Potter came to, Injun Joe <u>slyly</u> lied to him. [1] "You done murdered the doc," he <u>sneered</u>, "but I won't let on it was you, Muff."

Slyly: with cunning (intending to deceive)
Indent ¶ (time has passed)
Capitalize proper nouns, first word of sentences
Use lc for titles without a name ("the doc")
Capitalize first word of a quoted sentence
Use lc to continue interrupted quotations ("but")
Dress-ups: -ly adverb; strong verb
[!] Use commas after #5 Sentence Openers

---

the terrified boys fled in the dark as the **wan** Winter moon silently slipped behind the clouds. they scurried to the village, speechless with horror.

    [1] The <u>terrified</u> boys <u>fled</u> in the dark <u>as</u> the <u>wan</u> winter moon <u>silently</u> <u>slipped</u> behind the clouds. [1] They <u>scurried</u> to the village, <u>speechless</u> with horror.

Wan: lacking color; pale
Indent ¶ (new topic)
Capitalize first word of sentences
Use lc for names of seasons
Dress-ups: quality adjectives; strong verbs; adverb
    clause ("as …"); -ly adverb
[!] Alliteration: wan winter; silently slipped

"I, tom sawyer," the frightened boy whispered, "Swears never two tell what I know 'bout the murder, or injun joe might kill us." huck finn **vowed** the same.

[1] "I, Tom Sawyer," the <u>frightened</u> boy <u>whispered</u>, "swears never to tell what I know 'bout the murder, or Injun Joe might kill us." [1] Huck Finn <u>vowed</u> the same.

Vowed: promised; pledged
Capitalize proper nouns
Use lc to continue interrupted quotations ("swears")
Dress-ups: quality adjective; strong verbs
Homophones: to/two/too
[!] Use commas around nonessential phrases,
    including appositives (Tom Sawyer)

Chapter 5: Quotation Marks and End Marks

Instructions for students:
- Define bolded words with the definition that fits the context.
- Indent to start new paragraphs.
- Check for proper capitalization and correct as needed.
- Dress-ups: underline quality adjectives, -ly adverbs, strong verbs, and adverb clauses.
- Sentence Openers: mark [2] preposition, [3] -ly adverb, and [5] adverb clause (note: no need to keep marking #1).
- Correct faulty homophones.

Fix-Its and Corrections   ## *Grammar, Skills, and Vocabulary*

Week 14

one morning tom, huck, and they're comrade joe harper made a compact to be pirates. that night they met on the riverbank with a ham, bacon, and what **provisions** they could steel—as became pirates

    One morning Tom, Huck, and their comrade Joe Harper made a compact to be pirates. That night they met on the riverbank with a ham, bacon, and what provisions they could steal—as became pirates.

Provisions: a stock of necessary supplies, esp. food
Indent ¶ (new time/topic)
Periods at end of statements
Homophones: there/their/they're; steel/steal
[!] Commas with 3 or more items in a series
[!] SO #2, disguised (*During, In, At* morning, night)
[!] Use em-dashes to draw attention

---

with huck and joe at the oars, tom guided the small log raft that they had captured steadily the mighty mississippi river carried the pirates passed the sleeping town of st petersburg to an **uninhabited** island on the faraway shore

[2] With Huck and Joe at the oars, Tom <u>guided</u> the small log raft that they had <u>captured</u>. [3] Steadily the <u>mighty</u> Mississippi River carried the pirates past the <u>sleeping</u> town of St. Petersburg to an <u>uninhabited</u> island on the <u>faraway</u> shore.

Uninhabited: not lived on
Periods after abbreviations
Periods at end of statements
Dress-ups: strong verbs; quality adjectives
Homophones: passed/past

---

in a **dismal** forest the lads built a campfire and cooked some bacon. what wood the boys say if they could see us now tom asked excitedly

    [2] In a <u>dismal</u> forest the lads built a campfire and cooked some bacon. "What would the boys say <u>if</u> they could see us now?" Tom asked <u>excitedly</u>.

Dismal: gloomy; dreary; cheerless
Indent ¶ (new scene)
Use question marks at end of questions
Use quotation marks with direct quotations
Periods at end of statements
Dress-ups: quality adj.; adverb clause; -ly adverb
Homophones: wood/would

I **reckon** they'd just dye two be here boasted huck Joe wondered aloud if pirates really make men walk the plank and where they bury there treasure?

    "I reckon they'd just die to be here!" <u>boasted</u> Huck. Joe <u>wondered</u> aloud <u>if</u> pirates really make men walk the plank and <u>where</u> they bury their treasure.

Reckon: suppose; think
Indent ¶ (new speaker)
Periods at end of statements and indirect questions
Exclamation marks after exclamations
Use quotation marks with direct quotations
Dress-ups: strong verbs; adverb clauses
Homophones: dye/die; to/two/too; there/their

Week 15

tom and joe knew that stealing bacon and ham was wrong, so they couldn't rest. feeling the pangs of **remorse**, they resolved that they're piracies would never again include stealing

    Tom and Joe knew that stealing bacon and ham was wrong, so they couldn't rest. Feeling the pangs of remorse, they <u>resolved</u> that their piracies would never again include stealing.

Remorse: regret for wrongdoing
Indent ¶ (new topic)
Periods at end of statements
Dress-ups: strong verb
Homophones: there/their/they're
[!] Compound sentence: MC, cc (so) MC
[!] Sentence Opener #4 (-ing phrase + comma)

---

next morning the adventurous boys beheld bugs and birds while they happily **romped** through the woods did a breakfast of Fried Fish ever taste so delicious

    Next morning the <u>adventurous</u> boys <u>beheld</u> bugs and birds <u>while</u> they <u>happily</u> <u>romped</u> through the woods. Did a breakfast of fried fish ever taste so delicious?

Romped: played merrily
Indent ¶ (time has passed)
Periods at end of statements; "?" at end of questions
Dress-ups: quality adjective; strong verbs; adverb clause; -ly adverb
[!] SO #2, disguised (*During the* next morning)
[!] Alliteration: boys beheld bugs and birds

---

gradually tom, huck, and joe became aware of a **peculiar** booming sound in the distance they asked each other what it was?

    [3] Gradually Tom, Huck, and Joe became aware of a <u>peculiar</u> booming sound in the distance. They asked each other what it was.

Peculiar: unusual; strange; odd
Indent ¶ (new topic)
Periods at end of statements
Periods at end of indirect questions
Dress-ups: quality adjective

Peering out over the river, the boys watched as a jet of white smoke burst from the side of a ferryboat "somebody's drownded exclaimed tom their shooting a cannon too make him come up to the top".

Peering out over the river, the boys watched <u>as</u> a jet of white smoke <u>burst</u> from the side of a ferryboat. "Somebody's drownded!" <u>exclaimed</u> Tom. "They're shooting a cannon to make him come up to the top."

Peering: looking carefully and intently
Periods at end of statements
Exclamation marks after exclamations
Use quotation marks with direct quotations
Periods and commas go inside quotation marks
Dress-ups: adverb clause; strong verbs
Homophones: there/their/they're; to/two/too
[!] Sentence Opener #4 (-ing phrase + comma)

Week 16

Scratching his head, Huck **speculated** who it could be? "Boys, I know who's drownded. It's us" Tom realized!

    Scratching his head, Huck <u>speculated</u> who it could be. "Boys, I know who's drownded. It's us!" Tom realized.

Speculated: reflected on a subject; thought about
Indent ¶ (new speaker)
Periods at end of indirect questions and statements
Exclamation marks immediately after exclamation
Dress-ups: strong verb
[!] Discuss who's/whose, it's/its
[!] Sentence Opener #4 (-ing phrase + comma)

---

at home tom's cousin mary, aunt polly, and mrs harper were not enjoying the fakers' fine **frolic** they sobbed as if there hearts would brake

    [2] At home Tom's cousin Mary, Aunt Polly, and Mrs. Harper were not enjoying the fakers' fine frolic. They sobbed <u>as if their hearts would break.</u>

Frolic: playful behavior; prank
Indent ¶ (new scene)
Periods at end of statements
Periods after abbreviations
Homophones: there/their/they're; break/brake
[!] Alliteration: fakers' fine frolic
[!] Note use of plural possessive: fakers'

the next saturday, wearing deep black, aunt polly, mary, and sid slowly entered the church While the **low-spirited** congregation exhibited great weeping and wailing, the reverend mr sprague told touching tales about the dear departed youngsters

The next Saturday, wearing deep black, Aunt Polly, Mary, and Sid <u>slowly</u> entered the church. [5] While the <u>low-spirited</u> congregation exhibited great weeping and wailing, the Reverend Mr. Sprague told <u>touching</u> tales about the dear departed youngsters.

Low-spirited: poor in spirits; depressed
Indent ¶ (new scene and time has passed)
Periods at end of statements
Periods after abbreviations
Dress-ups: -ly adverb; quality adjectives
[!] SO #2, disguised (*During* the next)
[!] Commas with 3 or more items in a series
[!] Alliteration: weeping and wailing; told touching tales; dear departed

---

abruptly the Minister looked up from his soggy handkerchief and stood **transfixed** marching up the aisle came the three dead boys they had been hiding in the choir loft all along— listening to their own funeral sermon

[3] Abruptly the minister looked up from his <u>soggy</u> handkerchief and stood transfixed. Marching up the aisle came the three dead boys. They had been hiding in the choir loft all along—listening to their own funeral sermon!

Transfixed: with his attention frozen, as if in a spell
Indent ¶ (new topic)
Use lc for common nouns *(minister)*
Periods at end of statements
Exclamation marks after exclamatory statements
Dress-ups: quality adjective
[!] No comma before *and* to join 2 compound verbs ("looked up … and stood")

Chapter 6: Who/Which Clauses

Instructions for students:
- Define bolded words with the definition that fits the context.
- Indent to start new paragraphs.
- Check for proper capitalization, quotation marks, and end marks; correct as needed.
- Dress-ups: underline quality adjectives, -ly adverbs, strong verbs, and adverb clauses.
- Dress-ups: underline the *who* or *which* in who/which clauses and correct *who* or *which* as needed.
- Sentence Openers: mark [2] preposition, [3] -ly adverb, and [5] adverb clause.
- Correct faulty homophones.

Fix-Its and Corrections

Grammar, Skills, and Vocabulary

Week 17

summer vacation, which the students eagerly **anticipated**, was approaching

    Summer vacation, <u>which</u> the students <u>eagerly</u> anticipated, was approaching.

Anticipated: looked forward to
Indent ¶ (new topic)
Dress-ups: *which* clause; -ly adverb
Set off most who/which clauses with commas

---

the elderly schoolmaster, which wanted the class to make a **notable** showing on examination day, was becoming more strict every day the boys, who knew that he wore a wig, privately planned a prank.

The <u>elderly</u> schoolmaster, <u>who</u> wanted the class to make a <u>notable</u> showing on Examination Day, was becoming more strict every day. The boys, <u>who</u> knew that he wore a wig, <u>privately</u> planned a prank.

Notable: worthy of notice; distinguished
Use *who* for people, *which* for things
Dress-ups: *who* clauses with commas
Dress-ups: quality adjectives; -ly adverb
[!] *elderly* = imposter -ly (adjective, not adverb)
Capitalize names of special events and calendar items
[!] Alliteration: privately planned a prank

---

st petersburg's schoolhouse, which was beautifully decorated with wreaths and flowers, was filled with students, parents, and town **dignitaries** patiently the schoolmaster presided from his great chair, which rested on a raised platform

    St. Petersburg's schoolhouse, <u>which</u> was <u>beautifully</u> decorated with wreaths and flowers, was filled with students, parents, and town dignitaries. [3] Patiently the schoolmaster <u>presided</u> from his great chair, <u>which</u> rested on a raised platform.

Dignitaries: persons of high position or rank
Indent ¶ (time has passed)
Period after abbreviation
Periods at end of statements
Dress-ups: *which* clauses with commas
Dress-ups: -ly adverb; strong verb
[!] Commas with 3 or more items in a series

---

a shy, small girl who lisped recited "mary had a little lamb". with **conceited** confidence tom sawyer launched into the "give me liberty or give me death" speech, but he broke down in the middle of it

A shy, small girl <u>who</u> lisped recited "Mary Had a Little Lamb." [2] With <u>conceited</u> confidence Tom Sawyer <u>launched</u> into the "Give Me Liberty or Give Me Death" speech, but he broke down in the middle of it.

Conceited: vain; self-important
Dress-ups: *who* clause
[!] No commas with essential who/which clauses
Dress-ups: quality adjective; strong verb
Capitalize titles except for little words (e.g., articles and coordinating conjunctions)
Periods and commas go inside quotation marks
[!] Use commas between coordinate adjectives
[!] Compound sentence: MC, cc MC

Week 18

the headmaster, which intended to exercise the class's geography skills, rose from his chair, turned his back to the audience, and began drawing a map of america on the blackboard. when his hand, witch was unsteady, slipped, giggles **rippled** around the room

    The headmaster, <u>who</u> intended to <u>exercise</u> the class's geography skills, rose from his chair, turned his back to the audience, and began drawing a map of America on the blackboard. [5] When his hand, <u>which</u> was <u>unsteady</u>, slipped, giggles <u>rippled</u> around the room.

Rippled: rose and fell gently in tone and volume
Indent ¶ (new topic)
Use *who* for people, *which* for things
Dress-ups: *who* and *which* clauses with commas
Dress-ups: strong verbs; quality adjective
Homophones: witch/which
[!] Commas with 3 or more items in a series
[!] Use commas after #5 Sentence Openers

---

a **garret** happened to be right above the headmaster, and down threw the trapdoor emerged a cat suspended around its haunches by a string The cat, which had a rag tied around its jaws to keep it from mewing, swung wildly in the air

A garret happened to be right above the headmaster, and down through the trapdoor <u>emerged</u> a cat, suspended around its haunches by a string. The cat, <u>which</u> had a rag tied around its jaws to keep it from mewing, swung <u>wildly</u> in the air.

Garret: an attic, usually small and wretched
Dress-ups: *which* clause with commas
Dress-ups: strong verb; -ly adverb
Homophones: threw/through
Periods at end of statements
[!] Compound sentence: MC, cc MC
[!] Invisible *which* clause: "a cat, which was suspended …"
[!] *Its* = possessive form of *it*

---

the giggles, which were increasing, **flustered** the headmaster. "Give me just a moment, he called out, Won't you"

The giggles, <u>which</u> were increasing, <u>flustered</u> the headmaster.   "Give me just a moment," he called out, "won't you?"

Flustered: nervous and confused
Indent ¶, 2nd part (new speaker)
Dress-ups: *which* clause with commas; strong verb
Use quotation marks only around the part spoken
Use lc to continue interrupted quotations

---

down, down descended the cat, which clawed the air **frantically**. then it snagged the headmaster's wig with its desperate claws, clung to the headpiece, and was snatched up into the garret in an instant—with its shaggy trophy

    Down, down descended the cat, <u>which</u> <u>clawed</u> the air <u>frantically</u>. Then it <u>snagged</u> the headmaster's wig with its <u>desperate</u> claws, clung to the headpiece, and was <u>snatched</u> up into the garret in an instant—with its <u>shaggy</u> trophy!

Frantically: desperate or wild with fear
Indent ¶ (new topic)
Dress-ups: *which* clause with commas
Dress-ups: strong verbs; -ly adverb; quality adjectives
[!] Commas with 3 or more items in a series
[!] *Its* = possessive form of *it*
[!] Use em-dashes to draw attention
[!] Note that *which* is used with ordinary animals

Week 19

during the Summer muff potter's trial **vigorously** stirred the sleepy town all the gossiping kept tom in a cold shiver. "huck, have you ever told anybody that secret witch we been keepin' 'bout injun joe" Shuddering, huck answered, "tom sawyer, you know we wouldn't be alive to days if that got found out".

    [2] During the summer Muff Potter's trial <u>vigorously</u> <u>stirred</u> the <u>sleepy</u> town. All the gossiping kept Tom in a cold shiver.
    "Huck, have you ever told anybody that secret <u>which</u> we been keepin' 'bout Injun Joe?"
    Shuddering, Huck answered, "Tom Sawyer, you know we wouldn't be alive two days <u>if</u> that got found out."

Vigorously: forcefully; energetically
Indent ¶ (time has passed; new speakers)
Use lc for names of seasons
Periods and commas go inside quotation marks
Dress-ups: *which* clause
[!] No commas with essential who/which clauses
Dress-ups: quality adjective; -ly adverb; strong verb; adverb clause ("if")
Homophones: witch/which; to/two/too
[!] Comma: NDA (Huck; Tom Sawyer)
[!] Sentence Opener #4 (-ing + comma)
[!] Comma: direct quotation with verb of speaking

---

was muff potter guilty of the murder of doc robinson a **somber** jury filed into the courtroom shortly afterward, muff potter, who looked pail and hopeless, came in slowly with chains upon him With a grim expression injun joe watched it all

    Was Muff Potter guilty of the murder of Doc Robinson? A <u>somber</u> jury <u>filed</u> into the courtroom. [3] Shortly afterward, Muff Potter, <u>who</u> looked pale and hopeless, came in <u>slowly</u> with chains upon him. [2] With a <u>grim</u> expression Injun Joe watched it all.

Somber: extremely serious; grave
Indent ¶ (new scene; time has passed)
Dress-ups: *who* clause with commas
Dress-ups: quality adjectives; strong verb; -ly adverb
Homophones: pail/pale

---

first, counsel four the **prosecution** called up a witness which saw potter near the graveyard about the time of the murder after this testimony potter's lawyer didn't cross-examine, however. Explaining that he found a bloody knife at the gravesite, the second witness was not questioned buy potter's lawyer, either.

    First, counsel for the prosecution called up a witness <u>who</u> saw Potter near the graveyard about the time of the murder. [2] After this testimony Potter's lawyer didn't <u>cross-examine</u>, however. Explaining that he found a bloody knife at the gravesite, the second witness was not questioned by Potter's lawyer, either.

Prosecution: the officials who carry on legal proceedings against a person
Indent ¶ (new topic)
Use *who* for people, *which* for things
Period at end of statements
Dress-ups: *who* clause
Homophones: four/for; buy/by
[!] No commas with essential who/which clauses
Dress-ups: strong verb
[!] Sentence Opener T (transition)
[!] Sentence Opener #4 (-ing phrase + comma)

---

finally, a third witness testified that he had seen that knife in muff potter's possession I have no questions, said counsel for the defense Tom was **apprehensive**. muff potter had always been kind too him did this attorney mean two throw away his client's life without an effort

[3] Finally, a third witness <u>testified</u> that he had seen that knife in Muff Potter's possession.
    "I have no questions," said counsel for the defense.
    Tom was <u>apprehensive</u>. Muff Potter had always been kind to him. Did this attorney mean to throw away his client's life without an effort?

Apprehensive: anxious; uneasy
Indent ¶ (new speaker; new topic)
Period at end of statements
Use quotation marks with direct quotations
Question marks after questions
Homophones: to/two/too
Dress-ups: strong verb; quality adjective
[!] Comma: direct quotation with verb of speaking
[!] Sentence Opener #6 (**very short sentence**)
[!] Note that the final question is something Tom is wondering

Week 20

then potter's lawyer exclaimed unexpectedly, call thomas sawyer too the witness stand" after tom's oath, the lawyer asked, "Thomas sawyer, where were you on the seventeenth of june about midnight tom, who glanced at injun joe's iron face, **stammered**, "I-i-i-n the graveyard

Then Potter's lawyer <u>exclaimed</u> <u>unexpectedly</u>, "Call Thomas Sawyer to the witness stand." [2] After Tom's oath, the lawyer asked, "Thomas Sawyer, where were you on the seventeenth of June about midnight?"

Tom, <u>who</u> glanced at Injun Joe's <u>iron</u> face, <u>stammered</u>, "I-i-i-n the graveyard."

Stammered: spoke with involuntary pauses
Indent ¶ (new speakers)
Use quotation marks with direct quotations
Capitalize first word of a quoted sentence
Period at end of statements
Question marks after questions
Dress-ups: *who* clause with commas
Dress-ups: strong verbs; -ly adverb; quality adjective
Homophones: to/two/too
[!] Comma: direct quotation with verb of speaking
[!] Comma: NDA (Thomas Sawyer)

---

the audience listened breathlessly "were you hidden"? "I was hid behind the elms that's on the edge of the grave". injun joe gave a barely **perceptible** start

The audience listened <u>breathlessly</u>.
"Were you hidden?"
"I was hid behind the elms that's on the edge of the grave." Injun Joe gave a <u>barely</u> <u>perceptible</u> start.

Perceptible: easily perceived, seen, or noticed
Indent ¶ (new speakers)
Dress-ups: -ly adverbs; quality adjective
[!] Question inside " " if part of quoted material
[!] Periods and commas go inside quotation marks

---

now, my boy, tell us everything. Don't be afraid". beginning in a timid whisper, tom **recounted** the ghastly tail all eyes were fixed on him

"Now, my boy, tell us everything. Don't be afraid."
Beginning in a <u>timid</u> whisper, Tom <u>recounted</u> the <u>ghastly</u> tale. All eyes were fixed on him.

Recounted: told the facts and details of
Indent ¶ (new speakers)
Dress-ups: quality adjectives; strong verbs
[!] *ghastly* = imposter -ly (adjective, not adverb)
Use quotation marks with direct quotations
Periods and commas go inside quotation marks
Homophones: tail/tale
[!] Commas: NDA (my boy)
[!] Sentence Opener #4 (-ing phrase + comma)

---

the tension peaked when the boy revealed, as muff wrassled with the doctor, injun joe rushed at him with the knife and—" Crash! Madly injun joe sprang for a window, tore his way threw his **opponents**, and was gone!

The tension <u>peaked</u> <u>when</u> the boy revealed, "<u>As</u> Muff wrassled with the doctor, Injun Joe <u>rushed</u> at him with the knife and—"
Crash! [3] Madly Injun Joe <u>sprang</u> for a window, <u>tore</u> his way through his opponents, and was gone!

Opponents: those who were against, or opposed, him
Indent ¶ (new speaker; new topic)
Dress-ups: strong verbs; adverb clauses
Homophones: threw/through
Use quotation marks with direct quotations
[!] Comma: direct quotation with verb of speaking
[!] Use em-dashes to indicate interruption
[!] Commas with 3 or more items in a series

Chapter 7: Commas

Instructions for students:
- Define bolded words with the definition that fits the context.
- Indent to start new paragraphs.
- Correct comma errors.
- Check for proper capitalization, quotation marks, and end marks; correct as needed.
- Dress-ups: underline quality adjectives, -ly adverbs, strong verbs, adverb clauses, and who/which.
- Sentence Openers: mark [2] preposition, [3] -ly adverb, and [5] adverb clause.
- Correct faulty homophones.

Fix-Its and Corrections

Grammar, Skills, and Vocabulary

Week 21

Once again Tom was an honored hero. In st petersburg missouri the newspaper even featured him conspicuously on the front page although his days were happy at night he dreamed that Injun Joe looked at him with **vengeful** eyes

    Once again Tom was an <u>honored</u> hero. [2] In St. Petersburg, Missouri, the newspaper even <u>featured</u> him <u>conspicuously</u> on the front page. [5] Although his days were happy, at night he dreamed that Injun Joe looked at him with <u>vengeful</u> eyes.

Vengeful: seeking revenge; wanting to get even
Indent ¶ (new topic)
Use commas between city and state, and after state
Use commas after #5 Sentence Openers (introductory adverb clauses)
Dress-ups: quality adjectives; strong verb; -ly adverb

After the murder trial a sizeable reward for Injun Joe had been offered publicized and even doubled. Also the country had been **scoured** "i'm glad i saved Muff from the hangman Tom confided to Huck "But i won't breathe easy 'til they find Injun Joe".

[2] After the murder trial a <u>sizeable</u> reward for Injun Joe had been offered, publicized, and even doubled. Also, the country had been <u>scoured</u>.
    "I'm glad I saved Muff from the hangman," Tom <u>confided</u> to Huck, "but I won't breathe easy <u>'til</u> they find Injun Joe."

Scoured: thoroughly searched through
Indent ¶, 2nd part (new speaker)
Comma not needed after #2 SO of 4 words or fewer
Use commas with 3 or more items in a series
Use commas to set off transitional words and phrases
Use comma with verb of speaking & direct quotation
Use lc to continue interrupted quotations
Dress-ups: quality adjective; strong verbs; adverb clause (*'til=until*)
[!] Sentence Opener T (Also)

As time passed Tom's fear of Injun Joe lessened and that **inevitable** day came when he developed a raging desire to hunt for buried treasure somewhere

    [5] As time passed, Tom's fear of Injun Joe lessened, and that <u>inevitable</u> day came <u>when</u> he developed a <u>raging</u> desire to hunt for buried treasure somewhere.

Inevitable: sure to happen or come
Indent ¶ (time has passed)
Use commas after #5 Sentence Openers
Use a comma before *and* to link 2 main clauses
Dress-ups: quality adjectives; adverb clause

presently Tom stumbled upon Huck who was always willing to engage in an enterprise which offered entertainment and required no **capital** "bully idea" exclaimed Huck

[3] Presently Tom <u>stumbled</u> upon Huck, <u>who</u> was always willing to engage in an enterprise <u>which</u> offered entertainment and required no capital.
    "Bully idea!" exclaimed Huck.

Capital: wealth, in the form of money or property
Indent ¶, 2nd part (new speaker)
Use commas to set off most who/which clauses
    (when nonessential)
Use exclamation marks after exclamations
Dress-ups: strong verb; who clause; which clause

Week 22

Since Tom generally knew where to search for buried treasure Huck followed him to the **desolate** old haunted house just outside of st petersburg they brought along a pick and a shovel

    [5] Since Tom <u>generally</u> knew where to search for buried treasure, Huck followed him to the <u>desolate</u> old haunted house just outside St. Petersburg. They brought along a pick and a shovel.

Desolate: dreary, gloomy, and abandoned
Indent ¶ (new topic)
Use commas after #5 Sentence Openers
Dress-ups: -ly adverb; quality adjective
[!] No commas with cumulative adjectives
    (old haunted house)

---

trembling and talking in whispers Tom and Huck dropped there tools and climbed the creaky stairs to the second floor of the **dilapidated** house. after a few minutes two men entered and the boys noiselessly lied down with their eyes to knotholes in the termite-ridden floor

Trembling and talking in whispers, Tom and Huck dropped their tools and climbed the <u>creaky</u> stairs to the second floor of the <u>dilapidated</u> house. [2] After a few minutes two men entered, and the boys <u>noiselessly</u> lay down with their eyes to knotholes in the <u>termite-ridden</u> floor.

Dilapidated: fallen into ruin and decay
No comma before *and* to join 2 compound verbs
Use a comma before *and* to link 2 main clauses
Usage: *lay* = past of *lie (lie, lay, lain)*
Comma not needed after #2 SO of 4 words or fewer
Dress-ups: quality adjectives; -ly adverb
Homophones: there/their/they're
[!] Sentence Opener #4 (-ing phrase + comma)

"Well I've thought it over pardner" said one man "And it's dangerous for us to be carryin' around this money we stole". the **gruff** voice made the boys gasp and quake It was Injun Joe

    "Well, I've thought it over, pardner," said one man, "and it's dangerous for us to be carryin' around this money we stole." The <u>gruff</u> voice made the boys <u>gasp</u> and <u>quake</u>. It was Injun Joe!

Gruff: harsh; hoarse; rough; curt
Indent ¶ (new speaker)
Use commas to set off transitional words (Well)
Set off NDAs with commas (pardner)
Use commas w/ verb of speaking & direct quotation
Periods and commas go inside quotation marks
Dress-ups: quality adjective; strong verbs
[!] It's = it is

---

digging with his bowie knife, Injun Joe was about to bury the **loot** when his knife struck something—a box. He dug it out and opened it. Silently the men contemplated shiny gold coins

    Digging with his bowie knife, Injun Joe was about to bury the loot <u>when</u> his knife <u>struck</u> something—a box. He dug it out and opened it. [3] Silently the men <u>contemplated</u> <u>shiny</u> gold coins.

Loot: valuables taken by dishonesty or force
Indent ¶ (new topic)
No comma before *and* to join 2 compound verbs
Dress-ups: adverb clause; strong verbs; quality adj.
[!] Sentence Opener #4 (-ing phrase + comma)
[!] Use em-dashes to draw attention
[!] No commas with cumulative adj. (shiny gold)

Week 23

Injun Joe's **comrade** whispered greedily there's thousands of dollars hear. Let's bury it for ourselves"! Noticing a pick with fresh dirt on it, Injun Joe grumbled "somebody's coming back for this. if we bury it they'll see the ground disturbed. No we'll hide it under a cross in my den.

Injun Joe's comrade <u>whispered</u> <u>greedily</u>, "There's thousands of dollars here. Let's bury it for ourselves!"
Noticing a pick with fresh dirt on it, Injun Joe <u>grumbled</u>, "Somebody's coming back for this. [5] If we bury it, they'll see the ground disturbed. No, we'll hide it under a cross in my den."

Comrade: companion or associate
Indent ¶ (new speakers)
Use comma with verb of speaking & direct quotation
Use quotation marks around direct quotations
Capitalize 1st word of a quoted sentence
Homophones: hear/here
Exclamation inside " " if part of quoted material
Use commas after #5 Sentence Openers (If …)
Use commas to set off transitional words (No,)
Dress-ups: strong verbs; -ly adverb
[!] Sentence Opener #4 (-ing phrase + comma)

Injun Joe then unexpectedly wondered do you reckon theirs somebody upstairs Tom and Huck nearly fainted with terror Putting his murderous hand on his knife, Injun Joe turned toward the stairway the boys heard steps coming up the **creaky** stairs

Injun Joe then <u>unexpectedly</u> wondered, "Do you reckon there's somebody upstairs?"
Tom and Huck <u>nearly</u> fainted with terror.
Putting his <u>murderous</u> hand on his knife, Injun Joe turned toward the stairway. The boys heard steps coming up the <u>creaky</u> stairs.

Creaky: worn-down; having a rasping, grating sound
Indent ¶ (new speaker; new topics)
Use comma with verb of speaking & direct quotation
Use quotation marks around direct quotations
Capitalize 1st word of a quoted sentence
Homophones: there's/theirs
Question marks after questions (inside quotations)
Dress-ups: -ly adverbs; quality adjectives
[!] Sentence Opener #4 (-ing phrase + comma)

Panicking, they were about to spring for the closet when their was a crash of rotten timbers. Injun Joe landed on the ground amid the **debris**. His partner snarled "well if anybody's up they're, let 'em stay there It'll be dark soon so let 'em follow us. We'll be waiting for 'em

Panicking, they were about to <u>spring</u> for the closet <u>when</u> there was a crash of rotten timbers. Injun Joe landed on the ground amid the debris.
His partner <u>snarled</u>, "Well, <u>if</u> anybody's up there, let 'em stay there. It'll be dark soon, so let 'em follow us. We'll be waiting for 'em."

Debris: remains of something broken or destroyed
Indent ¶, 2nd part (new speaker)
[!] Sentence Opener #4 (-ing + comma)
Homophones: there/their/they're
Use comma with verb of speaking & direct quotation
Capitalize first word of a quoted sentence
Use commas to set off transitional words (Well,)
Use a comma before *so* to link 2 main clauses
Use quotation marks around direct quotations
Dress-ups: strong verbs; adverb clauses

Injun Joe agreed with his friend and they cautiously slipped away into the deepening twilight weakly Tom and Huck stood up They stared after the men threw the **chinks** between the logs of the house. Follow? Not they

Injun Joe agreed with his friend, and they <u>cautiously</u> <u>slipped</u> away into the <u>deepening</u> twilight.
[3] Weakly Tom and Huck stood up. They stared after the men through the chinks between the logs of the house. Follow? Not they!

Chinks: narrow openings or cracks
Indent ¶ (new topics)
Use a comma before *and* to link 2 main clauses
Homophones: threw/through
Exclamation marks after exclamations
Dress-ups: -ly adverb; strong verb; quality adjective

Chapter 8: Apostrophes

Instructions for students:
- Define bolded words with the definition that fits the context.
- Indent to start new paragraphs.
- Correct apostrophe and comma errors.
- Check for proper capitalization, quotation marks, and end marks; correct as needed.
- Dress-ups: underline quality adjectives, -ly adverbs, strong verbs, adverb clauses, and who/which.
- Sentence Openers: mark [2] preposition, [3] -ly adverb, and [5] adverb clause.
- Correct faulty homophones.

Fix-Its and Corrections

Grammar, Skills, and Vocabulary

Week 24

the glad **tidings** in st petersburg were that judge thatchers family was back in town. Beckys mother announced that theyd postponed the longed-for picnic long enough When Becky met Tom she confided weve been hearing how brave you were at the trial tom

The glad tidings in St. Petersburg were that Judge Thatcher's family was back in town. Becky's mother announced that they'd postponed the <u>longed-for</u> picnic long enough.
    [5] When Becky met Tom, she <u>confided</u>, "We've been hearing how brave you were at the trial, Tom."

Tidings: news or information
Indent ¶ (new topic; new speaker)
Capitalize proper nouns and titles used with names
Use apostrophes to show possession
Use apostrophes in contractions
Use commas after #5 Sentence Openers
Use comma with verb of speaking & direct quotation
Use quotation marks with direct quotations
Capitalize first word of a quoted sentence
Set off NDAs with commas (Tom)
Dress-ups: quality adjective; strong verb

She then confidently asked "will you **escort** me to the picnic Tom"? finally saturday morning arrived and the villages young folks gathered at the thatchers house

She then <u>confidently</u> asked, "Will you <u>escort</u> me to the picnic, Tom?"
    [3] Finally Saturday morning arrived, and the village's young folks <u>gathered</u> at the Thatchers' house.

Escort: to accompany or go with, as on a date
Indent ¶, 2nd part (time has passed)
Use comma with verb of speaking & direct quotation
Set off NDAs with commas (Tom)
Use a comma before *and* to link 2 main clauses
Use apostrophes to show possession
Discuss how to form plural possessives (Thatchers')
Dress-ups: -ly adverb; strong verbs

Judge Thatcher reassuringly explained to the childrens parents theyll be safe with several **chaperones** mrs thatcher told her daughter, Becky the ferryboat wont get back till late youd better stay overnight at Suzy Harpers".

Judge Thatcher <u>reassuringly</u> explained to the children's parents, "They'll be safe with several chaperones."
    Mrs. Thatcher told her daughter, "Becky, the ferryboat won't get back till late. You'd better stay overnight at Suzy Harper's."

Chaperone: an older person who attends and
    supervises a social gathering for young people
Indent ¶, 2nd part (new speaker)
Use apostrophes to show possession
Discuss how to form plural possessives (children's)
Use apostrophes in contractions
Set off NDAs with commas (Becky)
Note: *Harper* is possessive because *house* is implied
Periods and commas go inside quotation marks
Dress-ups: -ly adverb

Tying up three miles below town, the ferryboat waited during the lighthearted picnickers feast Somebody **jovially** shouted whos ready for the cave

      Tying up three miles below town, the ferryboat waited during the <u>lighthearted</u> picnickers' feast.
      Somebody <u>jovially</u> shouted, "Who's ready for the cave?"

Jovially: merrily and joyfully
Indent ¶ (new scene; new speaker)
Use apostrophes w/ plural possessives & contractions
Use comma + " " w/ speaking vb. + direct quotation
Capitalize first word of a quoted sentence
Dress-ups: quality adjective; -ly adverb
[!] Sentence Opener #4 (-ing phrase + comma)

Week 25

The caves massive oak door stood unbarred. dimly revealing the **lofty** rock walls, the childrens candles flickered

      The cave's <u>massive</u> oak door stood <u>unbarred</u>. [3] Dimly revealing the <u>lofty</u> rock walls, the children's candles <u>flickered</u>.

Lofty: high in the air; towering
Indent ¶ (new topic)
Use apostrophes to show possession
Dress-ups: quality adjectives; strong verb
[!] No commas with cumulative adjectives

No one fully understood the depths of the cave. a young man whispered if a person was to go to far into mcDougals cave, hed wander in the **labyrinth** and never find the end

No one fully understood the depths of the cave.
      A young man <u>whispered</u>, "If a person was to go too far into McDougal's Cave, he'd <u>wander</u> in the labyrinth and never find the end."

Labyrinth: a confusing combination of passages, in which it is hard to find one's way or reach the exit
Indent ¶, 2nd part (new speaker)
Use comma with verb of speaking & direct quotation
Capitalize first word of a quoted sentence
Use quotation marks around direct quotations
Use apostrophes in contractions. Homophones: to/too
Dress-ups: strong verbs; adverb clause

Couples ducked into shadowy **recesses** in the walls, and shouted "Boo"! at there friends By and by the groups who were panting laughing and growing weary returned to the mouth of the cave

      Couples <u>ducked</u> into <u>shadowy</u> recesses in the walls and shouted "Boo!" at their friends. By and by, the groups, <u>who</u> were panting, laughing, and growing weary, returned to the mouth of the cave.

Recess: secluded place; indentation or small hollow
Indent ¶ (new topic)
No comma before *and* to join 2 compound verbs
Exclamation inside quotation marks
Homophones: there/their/they're
Use commas after introductory transitional phrases
Use commas to set off most who/which clauses
Use commas with 3 or more items in a series
Dress-ups: strong verb; quality adjective; who clause

---

they were amazed to find that theyd been in mcDougals cave all day eventually the **blithe** picnickers headed slowly up the river, and back to town on the old ferryboat

They were amazed to find that they'd been in McDougal's Cave all day. [3] Eventually the <u>blithe</u> picnickers headed <u>slowly</u> up the river and back to town on the old ferryboat.

Blithe: cheerful; joyous; merry
Use apostrophes in contractions; to show possession
Capitalize proper nouns
Use periods to separate 2 main clauses
No comma before *and* to join 2 items in a series
("up … and back")
Dress-ups: quality adjective; -ly adverb

Week 26

On sunday morning Becky wasnt at church. neither was Tom. when the sermon was finished Judge Thatchers wife **strode** up to Suzy Harpers mother. Is my Becky going to sleep all day she half-jokingly inquired. "your Becky"?

    [2] On Sunday morning Becky wasn't at church. Neither was Tom. [5] When the sermon was finished, Judge Thatcher's wife strode up to Suzy Harper's mother.
    "Is my Becky going to sleep all day?" she <u>half-jokingly</u> inquired.
    "Your Becky?"

Strode: (past of *stride*) walked with long steps, as with haste or impatience
Indent ¶ (time has passed; new speakers)
Use apostrophes in contractions
Use commas after #5 sentence openers
Use apostrophes to show possession
Use quotation marks around direct quotations
Question marks after questions
Dress-ups: -ly adverb
[!] Sentence Opener #6 (V.S.S.)

Yes didnt she stay with you last night" "why no I havent seen her. mrs Thatcher turned pail, and sank into a pew just as Aunt Polly **strolled** up to the to lady's. Smiling, she observed "I reckon my Tom stayed with one of you last night since he hasnt been home

    "Yes, didn't she stay with you last night?"
    "Why, no, I haven't seen her."
    Mrs. Thatcher turned pale and sank into a pew <u>just as</u> Aunt Polly <u>strolled</u> up to the two ladies. Smiling, she observed, "I reckon my Tom stayed with one of you last night <u>since</u> he hasn't been home."

Strolled: walked along at a leisurely pace
Indent ¶ (new speakers)
Use quotation marks around direct quotations
Use commas to set off transitions (Yes, Why, no)
Use apostrophes in contractions
Capitalize first word of a quoted sentence
No comma before *and* to join 2 compound verbs
Plural, not possessive: *ladies*
Use comma with verb of speaking & direct quotation
Dress-ups: adverb clauses; strong verb
Homophones: pail/pale; to/two/too
[!] Sentence Opener #4 (-ing phrase + comma)

He didnt stay with us said mrs harper, shaking her head uneasily Mrs thatcher also shook her head, and turned paler than ever. Joe Harper, Aunt Polly asked, When did you see Tom last Joe couldnt say. All three lady's fell to **lamenting** and wringing there hands.

    "He didn't stay with us," said Mrs. Harper, shaking her head <u>uneasily</u>. Mrs. Thatcher also shook her head and turned paler than ever.
    "Joe Harper," Aunt Polly asked, "when did you see Tom last?"
    Joe couldn't say. All three ladies fell to <u>lamenting</u> and <u>wringing</u> their hands.

Lamenting: expressing grief for; regretting deeply
Indent ¶ (new speakers; new topic)
Use quotation marks around direct quotations
Use apostrophes in contractions
Use comma with verb of speaking & direct quotation
Use periods at ends of statements
No comma before *and* to join 2 compound verbs
Use lc to continue interrupted quotations
Plural, not possessive: *ladies*
Homophones: there/their/they're
Dress-ups: -ly adverb; strong verbs

Children and chaperone's were questioned They all said they hadnt noticed whether Tom and Becky were on board the ferryboat on the homeward trip It was dark; no one had thought of inquiring if anyone was missing Finally one young man fearfully **blurted** out what all were thinking they must still be in the cave"!

Children and chaperones were questioned. They all said they hadn't noticed whether Tom and Becky were on board the ferryboat on the homeward trip. It was dark; no one had thought of inquiring <u>if</u> anyone was missing.
    [3] Finally one young man <u>fearfully</u> <u>blurted</u> out what all were thinking. "They must still be in the cave!"

Blurted: uttered suddenly and impulsively
Indent ¶, 2nd part (new speaker)
Do not use apostrophes for plurals (chaperones)
Use periods at ends of statements
Use apostrophes in contractions
[!] Use semicolons to separate 2 main clauses
Use quotation marks around direct quotations
Capitalize first word of a quoted sentence
Exclamation inside " " if part of quoted material
Dress-ups: adverb clause; -ly adverb; strong verb

Chapter 9: V.S.S. and Commonly Misused Words

Instructions for students:
- Bolded words in this chapter are misused; find the intended word and explain the correct usage of both.
- Correct misuse of contractions and possessives.
- Indent to start new paragraphs.
- Correct apostrophe and comma errors.
- Check for proper capitalization, quotation marks, and end marks; correct as needed.
- Dress-ups: underline quality adjectives, -ly adverbs, strong verbs, adverb clauses, and who/which.
- Sentence Openers: mark [2] preposition, [3] -ly adverb, [5] adverb clause, and [6] V.S.S. (very short sentence).

Fix-Its and Corrections | ## *Grammar, Skills, and Vocabulary*

Week 27

Now lets go **foreword** and see what happened to Tom and Becky in McDougal's cave. for a while the chaperones and children stayed **altogether**, exploring the wondrous **cite**

Now let's go forward and see what happened to Tom and Becky in McDougal's Cave. [2] For a while the chaperones and children stayed all together, exploring the <u>wondrous</u> site.

Indent ¶ (new topic)
Use apostrophes in contractions (let's = let us)
Foreword: a short introductory note in a book
Forward: ahead; toward a time in the future
Altogether: entirely; *all together*: everyone together
Cite: to mention or quote a passage as an authority
Site: the location of some building, structure, or city

Toms **capitol** idea—he thought—was to make candle-smoke marks on the walls so they could find there way back to the group. He and Becky wandered **further** into the caves depths **then** ever before

Tom's <u>capital</u> idea—he thought—was to make candle-smoke marks on the walls so they could find their way back to the group. He and Becky wandered farther into the cave's depths than ever before.

Capitol: a building occupied by a state legislature
Capital: (noun) the city that's the seat of government
Capital: (adjective) first-rate or excellent (used here)
  Also: *capital letter* = uppercase letter
Farther refers to physical distance, whereas *further* refers to abstract relationships of degree or quality
Than is the conjunction used for comparison
Their = possessive; apostrophe for possession: *cave's*
[!] Use em-dashes to draw attention

Tom and Becky **past** through spacious caverns, from who's ceilings hung huge stalactites. Disturbed by the childrens lights, hundreds of bats **alternatively** squeaked and darted at them. Becky shrieked.

Tom and Becky passed through <u>spacious</u> caverns, from whose ceilings hung huge stalactites. Disturbed by the children's lights, hundreds of bats <u>alternately</u> <u>squeaked</u> and <u>darted</u> at them. [6] Becky <u>shrieked</u>.

Past: (noun or adj.) the time gone by; ago or gone by
Passed: moved on or ahead; proceeded
Alternatively: having a choice of 2 or more things
Alternately: interchanged or switched for each other
Whose = possessive form of *who*; *who's* = who is
Dress-ups: quality adjective; -ly adverb; strong verbs
[!] Sentence Opener 7 (advanced -ed opener)
New: Sentence Opener #6, V.S.S. (2 – 5 words)

The bats chased Tom and Becky a long way so the children thought it wise **council** to start back Nervously Becky was watching Toms face "can you find the way Tom. Its all a mixed-up crookedness to me" "oh it's **alright** Becky Well soon find the way"

The bats chased Tom and Becky a long way, so the children thought it wise counsel to start back.
  [3] Nervously Becky was watching Tom's face. "Can you find the way, Tom? It's all a <u>mixed-up</u> crookedness to me."
    "Oh, it's all right, Becky. We'll soon find the way."

Indent ¶, 2nd part (new speakers)
Council: assembly of persons for advice, consultation
Counsel: advice or plan
Alright/All right: both are now acceptable
Use a comma before *so* to link 2 main clauses
Use apostrophes to show possession
Set off NDAs with commas
Use question marks after questions
It's = it is   We'll = we will
Use commas after introductory interjections (Oh,)
Dress-ups: quality adjective

Week 28

Hunger and fatigue began to **effect** Tom and Becky so they drank from a nearby spring **set** on it's banks and ate some cake that Tom had saved from the picnic. exhausted, they **laid** down, and immediately fell asleep

      Hunger and fatigue began to affect Tom and Becky, so they drank from a nearby spring, sat on its banks, and ate some cake that Tom had saved from the picnic. Exhausted, they lay down and <u>immediately</u> fell asleep.

Indent ¶ (new topic)
Affect is the verb and *effect* the noun
You *set* an object down but *sit (sat, sat)* yourself
You *lay* an object down but *lie (lay, lain)* yourself
Use a comma before *so* to link 2 main clauses
Use commas with 3 or more items in a series
Its = possessive form of *it*
No comma before *and* to join 2 compound verbs
[!] Sentence Opener #7 (advanced -ed opener)

After what seemed a mighty stretch of time both awoke out of a dead stupor of sleep. **Sense** it was too cold too remain **stationery** for very long Becky suggested they move on. "Well Becky" explained Tom "We must stay here where theirs water to drink. **Beside** that, this little piece of candle is all we have left"

[2] After what seemed a mighty stretch of time, both awoke out of a dead stupor of sleep. [5] Since it was too cold to remain <u>stationary</u> for very long, Becky suggested they move on.
      "Well, Becky," explained Tom, "we must stay here <u>where</u> there's water to drink. Besides that, this little piece of candle is all we have left."

Indent ¶, 2nd part (new speaker)
Since is the conjunction and *sense* the noun
Stationary: standing still; not moving (adjective)
Stationery: writing paper (noun)
Beside: near (prep.) or along the side of (adv.)
Besides: in addition to
Comma needed after #2 SO of 5 or more words
Use commas after #5 SO
Use commas after introductory transitional words
Use comma with verb of speaking & direct quotation
Use lc to continue interrupted quotations
Use apostrophes in contractions *(there's = there is)*

Horrified, the children watched as there candle melted and the wick could burn no **further**. In a moment, their **principle** fear—being in utter darkness—came true. Becky shuddered.

      Horrified, the children watched <u>as</u> their candle melted and the wick could burn no farther. [2] In a moment their <u>principal</u> fear—being in utter darkness—came true. [6] Becky shuddered.

Indent ¶ (new topic)
Their = possessive of *they*
Further/farther confusion (see Week 27)
Principle (n.): accepted rule of conduct; basic truth
Principal (adj.): most important, chief
[!] Sentence Opener #7 (advanced -ed opener)
Comma not needed after #2 SO of 4 words or fewer
SO #6, V.S.S.

Tom took a kite line from his pocket tied it around a pillar and slowly led Becky **foreword** along a pitch-black corridor Suddenly a human hand who was holding a candle appeared from behind a rock

      Tom took a kite line from his pocket, tied it around a pillar, and <u>slowly</u> led Becky forward along a <u>pitch-black</u> corridor. [3] Suddenly a human hand, <u>which</u> was holding a candle, appeared from behind a rock!

Indent ¶ (new topic)
Foreword/forward confusion (see Week 27)
Use commas with 3 or more items in a series
Use *who* for people but not parts of people
Use commas to set off most who/which clauses
Exclamation marks after exclamatory statements
Dress-ups: -ly adverb; quality adj.; which clause

Week 29

Tom lifted up a startled shout and instantly the hand was followed by its body—Injun Joes! Tom froze was it an **allusion** Gratefully Tom observed Injun Joe take to his heel's Joe hadnt recognized him

Tom lifted up a startled shout, and <u>instantly</u> the hand was followed by its body—Injun Joe's! [6] Tom froze. [6] Was it an illusion? [3] Gratefully Tom observed Injun Joe take to his <u>heels</u>. [6] Joe hadn't recognized him.

Allusion: a reference to something
Illusion: a false impression of reality
Use a comma before *and* to link 2 main clauses
Its = possessive (correct this time)
Use apostrophes to show possession
SO #6, V.S.S.
Heels is plural, not possessive
Use apostrophes in contractions
Dress-ups:-ly adverb

The **affect** of the awful adversarys appearance left Tom weak. distressed with hunger and fear, he continued to lead Becky by the hand as they groped there way in the clammy, black cave

The effect of the awful adversary's appearance left Tom weak. Distressed with hunger and fear, he continued to lead Becky by the hand <u>as</u> they <u>groped</u> their way in the <u>clammy</u>, black cave.

Affect is the verb and *effect* the noun
Use apostrophes to show possession
Their = possessive of *they*
Dress-ups: adverb clause; strong verb; quality adjective
[!] Sentence Opener #7 (advanced -ed opener)
[!] Alliteration: awful adversary's appearance

Three days **past**. Tom and Becky were still lost and the searchers had given up the quest Mrs Thatcher just **laid** in her bed. Aunt Polly who's hair had turned white sank **farther** into melancholy.

[6] Three days passed. Tom and Becky were still lost, and the searchers had given up the quest. Mrs. Thatcher just lay in her bed. Aunt Polly, <u>whose</u> hair had turned white, sank further into melancholy.

Indent ¶ (time has passed and new scene)
Past/passed confusion (see Week 27)
You *lay* an object down but *lie (lay, lain)* yourself
Further/farther confusion (see Week 27)
Whose = possessive of *who*
SO #6, V.S.S.
Use a comma before *and* to link 2 main clauses
Use commas to set off most who/which clauses
Dress-ups: who/which

Since the tragedy **effected** the whole village folk's went to there rest on tuesday night sad, and forlorn. In the middle of the night however the bells suddenly pealed. They were found For two weeks afterward Tom regaled listeners with the tale of his **capitol** adventure.

[5] Since the tragedy affected the whole village, folks went to their rest on Tuesday night sad and <u>forlorn</u>. [2] In the middle of the night, however, the bells <u>suddenly</u> <u>pealed</u>. [6] They were found!
[2] For two weeks afterward Tom <u>regaled</u> listeners with the tale of his <u>capital</u> adventure.

Indent ¶, 2nd part (time has passed)
Affect is the verb and *effect* the noun
Capitol/capital confusion (see Week 27)
Use commas after #5 Sentence Openers
Folks is plural, not possessive
Their = possessive of *they*
Capitalize names of calendar items
No comma before *and* joining two adjectives
Use commas to set off transitional words *(however)*
SO #6, V.S.S.
Exclamation marks after exclamatory statements
Dress-ups: quality adj's; -ly adverb; strong verbs

Week 30

One day members of the town **counsel** and the school **principle set besides** Tom in the Judges house. When someone asked if Tom would visit the cave ever again the Judge had occasion to reassure him.

One day members of the town council and the school principal sat beside Tom in the judge's house. [5] When someone asked <u>if</u> Tom would visit the cave ever again, the judge had occasion to reassure him.

Counsel/council confusion (see Week 27)
Principal (n.): the head or director of a school (see also Week 28)
You *set* an object down but *sit (sat, sat)* yourself
Beside/besides confusion (see Week 28)
Use lc for titles without a name (the judge)
Use apostrophes to show possession
Use commas after #5 Sentence Openers
Dress-ups: adverb clause

"Nobody will get lost in that cave anymore Tom" Judge Thatcher promised him. "why" "I had it's door sheathed with iron and triple locked and ive got the keys Tom turned white He stood **stationery** and silent for several moments.

"Nobody will get lost in that cave anymore, Tom," Judge Thatcher promised him.

"Why?"

"I had its door <u>sheathed</u> with iron and triple locked, and I've got the keys."

[6] Tom turned white. He stood <u>stationary</u> and silent for several moments.

Indent ¶, 2nd part (new speakers; new topic)
Stationary/stationery confusion (see Week 28)
Set off NDAs with commas
Use comma with verb of speaking & direct quotation
Capitalize first word of quotation
Question marks after questions
Its = possessive form of *it*
Use a comma before *and* to link 2 main clauses
SO #6, V.S.S.
Dress-ups: strong verb; quality adjective
[!] Alliteration: stood stationary and silent

Finally Judge Thatcher exclaimed Tom whats the matter boy Are you **alright**" "oh judge Injun Joes in the cave" When the cave door was consequently unlocked a sorrowful **site** presented itself. Injun Joe **lied** stretched upon the ground, dead

[3] Finally Judge Thatcher exclaimed, "Tom, what's the matter, boy? Are you all right?"

"Oh, Judge, Injun Joe's in the cave!"

[5] When the cave door was <u>consequently</u> unlocked, a sorrowful sight presented itself. Injun Joe lay stretched upon the ground, dead.

Indent ¶ (new speakers; new topic)
Alright/All right: both are now acceptable
Site: the location of some building, structure, or city
Sight: something seen
Lie (telling falsehoods)/ *lie* (reclining) confusion
Use comma with verb of speaking & direct quotation
Set off NDAs with commas (Tom, Judge)
Use apostrophes in contractions
Use commas after introductory interjections (Oh,)
Capitalize titles when used as NDAs (Judge)
Use commas after #5 Sentence Openers

Joes face **laid** close to the crack of the door. Tom was touched He knew that Joes hunger and suffering had been far worse **then** their's. Nevertheless Tom felt an abounding **since** of relief because he didnt need to fear Injun Joes wrath any longer

Joe's face lay close to the crack of the door. [6] Tom was touched. He knew that Joe's hunger and suffering had been far worse than theirs. Nevertheless, Tom felt an <u>abounding</u> sense of relief <u>because</u> he didn't need to fear Injun Joe's wrath any longer.

You *lay* an object down but *lie (lay, lain)* yourself
Than is the conjunction used for comparison
Since is the conjunction and *sense* the noun
Use apostrophes to show possession
SO #6, V.S.S.
Theirs = possessive of *their*
Use apostrophes in contractions
Dress-ups: quality adjective; adverb clause
[!] Sentence Opener T (transition)

Chapter 10: Agreement

Instructions for students:
- Define bolded words with the definition that fits the context.
- Correct agreement errors (subject/verb or noun/pronoun).
- Correct misuse of tricky words, homophones, contractions, and possessives.
- Indent to start new paragraphs.
- Correct grammar and punctuation covered in prior chapters.
- Dress-ups: underline quality adjectives, -ly adverbs, strong verbs, adverb clauses, and who/which.
- Sentence Openers: mark [2] preposition, [3] -ly adverb, [5] adverb clause, and [6] V.S.S.

Fix-Its and Corrections

Grammar, Skills, and Vocabulary

Week 31

After Injun Joes funeral, Tom whispered to Huck that they're was some things they needed to discuss "Huck remember that day in the haunted house when Injun Joe planned to hide the treasure in his **den** under a cross"?

   [2] After Injun Joe's funeral Tom whispered to Huck that there were some things they needed to discuss. "Huck, remember that day in the haunted house <u>when</u> Injun Joe planned to hide the treasure in his den under a cross?"

Den: a cave used for concealment; a vile place
Indent ¶ (new topic)
Use apostrophes to show possession
Comma optional after #2 SO of 4 words or fewer
They're/there confusion
Subject/verb agreement: "things...were" (*there* isn't the subject, which follows the verb here)
Set off NDAs with commas
Question inside " " if part of quoted material

Keenly Huck searched his comrades face and asked "Tom, is you still on the sent of that treasure"? grinning, Tom exclaimed its in McDougals Cave

   [3] <u>Keenly</u> Huck searched his comrade's face and asked, "Tom, are you still on the scent of that treasure?"
      Grinning, Tom exclaimed, "It's in McDougal's Cave!"

Keenly: intensely; with sensitive perception
Indent ¶ (new speakers)
Use apostrophes to show possession
Use comma with verb of speaking & direct quotation
Subject/verb agreement: "are you"
Tricky words: sent/scent; its/it's
[!] Sentence Opener #4 (-ing + comma)

Tom—truthfully, now—is this for fun, or **earnest**? For earnest Huck All we needs to do is climb through that hole Becky and me escaped from, and dig it up

   "Tom—truthfully, now—is this for fun or earnest?"
   "For earnest, Huck. All we need to do is climb through that hole Becky and I escaped from and dig it up."

Earnest: serious in intention
Indent ¶ (new speakers)
No comma before *or* & *and* to join 2 items in a series
Set off NDAs with commas
Subject/verb agreement: "we need"
Pronoun usage: "Becky and I escaped"
[!] Use em-dashes to indicate interruption

After borrowing a **skiff** who's owner was absent the eager boys reached and entered the cave a trifle before noon. by and by Tom excitedly cried "looky-here Huck. There's lots of footprints and theirs the cross—done with candle-smoke

   [2] After borrowing a skiff <u>whose</u> owner was absent, the eager boys reached and entered the cave a trifle before noon.
      By and by Tom <u>excitedly</u> cried, "Looky-here, Huck. There are lots of footprints, and there's the cross—done with candle-smoke."

Skiff: a type of boat small enough for sailing or rowing by one person
Indent ¶ (new scene; new speaker)
Comma needed after #2 SO of 5 or more words
   [!] #2 because *borrowing* = prep. object here
Tricky words: who's/whose; theirs/there's
Use comma with verb of speaking & direct quotation
Set off NDAs with commas
Subject/verb agreement: "lots...are there"
Close quotation with quotation marks
Dress-ups: who/which (whose); -ly adverb

Week 32

After digging and scratching then removing some boards the boys uncovered the treasure box. my, but we's rich Tom exclaimed Huck, plowing among the **tarnished** coins with his hands

[2] After digging and scratching then removing some boards, the boys <u>uncovered</u> the treasure box. "My, but we're rich, Tom!" exclaimed Huck, <u>plowing</u> among the <u>tarnished</u> coins with his hands.

Tarnished: discolored; with the shine gone
Indent ¶ (new topic)
Comma needed after #2 SO of 5 or more words
    [!] #2 because -*ing* words = prep. objects here
Use quotation marks with direct quotations
Subject/verb agreement: "we're"
Set off NDAs with commas
Use exclamation marks after exclamatory statements
Dress-ups: strong verb; quality adjectives

No sooner does Tom and Huck get back to town with his treasure then the widow Douglas invited the villager's altogether for a grand party. Thats when the Widow announced that she meant to give Huck a home educate him and start him in a **modest** business.

No sooner did Tom and Huck get back to town with their treasure than the Widow Douglas invited the villagers all together for a grand party. That's when the widow announced that she meant to give Huck a home, educate him, and start him in a <u>modest</u> business.

Modest: limited in amount; free from extravagance
Indent ¶ (new scene)
Subject/verb agreement: "Tom & Huck *do*," but past tense here, so "did"
Noun/pronoun agreement: "Tom and Huck … their"
Tricky words: then/than; altogether/all together
Villagers is plural, not possessive
Use apostrophes for contractions
Use lc for titles without a name (widow)
Use commas with 3 or more items in a series
Dress-ups: quality adjective

Huck don't need money declared Tom. Maybe you don't believe it but he's gots lots of them. Then he poured there **princely** fortune out onto the widows table Look at them he exclaimed

"Huck doesn't need money," <u>declared</u> Tom. "Maybe you don't believe it, but he has lots of it." Then he <u>poured</u> their <u>princely</u> fortune out onto the widow's table. "Look at it!" he exclaimed.

Princely: magnificent; befitting a prince
Indent ¶ (new speaker)
Subject/verb agreement: "Huck doesn't"
"He's gots" should be "he has"; *there/their* confusion
Noun/pronoun agr.: "money" and "fortune" = "it"
Use comma with verb of speaking & direct quotation
Use a comma before *but* to link 2 main clauses
Use apostrophes to show possession
Use exclamation marks after exclamations

Everybody were **astounded** The boys gold coins amounted to a little over twelve thousand dollars The sum were more then anyone present have ever seen at one time before, although some persons there was worth more than that in property.

[6] Everybody was <u>astounded</u>. The boys' gold coins amounted to a little over twelve thousand dollars. The sum was more than anyone present had ever seen at one time before, <u>although</u> some persons there were worth more than that in property.

Astounded: astonished and bewildered
Indent ¶ (new topic)
Subject/verb agreement: "everybody was"; "sum was"; "anyone has" (but past); "persons were"
Use apostrophes to form plural possessives
Tricky words: then/than
[!] Don't switch tenses
Dress-ups: quality adjective; adverb clause

Week 33

The widow Douglas and aunt Polly put the two boys money in the bank, where it would be safe for him. They're **windfall** made a mighty stir in the little village of st Petersburg. whenever folks announced that Tom or Huck were appearing he was sure to be stared at admired and courted

The Widow Douglas and Aunt Polly put the two boys' money in the bank, <u>where</u> it would be safe for them.

    Their windfall made a mighty stir in the little village of St. Petersburg. [5] Whenever folks announced that Tom or Huck was appearing, he was sure to be stared at, admired, and <u>courted</u>.

Windfall: an unexpected gain
Indent ¶, 2nd part (time has passed)
Capitalize titles used with names
Use apostrophes to form plural possessives
Noun/pronoun agreement: "boys … them"
Homophones: there/their/they're
2 singular subjects joined by *or* take a singular verb
Use commas after #5 Sentence Openers
Use commas with 3 or more items in a series
Dress-ups: adverb clause; strong verb

Adoption had an **intolerable** affect on Huck. "I are bein' smothered" he complained Hucks suffering's was almost more then he could bear He bravely bore his miseries three weeks and than one day turned up missing

    Adoption had an <u>intolerable</u> effect on Huck. "I am bein' smothered," he complained. Huck's sufferings were almost more than he could bear. He <u>bravely</u> bore his miseries three weeks and then one day turned up missing.

Intolerable: impossible to tolerate or endure
Indent ¶ (new topic)
Tricky words: affect/effect; then/than
Subject/verb agreement: "I am"; "sufferings were"
Use comma with verb of speaking & direct quotation
Use apostrophes to show possession
Sufferings is plural, not possessive
Dress-ups: quality adjective; -ly adverb

Tom Sawyer wisely went poking around among some animal pens and in it he found the **refugee**. "Ive tried it" said Huck "And it don't work. them fancy clothes smothers me. The Widow wont let me smoke or scratch and doggone it she pray all the time! Bein' rich aren't what its cracked up too be.

Tom Sawyer <u>wisely</u> went poking around among some animal pens, and in them he found the refugee.

    "I've tried it," said Huck, "and it doesn't work. Those fancy clothes <u>smother</u> me. The widow won't let me smoke or scratch, and, doggone it, she prays all the time! Bein' rich isn't what it's cracked up to be."

Refugee: someone who flees for refuge or safety
Indent ¶, 2nd part (new speaker)
Use comma before *and* to link 2 main clauses (twice)
Noun/pronoun agreement: "pens … them"
Use apostrophes in contractions
Use commas w/ verb of speaking & direct quotation
Use lc to continue interrupted quotations
Subject/verb agreement: "it doesn't"; "clothes smother"; "she prays"; "Being isn't"
Tricky words: them/those; its/it's; too/to
Use commas to set off interjections
Dress-ups: -ly adverb; strong verb

Conclusion
Thus ends this **chronicle** Most of the characters in this story still lives, and is prosperous and happy Someday it may seem worthwhile two take up the younger ones again, and see how he turned out but those are another book entirely

Conclusion
    [6] Thus ends this chronicle. Most of the characters in this story still live and are prosperous and happy. Someday it may seem worthwhile to take up the younger ones again and see how they turned out, but that is another book <u>entirely</u>.

Chronicle: a record of events, or history
Indent ¶ (new topic)
Subject/verb agreement: "Most live … are"
No comma before *and* to join 2 compound verbs
Homophones: to/two/too
Noun/pronoun agreement: "ones … they"; "that is … another book"
Dress-ups: -ly adverb

The Frog Prince, or Just Desserts

Introduction

Recommended for grades four through eight, the Frog Prince Fix-Its are divided into thirty-three weeks, with four passages to rewrite and correct each week. See the Introduction under Teaching Procedure for instructions.

In the notes beside the Fix-Its, exclamations in brackets [!] will alert you to advanced concepts you may wish to explain to your students, depending on their ability. These often have corresponding errors for students to locate, but do not necessarily expect students to find them. In the Appendix you will find a fuller discussion of the dress-ups and sentence openers as well as most grammar issues. Starting with Week 7, I stop marking #1 Subject Openers. If your students are having trouble recognizing them, however, you may wish to continue marking these.

Because the Fix-It stories are usually taught over the course of a school year, students may sometimes have trouble following the storyline. As you discuss the sentences each week, I recommend you check students' reading comprehension first, discussing the events leading up to and including that week's reading.

Background

You may wish to read the original tale to your students by way of introduction to my version. While mine follows the overall plot, it is a radical departure from the basic story, stemming from my distaste for the ending. Why should the princess get to marry the prince when she is decent to him only after discovering his true identity? Fairy tales ought to end with characters receiving their just deserts.

The story originates as a tale by the Brothers Grimm about a princess's refusal to honor her promise to a frog. The version printed below is a popular variation of the story.

The Frog Prince

One fine evening a young princess put on her bonnet and clogs and went out to take a walk by herself in a wood. When she came to a cool spring of water that rose in the midst of it, she sat herself down to rest a while. Now, she had a golden ball in her hand, which was her favorite plaything, and she was always tossing it up into the air and catching it again as it fell. After a time she threw it up so high that she missed catching it as it fell, and the ball bounded away and rolled along upon the ground, till at last it fell down into the spring. The princess looked into the spring after her ball, but it was very deep, so deep that she could not see the bottom of it.

Then she began to bewail her loss and said, "Alas! If only I could get my ball again, I would give all my fine clothes and jewels and everything that I have in the world."

While she was speaking, a frog put its head out of the water and said, "Princess, why do you weep so bitterly?"

"Alas!" said she. "What can you do for me, you nasty frog? My golden ball has fallen into the spring."

The frog said, "I want not your pearls and jewels and fine clothes, but if you will love me and let me live with you, eat from off your golden plate and sleep upon your bed, I will bring you your ball again."

"What nonsense," thought the princess, "this silly frog is talking! He can never even get out of the spring to visit me, though he may be able to get my ball for me, and therefore I will tell him he shall have what he asks." So she said to the frog, "Well, if you will bring me my ball, I will do all you ask."

Then the frog put his head down and dived deep under the water. After a little while he came up again, with the ball in his mouth, and threw it on the edge of the spring. As soon as the young princess saw her ball, she ran to pick it up, and she was so overjoyed to have it in her hand again that she never thought of the frog but ran home with it as fast as she could. The frog called after her, "Stay, Princess, and take me with you as you said," but she did not stop to hear a word.

The next day, just as the princess had sat down to dinner, she heard a strange noise—tap, tap—plash, plash—as if something was coming up the marble staircase. Soon afterward there was a gentle knock at the door and a little voice cried out and said:

> Open the door, my princess dear.
> Open the door to thy true love here!
> And mind the words that thou and I said,
> By the fountain cool, in the greenwood shade.

Then the princess ran to the door and opened it, and there she saw the frog, whom she had quite forgotten. At this sight she was sadly frightened, and shutting the door as fast as she could, she came back to her seat. The king, her father, seeing that something had frightened her, asked her what was the matter. "There is a nasty frog at the door," said she, "who lifted my ball for me out of the spring this morning. I told him that he should live with me here, thinking that he could never get out of the spring, but there he is at the door, and he wants to come in."

While she was speaking the frog knocked again at the door and said:

> Open the door, my princess dear.
> Open the door to thy true love here!
> And mind the words that thou and I said,
> By the fountain cool, in the greenwood shade.

Then the king said to the young princess, "As you have given your word, you must keep it, so go let him in." She did so, and the frog hopped into the room and then straight on—tap, tap—plash, plash—from the bottom of the room to the top, till he came up close to the table where the princess sat.

"Pray lift me upon the chair," said he to the princess, "and let me sit next to you." As soon as she had done this, the frog said, "Put your plate nearer to me, that I may eat out of it." This she did, and when he had eaten as much as he could, he said, "Now I am tired. Carry me upstairs and put me into your bed." And the princess, though very unwilling, took him up in her hand and put him upon the pillow of her own bed, where he slept all night long. As soon as it was light, he jumped up, hopped downstairs, and went out of the house.

"Now, then," thought the princess, "at last he is gone, and I shall be troubled with him no more."

But she was mistaken, for when night came again she heard the same tapping at the door. The frog came once more and said:

> Open the door, my princess dear.
> Open the door to thy true love here!
> And mind the words that thou and I said,
> By the fountain cool, in the greenwood shade.

When the princess opened the door, the frog came in and slept upon her pillow as before, till the morning broke. The third night he did the same. When the princess awoke on the following morning, however, she was astonished to see, instead of the frog, a handsome prince, gazing on her with the most beautiful eyes she had ever seen and standing at the head of her bed.

He told her that he had been enchanted by a spiteful fairy, who had changed him into a frog, and that he had been fated so to abide till some princess should take him out of the spring, let him eat from her plate, and let him sleep upon her bed for three nights. "You," said the prince, "have broken his cruel charm, and now I have nothing to wish for but that you should go with me into my father's kingdom, where I will marry you and love you as long as you live."

The young princess, you may be sure, was not long in saying "Yes" to all this. As they spoke, a gay coach drove up, with eight beautiful horses decked with plumes of feathers and a golden harness. Behind the coach rode the prince's servant, faithful Heinrich, who had bewailed the misfortunes of his dear master during his enchantment so long and so bitterly that his heart had well-nigh burst.

They then took leave of the king, got into the coach with eight horses, and all set out, full of joy and merriment, for the prince's kingdom, which they reached safely. There they lived happily a great many years.

Background to the Brothers Grimm

Born near Frankfurt, Germany, the Hessian brothers Jacob (1785–1863) and Wilhelm Grimm (1786–1859) are best known today for their collection and adaptation of German and other European folktales. "The Frog Prince" has sparked numerous modern adaptations, often with a kiss from the princess the catalyst for the frog's transformation back into a prince. In the version from the Brothers Grimm, the spell is broken when the princess throws the frog against a wall in revulsion.

The Frog Prince, or Just Desserts

Fix-Its and Corrections

Grammar, Skills, and Vocabulary

Week 1

Several hundred years ago, in an obscure kingdom, tucked away among the alps, rained a **decorous** and dignified King. Ruling Monarch in a line of Monarchs that stretched back to the middle ages.

[2] Several hundred years ago in an <u>obscure</u> kingdom <u>tucked away</u> among the Alps, reigned a <u>decorous</u> and dignified king, ruling monarch in a line of monarchs that stretched back to the Middle Ages.

Decorous: with proper dignity in conduct & manners
Indent ¶ (new topic)
[!] Disguised #2 (*During, In,* or *At* that time period)
[!] With several intro. phrases, comma after last only
Capitalize proper nouns (Alps, Middle Ages)
Homophone: rained/reigned
Use lc for common nouns and titles without a name
Correct fragment by joining phrase to main clause
Dress-ups: quality adjectives; strong verb

King Morton esteemed values, and he would have none of this recent **drivel** of dropping "Sir" and Madam when addressing ones elders. Nor could he tolerate modern jargon "sweet" should refer to pastry's; cool ought too refer too the temperature; good night should be a nighttime parting.

[1] King Morton <u>esteemed</u> values. [1] He would have none of this recent drivel of dropping "Sir" and "Madam" when addressing one's elders. [1] Nor could he <u>tolerate</u> modern jargon. [1] "Sweet" should refer to pastries; "cool" ought to refer to the temperature; "good night" should be a nighttime parting.

Drivel: nonsense; meaningless talk or thinking
Indent ¶ (new topic)
[!] Avoid stringing together sentences with *and*
[!] Use quotation marks around words used as words
   (adv., but students may see the pattern provided)
Use apostrophes to show possession
Fused: use a period to separate 2 main clauses
Pastries should be plural, not possessive
Homophone: too/to
[!] Note use of semicolons to separate main clauses
Dress-ups: strong verbs

He became livid on the subject of modern gadgets. Just so much **folderol** in his opinion. Because downloading movies on iPods would guarantee eye problem's when children reached *his* distinguished age.

[1] He became <u>livid</u> on the subject of modern gadgets—just so much folderol, in his opinion. [1] Downloading movies on iPods would guarantee eye problems <u>when</u> children reached *his* <u>distinguished</u> age.

Folderol: foolish talk or ideas; nonsense
Indent ¶ (new topic)
Correct 1st fragment by joining phrase to main clause
Use commas to set off transitional phrases
Correct 2nd fragment by dropping *Because*
Problems is plural, not possessive
[!] Tricky -ing opener: a #1 (imposter #4)
[!] Note use of italics for emphasis (use sparingly)
Dress-ups: quality adjectives; adverb clause

Moreover didnt they realize cell phones were intended for emergencies only. Only yesterday the palace accountant had **vehemently**, complained two him that the youngest of his 2 daughters had racked up 1000 text messages on her cell phone—in a single month!

[T] Moreover, didn't they realize cell phones were intended for emergencies only? [3] Only yesterday the palace accountant had <u>vehemently</u> complained to him that the younger of his two daughters had <u>racked up</u> one thousand text messages on her cell phone—in a single month!

Vehemently: forcefully; with strong emotion
[!] Transitional Opener (mark as "T")
Use commas after introductory transitional words
Use apostrophes in contractions
Use a question mark after question
No comma between an adverb and verb it describes
Homophone: two/to
Spell out numbers written as one or two words
[!] Note use of dash and exclamation for emphasis
Dress-ups: -ly adverb; strong verb

Week 2

Worst, she was texting for amusement too her own sister, Maribella—in the same palace! And when he demanded it back Dorinda had **inarticulately** mumbled something about not being able to locate it

Worse, she was texting for amusement to her own sister, Maribella—in the same palace! [5] When he demanded it back, Dorinda had <u>inarticulately</u> <u>mumbled</u> something about not being able to locate it.

Inarticulately: unable to express herself clearly
Use *worse* since only 2 things are compared
Homophone: too/to
[!] Avoid starting sentences with coord. conjunctions
Use commas after #5 Sentence Openers
Use a period at end of statements
Dress-ups: -ly adverb; strong verb

His youngest daughter—now there was another topic that brought red to his face unlike her only sister princess Dorinda had been an **obstinate** child from toddlerhood.

    His younger daughter—now there was another topic that brought red to his face. [2] Unlike her only sister, Princess Dorinda had been an <u>obstinate</u> child from toddlerhood.

Obstinate: stubborn; inflexible (quality adjective)
Indent ¶ (new topic)
[!] Use the comparative adjective when comparing 2
[!] Use em-dashes to indicate a break in thought
Fused: use a period to separate 2 main clauses
[!] Comma after *sister* to avoid misreading
Capitalize titles used with names

Never one to obey anyone to say nothing of His Royal Highness himself she would escape from the nursery to find mischief wherever she could. Once she stealed into the throne room, swinging on the chandelier's, and landing at the feet of the scandalized **courtiers**.

Never one to obey anyone, to say nothing of his Royal Highness himself, she would escape from the nursery to find mischief <u>wherever</u> she could. [T] Once she stole into the throne room, swinging on the chandeliers and landing at the feet of the <u>scandalized</u> courtiers.

Courtiers: people in attendance at the court of a king
[!] Use commas around nonessential phrases
His is not part of the title so should be lowercase
Spelling: *mischief*—"i before e" rule
[!] Transitional Opener [T]
Stole is the past tense of *steal*, not *stealed*
Chandeliers is plural, not possessive
No comma before *and* to join 2 items in a series
    ("swinging … and landing")
Dress-ups: adverb clause; quality adjective

And another time, she upset the **prestigious** new employee in the kitchen the Iron Chef himself, he was experimenting with sturgeon roe ice cream when she sneaked a taste making a wry face at the concoction.

[2] Another time she upset the <u>prestigious</u> new employee in the <u>kitchen, the</u> Iron Chef himself. [1] He was experimenting with sturgeon roe ice cream <u>when</u> she <u>sneaked</u> a taste, making a <u>wry</u> face at the concoction.

Prestigious: respected; distinguished; honored
Sturgeon roe: the eggs (roe) of a type of fish
    (sturgeon) prized for its caviar
[!] Avoid starting sentences with coord. conjunctions
[!] Disguised #2 (*During, In,* or *At* that time period)
Comma not needed after #2 SO of 4 words or fewer
[!] Use commas around nonessential phrases (2 here)
[!] Invisible *who* clause: "kitchen, who was the Iron"
[!] Comma splice: needs period, not comma (2 MC)
Snuck is also correct but *sneaked* preferred
Dress-ups: quality adjectives; adv. clause; strong verb

Week 3

King Mortons greatest **mortification** had occured 2 years earlier at a dinner party for the ambassador of nordicland. Taking an instant dislike to the ambassadors son whom, truth be told, was a bit of a brat Dorinda squirted mouthwash into his sturgeon roe soup from a travel bottle she carried in her purse.

[1] King Morton's greatest mortification had occurred two years earlier at a dinner party for the Ambassador of Nordicland. [4] Taking an instant dislike to the ambassador's son, <u>who</u>, truth be told, was a bit of a brat, Dorinda <u>squirted</u> mouthwash into his sturgeon roe soup from a travel bottle she carried in her purse.

Mortification: a feeling of humiliation or shame
Indent ¶ (flashback)
Use apostrophes to show possession (twice)
Spelling: *occurred*
Spell out numbers written as one or two words
Capitalize titles and proper nouns
[!] Use *who* for nominative case (*he* was, so *who*)
Use commas after #4 SO (-ing phrase)
Use commas to set off most who/which clauses
[!] "truth be told" nonessential, so commas correct
Dress-ups: who clause; strong verb

Despite the fact that the youngster from nordicland felt quite **queasy** she had no mercy. During the obligatory dance following the dinner rapidly and repeatedly she twirled him around. Last scene, he was rushing to the royal restroom's noticeably green.

[2] Despite the fact that the youngster from Nordicland felt quite <u>queasy</u>, she had no mercy. [2] During the <u>obligatory</u> dance following the dinner, <u>rapidly and repeatedly</u> she <u>twirled</u> him around. Last seen, he was <u>rushing</u> to the royal restroom, <u>noticeably</u> green.

Queasy: feeling sick to the stomach; nauseous
Capitalize proper nouns
Commas needed after #2 SOs of 5+ words (twice)
Homophone: scene/seen
Restroom should be singular, not possessive
[!] Use commas to set off nonessential phrases
[!] Alliteration: quite queasy; rapidly and repeatedly; rushing to the royal restroom
[!] Advanced style: dual -ly adverbs
Dress-ups: quality adj's; strong verbs; -ly adverb

Threatening to **sever** diplomatic ties the Ambassador quit the palace the following morning in a fury. As he expressed it to his attaché the King can hardly run a country if he can't rule his own daughter

[4] Threatening to <u>sever</u> <u>diplomatic</u> ties, the ambassador <u>quit</u> the palace the following morning in a fury. [5] As he expressed it to his attaché, "The king can hardly run a country <u>if</u> he can't rule his own daughter."

Sever: break off or dissolve; cut off
Indent ¶ (new speaker)
Use commas after #4 SO (-ing phrase)
Use lc for titles without a name (twice)
Use commas after #5 Sentence Openers and to set up direct quotation
Use quotation marks with direct quotations
Capitalize the first word of a quoted sentence
Use a period at end of statements
Dress-ups: strong verbs; quality adj.; adverb clause

King Morton still blushed when he recalled that day, it took several months' of **diplomatic** negotiations to smooth over the episode. Worst Dorinda never seemed to understand that she was responsible.

[1] King Morton still <u>blushed</u> <u>when</u> he recalled that day. [1] It took several months of diplomatic negotiations to smooth over the episode. Worse, Dorinda never seemed to understand that she was responsible.

Diplomatic: skillful, tactful in handling negotiations and other relations with foreign countries
Indent ¶ (new topic)
[!] Comma splice: needs period, not comma (2 MC)
Months is plural, not possessive
Use *worse* since only 2 things are compared
Use comma after introductory transitional expression
Dress-ups: strong verb; adverb clause

Week 4

Older now, Princess Dorinda had earned a name for beauty reaching into the furthest kingdoms. With the latest fad—a beauty spot—perched high on her cheek, and her hair twisted into a powdered **pompadour** Princess Dorinda fancied herself quiet chic.

Older now, Princess Dorinda had earned a name for beauty reaching into the farthest kingdoms. [2] With the latest fad—a beauty spot—<u>perched</u> high on her cheek and her hair <u>twisted</u> into a powdered pompadour, Princess Dorinda <u>fancied</u> herself quite <u>chic</u>.

Pompadour: woman's hairstyle in which her hair is raised over her forehead in a roll; a puffy hairstyle
Indent ¶ (new time and new topic)
Usage: *furthest/farthest* (use *farthest* for distances)
[!] Note use of em-dashes to draw attention
No comma before *and* to join 2 items in a series (fad … and … hair)
Comma needed after #2 SO of 5 or more words (ends after *pompadour*)
Spelling: *quite*, not *quiet*
Dress-ups: strong verbs; quality adjective

Alas her beauty was flawed by her reputation for **finickiness**, and, dare I mention it, self-centeredness. Time and again king Morton had urged her to consider 1 or another young suitor, time and again she had refused all the eligible, young men.

[T] Alas, her beauty was <u>flawed</u> by her reputation for finickiness and, dare I mention it, self-centeredness. Time and again King Morton had <u>urged</u> her to consider one or another young suitor. Time and again she had refused all the <u>eligible</u> young men.

Finickiness: being difficult to please
Indent ¶ (new topic)
Use comma after introductory interjection
No comma before *and* to join 2 items in a series (here, 2 objects of a prep.: finickiness and self-c.)
Capitalize titles used with names
Spell out numbers written as one or two words
[!] Comma splice: needs period, not comma (2 MC)
[!] No commas with cumulative adjectives
Dress-ups: strong verbs; quality adjective

None are wealthy enough, or titled enough to suite her all too high Highness. During these reflections, King Morton shakes his head in **abject** despair dislodging his jewel encrusted crown.

[1] None were wealthy enough or titled enough to suit her all-too-high Highness. [2] During these reflections, King Morton shook his head in <u>abject</u> despair, <u>dislodging</u> his <u>jewel-encrusted</u> crown.

Abject: utterly hopeless; miserable
Don't switch tenses
No comma before *or* to join 2 items in a series (adj's)
Usage: *suite/suit* confusion
Join words w/ a hyphen that function as a single adj.
[!] Use commas to set off nonessential phrases
Dress-ups: quality adjectives

He wasn't the only 1 clucking his tongue in **consternation** over princess Dorinda, lady Constance her elder companion since childhood had virtually given up on training her young charge in true, courtly behavior.

[1] He wasn't the only one <u>clucking</u> his tongue in consternation over Princess Dorinda. [1] Lady <u>Constance,</u> her elder companion since childhood, had virtually given up on training her young charge in true <u>courtly</u> behavior.

Consternation: dismay; alarm; horror
Indent ¶ (new topic)
Spell out numbers written as one or two words
Capitalize titles used with names
[!] Comma splice: needs period, not comma (2 MC)
[!] Use commas around nonessential phrases
[!] No commas with cumulative adjectives
Dress-ups: strong verb; [!] invisible *who* clause: "Constance, who was"; quality adj. (*courtly*)

Week 5

Years of indulgence had spoiled her beyond recognition however she recalled a time in her childhood when her charge had seemed a lovable **tractable** and contented child.

[1] Years of indulgence had spoiled her beyond recognition. [T] However, Lady Constance recalled a time in Dorinda's childhood <u>when</u> her charge had seemed a lovable, <u>tractable,</u> and contented child.

Tractable: easily controlled; manageable; willing
Fused: use a period to separate 2 main clauses
Use commas after introductory transitional words
[!] Pronouns *she* and *her*: unclear antecedents
Use commas with 3 or more items in a series
Dress-ups: adverb clause; quality adjective

She use to bring pictures she had drawn two Lady Constance and she had cuddled in her lap in the evenings. Sadly, when Dorindas mother was alive no expense had been spared too **gratify** the princess's.

[1] She used to bring pictures she had drawn to Lady Constance, and she had <u>cuddled</u> in her lap in the evenings.

    [3] Sadly, <u>when</u> Dorinda's mother was alive, no expense had been spared to gratify the princesses.

Gratify: indulge; give pleasure to
Indent ¶, 2nd part (new topic)
Usage: *use/used* confusion; *two/too/to* (twice)
Compound sentence needs comma: MC, cc MC
Use apostrophes to show possession
Use commas after #5 SO (here, the intro adverb
    clause immediately follows the -ly adverb)
Princesses is plural, not possessive
Dress-up: strong verb; adverb clause

No extravagance was to grate: Disneys Princess Castle Ground became thier playground, they each owned a personal set of the European Girl dolls and thier friends, with thier complete wardrobes, and **ubiquitous** furniture and accessories.

[1] No extravagance was too great: Disney's Princess Castle Ground became their playground; they each owned a personal set of the European Girl dolls and their friends, with their complete wardrobes and <u>ubiquitous</u> furniture and accessories.

Ubiquitous: being everywhere at the same time
Homophone: to/too; grate/great
[!] Note correct use of colon (see Appendix)
Use apostrophes to show possession
Spelling: *their* (an exception to the "*i* before *e*" rule)
Use semicolons to separate 2 main clauses
No comma before *and* to join 2 items in a series
Dress-ups: quality adjective

Shaking her head in dismay Lady Constance one day clucked to Lady Inwaiting its no wonder that child has turned out so **blemished.** *[quotation continues]*

    [4] Shaking her head in dismay, Lady Constance one day <u>clucked</u> to Lady Inwaiting, "It's no wonder that child has turned out so <u>blemished</u>. *[quotation continues]*

Blemished: marred or spoiled by imperfections
Indent ¶ (new speaker)
Use commas after #4 SO (-ing phrase)
Use comma with verb of speaking & direct quotation
Use quotation marks with direct quotations
Capitalize 1st word of a quoted sentence. *It's = it is*
Dress-ups: strong verb; quality adjective

Week 6

She had only too pout that her plasma TV was **minuscule**, and queen Magnifica told the Palace Accountant too order her a projection TV, complete with multimedia accessory's two.

[1] She had only to <u>pout</u> that her plasma TV was <u>miniscule</u>, and Queen Magnifica told the palace accountant to order her a projection TV, complete with multimedia accessories, too."

Minuscule: very small
No open " " b/c quotation continues, but close "
Homophone: too/to/two (three times)
Use UC for titles w/ names, lc for titles w/o a name
Accessories is plural, not possessive
Use commas to set off transitional words
Dress-ups: strong verb; quality adjective

Although they agonized, and **fretted** Princess Dorindas companions saw no remedy. One crisp spring morning when the cherry blossoms were just beginning to appear Princess Dorinda was distracted by her latest plaything a golden ball.

[5] Although they <u>agonized and fretted</u>, Princess Dorinda's companions saw no remedy.

    [2] One <u>crisp</u> spring morning <u>when</u> the cherry blossoms were just beginning to appear, Princess Dorinda was <u>distracted</u> by her latest plaything, a golden ball.

Fretted: felt worry or annoyance
Indent ¶, 2nd part (time has passed)
No comma before *and* to join 2 items in a series
Use commas after #5 Sentence Openers
Use apostrophe to show possession
[!] Disguised #2 (*During, In,* or *At* that time period)
[!] No comma b/t "crisp" & "spring": cumulative adj.
Comma needed after several introductory elements
[!] Use commas to set off nonessential phrases
Dress-ups: dual verbs; quality adj.; adverb clause

She tossed it up as she wandered between the exotic, botanical species in the regal conservatory. Where her father had found haven from his **monarchial** cares

[1] She tossed it up <u>as</u> she wandered among the <u>exotic</u> botanical species in the regal conservatory, <u>where</u> her father had found haven from his <u>monarchial</u> cares.

Monarchial: pertaining to a monarch (king)
Use *between* to compare 2 items; *among*, 3 or more
[!] No commas with cumulative adjectives
Correct fragment by joining DC to MC
[!] Comma: "where…" is a nonessential adj. clause
Use a period at end of statements
Dress-ups: adverb clauses; quality adjectives

Eyeing with **trepidation** the glass windows surrounding them King Morton suggested why don't you toss that ball out in the garden

[4] Eyeing with trepidation the glass windows surrounding them, King Morton suggested, "Why don't you toss that ball out in the garden?"

Trepidation: alarm; agitation
Indent ¶ (new speaker)
Use commas after #4 SO (-ing phrase)
Use comma with verb of speaking & direct quotation
Use quotation marks with direct quotations
Capitalize the first word of a quoted sentence
Use a question mark after question (inside " ")

Week 7

"Sweet" Princess Dorinda responded not noticing her fathers grimace. "Its like nice enough outside you know. Might be a like cool idea." "Precisely." What else could he say to such **twaddle**

"Sweet," Princess Dorinda responded, not noticing her father's grimace. "It's, like, nice enough outside, you know. Might be a, like, cool idea."
"Precisely." What else could he say to such twaddle?

Twaddle: trivial, silly talk; drivel
Indent ¶ (new speakers)
Use comma with verb of speaking & direct quotation
[!] Use commas around nonessential phrases and to avoid confusion (*responded not*, or *not noticing*?)
Use apostrophes to show possession
It's = it is
Use commas to set off interrupters (*like, you know*)
Legal fragments (casual conversation)
Use a question mark after a question

Beyond the imperial patio Princess Dorinda **meandered** aimlessly through the stately gardens tossing her ball up up up yet again, and catching it repeatedly with slick confidence.

[2] Beyond the imperial patio, Princess Dorinda <u>meandered</u> <u>aimlessly</u> through the <u>stately</u> gardens, tossing her ball up, up, up yet again and catching it <u>repeatedly</u> with <u>slick</u> confidence.

Meandered: rambled; took a winding course
Indent ¶ (new scene)
Comma optional after #2 SO of 4 words or fewer
[!] Use commas to set off nonessential phrases
Use commas with 3 or more items in a series
No comma before *and* to join 2 items in a series (tossing … and catching)
Dress-ups: strong verb; -ly adv.; adj's (*stately*=adj.)

At the corner of the well however a most regrettable event **transpired**. Up went her golden ball, then down with a splash, because she failed to catch it the heavy orb sinked to the bottom of the well

[2] At the corner of the well, however, a most <u>regrettable</u> event <u>transpired</u>. Up went her golden ball, then down with a splash. [5] Because she failed to catch it, the heavy orb sank to the bottom of the well.

Transpired: took place; occurred
Use commas around transitional words and after long introductory prepositional phrases (#2 SO)
[!] Comma splice: needs period, not comma (2 MC)
Use commas after #5 Sentence Openers
Usage: *Sank* is the past of *sink*
Use a period at end of statements
Dress-ups: quality adjective; strong verb

Tears flowed **copiously** and huge drops splashed her golden dress. "Ooh my golden baaall! Dorinda wailed if only I could have my ball back I would bestow a handsome reward on my benefactor!"

[6] Tears flowed <u>copiously</u>. [1] Huge drops <u>splashed</u> her golden dress.

   "Ooh, my golden baaall!" Dorinda <u>wailed</u>. [5] "If only I could have my ball back, I would <u>bestow</u> a <u>handsome</u> reward on my benefactor!"

Copiously: abundantly; plentifully
Indent ¶, 2nd part (new speaker)
Needs comma before cc to link 2 main clauses, but
   discuss poor choice of *and* to join clauses
Use commas after introductory interjections
Discuss quotation marks with interrupted speech
Acceptable fragment: "Ooh, my golden baaall!"
Capitalize the first word of a quoted sentence
Use commas after #5 Sentence Openers
Dress-ups: -ly adverb; strong verbs; quality adjective

Week 8

If you would permit me madam I should be honored to rescue your plaything", a **throaty** voice offered. And Dorindas tears dried instantly as she looked around for the person belonging to the voice.

   [5] "If you would <u>permit</u> me, Madam, I should be <u>honored</u> to <u>rescue</u> your plaything," a <u>throaty</u> voice offered.
   [1] Dorinda's tears dried <u>instantly</u> <u>as</u> she looked around for the person belonging to the voice.

Throaty: husky; hoarse; guttural
Indent ¶ (new speaker; new topic)
Open quotation with quotation marks
Use commas after #5 Sentence Openers
Comma: NDA (Madam) & UC titles used as NDAs
Periods and commas go inside quotation marks
[!] Avoid starting sentences with coord. conjunctions
Use apostrophes to show possession
Dress-ups: strong verbs and adj.; -ly adv.; adv. clause

A little flustered when sighting no one, she inquired "pray tell, who has **tendered** such a thoughtful offer Groomed in courtly speech Dorinda could talk as a princess when convenient.

[7] A little <u>flustered</u> <u>when</u> sighting no one, she <u>inquired</u>, "Pray tell, <u>who</u> has <u>tendered</u> such a thoughtful offer?" [7] Groomed in <u>courtly</u> speech, Dorinda could talk like a princess <u>when</u> <u>convenient</u>.

Tendered: offered formally
Use comma with verb of speaking & direct quotation
Capitalize the first word of a quoted sentence
Use a question mark after a question
[!] Use commas after #7 Sentence Openers (-ed)
Usage: *like* vs. *as*
Dress-ups: quality adjectives; adverb clauses;
   strong verbs; who clause

When a slimy putrid green amphibian hopped toward her on the rim of the well, croaking, "It was me Dorinda let lose a spine tingling shriek and nearly ran away, her **inquisitiveness** got the better of her however.

   [5] When a <u>slimy</u>, <u>putrid-green</u> amphibian hopped toward her on the rim of the well, croaking, "It was I," Dorinda let loose a <u>spine-tingling</u> shriek and nearly ran away.
   [1] Her inquisitiveness got the better of her, however.

Inquisitiveness: a state of active curiosity
Indent ¶ (new speaker; new topic)
Use commas with coordinate adjectives
Join words w/ a hyphen that function as a single adj.
[!] Use *I* for predicate nominatives, not *me*
Spelling: *loose*, not *lose*
[!] Comma splice: needs period, not comma (2 MC)
Use commas to set off transitional words
Dress-ups: quality adjectives

"How is it you can talk Mr Frog" "Its a dull story but maybe I'll tell it to you one day, for the present, would you like me to **salvage** your ball?"

"How is it you can talk, Mr. Frog?"
   [1] "It's a dull story, but maybe I'll tell it to you one day. [2] For the present, would you like me to <u>salvage</u> your ball?"

Salvage: to save from loss (strong verb)
Indent ¶, 2nd part (new speaker)
Comma: NDA (Mr. Frog)
Use periods after abbreviations
Use a question mark after a question
It's = it is
Compound sentence needs comma: MC, cc MC
[!] Comma splice: needs period, not comma (2 MC)

Week 9

"Oh yes **benevolent** frog!" (Notice that in fairy tales, character's don't have great curiosity about such oddities as talking frogs—or, maybe Dorinda was to self-centered to think about any one other than her.

[T] "Oh, yes, benevolent frog!"
(Notice that in fairy tales, characters don't have great curiosity about such oddities as talking frogs—or maybe Dorinda was too self-centered to think about anyone other than herself.)

Benevolent: charitable; kindly
Indent ¶ (new speaker; new topic)
Use commas to set off transitions and interjections
Characters is plural, not possessive
[!] Use em-dashes to indicate a break in thought
No comma after cc's, sometimes before
Usage: *to/too; her/herself; anyone* is one word
Close parentheses
Dress-ups: quality adjectives
Note: SO #1 no longer marked; continue if needed

"I'll gladly do so, with one **stipulation** the frog responded. "Anything! My dad'll kill me if I loose that ball, which cost him a Royal Fortune. Its gold you know.

"I'll gladly do so, with one stipulation," the frog responded.
"Anything! My dad'll kill me if I lose that ball, which cost him a royal fortune. It's gold, you know."

Stipulation: condition; demand
Indent ¶ (new speakers)
Use comma with verb of speaking & direct quotation
Close quotations with quotation marks
Usage: *loose/lose; its/it's* (*dad'll* okay, colloquialism)
Use lc for common nouns (royal fortune)
Use commas to set off interrupters (you know)
Dress-ups: adverb clause; which clause

"Well I didn't know anything of the sort but I do think I could **dexterously** retrieve it. Here are my terms I'll bring you the ball if you'll treat me at your table in the castle let me dine from your very own plate and allow me to dwell one night in the palace".

[T] "Well, I didn't know anything of the sort, but I do think I could dexterously retrieve it. Here are my terms: I'll bring you the ball if you'll treat me at your table in the castle, let me dine from your very own plate, and allow me to dwell one night in the palace."

Dexterously: skillfully (in using his hands)
Indent ¶ (new speaker)
[!] Transitional Opener [T]
Use commas after introductory transitions
Compound sentence needs comma: MC, cc MC
[!] Use colon after MC to introduce a list or give an explanation
[!] No comma w/ mid-sentence adv. clause ("if…")
Use commas with 3 or more items in a series
Periods and commas go inside quotation marks
Dress-ups: -ly adverb; adverb clause; strong verb

Sure thing Dorinda responds hastily perhaps a little to **curtly**. With that, the frog hops back into the water disappears four a few moments then returns, panting as only frogs can pant with the ball.

"Sure thing," Dorinda responded hastily, perhaps a little too curtly.
[2] With that, the frog hopped back into the water, disappeared for a few moments, then returned with the ball, panting as only frogs can pant.

Curtly: briefly, to the point of rudeness
Indent ¶ (new speaker; new topic)
Use quotation marks with direct quotations
Use comma with verb of speaking & direct quotation
Don't switch tenses
[!] Use commas to set off nonessential phrases
Homophones: to/too; four/for
Use commas with 3 or more items in a series
Misplaced prep. phrase (he's not panting w/ the ball)
Dress-ups: -ly adverbs; adverb clause

Week 10

You didnt tell me it was solid gold he **wheezed**. Princess Dorinda didnt hear him, she had all ready skipped back to the palace, tickled with the return of her treasure.

"You didn't tell me it was solid gold," he wheezed.
Princess Dorinda didn't hear him. She had already skipped back to the palace, tickled with the return of her treasure.

Wheezed: breathed w/ difficulty & a whistling sound
Indent ¶, 2nd part (new topic)
Use quotation marks with direct quotations
Use apostrophes in contractions
Use comma with verb of speaking & direct quotation
[!] Comma splice: needs period, not comma (2 MC)
Usage: *all ready* should be *already*
Dress-ups: strong verbs; quality adjective

That evening while the royal family dined **sumptuously** they heard a faint tapping at the castle door, moments later, the footman appeared, with a message for Princess Dorinda.

[2] That evening <u>while</u> the royal family dined <u>sumptuously</u>, they heard a <u>faint</u> tapping at the castle door. Moments later, the footman appeared with a message for Princess Dorinda.

Sumptuously: magnificently; luxuriously
Indent ¶ (time has passed)
Use commas after long introductory elements (here, a disguised #2 followed by an adverb clause)
[!] Comma splice: needs period, not comma (2 MC)
[!] No commas with essential phrases ("with …")
Dress-ups: adverb clause; -ly adverb; quality adj.

"Princess" he began. You have a visitor at the door excusing herself from the table Dorinda hastened away. When she opened the door however blood drained from her face, their squatted the **forbearing** frog.

"Princess," he began, "you have a visitor at the door."
[4] Excusing herself from the table, Dorinda <u>hastened</u> away. [5] When she opened the door, however, blood <u>drained</u> from her face. There <u>squatted</u> the <u>forbearing</u> frog.

Forbearing: patient & self-controlled when provoked
Indent ¶, 2nd part (new topic)
Use commas w/ verb of speaking & direct quotation
Use " and lc to continue interrupted quotations
Fused: use a period to separate 2 main clauses
Use commas after #4 SO (-ing phrase)
Use commas after #5 Sentence Openers & transitions
[!] Comma splice: needs period, not comma (2 MC)
Homophone: *their/there*
Dress-ups: strong verbs; quality adjective

"You forgot you're pledge to treat me **hospitably** at the palace" he croaked she slammed the door in his face. Dorinda who was at the door, King Morton inquired when she returned to the table.

"You forgot your pledge to treat me <u>hospitably</u> at the palace," he <u>croaked</u>.
She <u>slammed</u> the door in his face.
"Dorinda, <u>who</u> was at the door?" King Morton <u>inquired</u> <u>when</u> she returned to the table.

Hospitably: treating guests warmly and generously
Indent ¶ (new topic; new speaker)
Your is the possessive; *you're = you are*
Use comma with verb of speaking & direct quotation
Fused: use a period to separate 2 main clauses
Use quotation marks with direct quotations
Comma: NDA (Dorinda)
Use a question mark after a question
Dress-ups: -ly adverb; strong verbs; who clause, adverb clause

---

Week 11

Dorinda may have had her **deficiencies** but she did tell the truth when asked directly "A frog". "What did he want"?

Dorinda may have had her deficiencies, but she did tell the truth when asked <u>directly</u>. "A frog."
"What did he want?"

Deficiencies: inadequacies; faults
Indent ¶ (new speakers)
Compound sentence needs comma: MC, cc MC
Use a period at end of statements
Periods and commas go inside quotation marks
Question inside " " if part of quoted material
Dress-up: -ly adverb

(Now you and me might have trouble with King Mortons **rejoinder**—why didn't he think it unusual that a frog would knock at the castle door? but remember, this is a fairy tale which is allowed to be bizarre.

(Now you and I might have trouble with King Morton's rejoinder—why didn't he think it unusual that a frog would knock at the castle door?—but remember, this is a fairy tale, <u>which</u> is allowed to be <u>bizarre</u>.)

Rejoinder: response; answer to a reply
Indent ¶ (new topic)
Usage: *I*, not *me* (Now *we* might …, so *I*)
Use apostrophes to show possession
[!] Complete em-dashes to indicate a break in thought
Note: " ? " or " ! " may be used with a dash
Use commas to set off most who/which clauses
Close parentheses
Dress-ups: which clause; quality adjective

Gushing tears yet again which Dorinda could **expediently** turn on and off like a faucet she sobbed the story of the frogs rescue of her ball, and the promises she had foolishly made.

[4] Gushing tears yet again, <u>which</u> Dorinda could <u>expediently</u> turn on and off like a faucet, she <u>sobbed</u> the story of the frog's rescue of her ball and the promises she had <u>foolishly</u> made.

Expediently: to her advantage; out of self-interest
Indent ¶ (new topic)
Use commas after #4 SO (-ing phrase)
Use commas to set off most who/which clauses
[!] Simile: "like a faucet"
Frogs is possessive, not plural
No comma before *and* to join 2 items in a series
Dress-ups: which clause; -ly adverbs; strong verb

Surely you wouldn't make me like, touch that slimy, old thing? she groaned **piteously**. "Daughter you are a royal princess, your word, of all peoples, must be trustworthy.

[3] "Surely you wouldn't make me like, touch that <u>slimy</u> old thing?" she <u>groaned</u> piteously.
"Daughter, you are a royal princess. Your word, of all people's, must be <u>trustworthy</u>."

Piteously: sorrowfully; in a way that arouses pity
Indent ¶, 2nd part (new speaker)
Use quotation marks with direct quotations
[!] No commas with cumulative adjectives
Comma: NDA (Daughter)
[!] Comma splice: needs period, not comma (2 MC)
People's is possessive (of all people's words)
Dress-ups: quality adjectives; strong verb; -ly adverb

Week 12

Princess Dorinda reluctantly slank to the door and opened it a crack just wide enough for the frog to squeeze through. I guess you can come in she sighed **audibly**.

Princess Dorinda <u>reluctantly</u> <u>slunk</u> to the door and opened it a crack, just wide enough for the frog to <u>squeeze</u> through. "I guess you can come in," she <u>sighed</u> audibly.

Audibly: loudly enough to be heard
Indent ¶ (new topic)
Spelling: *slunk* is preferred but *slinked* is also correct
[!] Use commas to set off nonessential phrases
Use quotation marks with direct quotations
Use comma with verb of speaking & direct quotation
Dress-ups: -ly adverbs; strong verbs

Hopping, she let him traipse behind her to the **resplendent** dinning hall. "Thank you for you're hospitality sire I'm Arthur," the frog introduced himself.

[4] Hopping, he <u>traipsed</u> behind her to the <u>resplendent</u> dining hall.
"Thank you for your hospitality, Sire. I'm Arthur," the frog introduced himself.

Resplendent: splendid; magnificent; dazzling
Indent ¶, 2nd part (new speaker)
[!] Illegal #4: word after " , " should do the *inging*
Spelling: *dining*, not *dinning*
Homophone: you're/your
Capitalize titles when used as NDAs
Comma: NDA (Sire)
Fused: use a period to separate 2 main clauses
Dress-ups: strong verb; quality adjective

Dorinda, her father commanded Pick Arthur up and let him feast **unstintingly** from you're golden plate. Yuck I won't touch another bite she moaned again. "Be that as it may— a promise is a promise," King Morton reminded him.

"Dorinda," her father <u>commanded</u>, "pick Arthur up and let him feast <u>unstintingly</u> from your golden plate."
"Yuck! I won't touch another bite," she <u>moaned</u> again.
"Be that as it may—a promise is a promise," King Morton reminded her.

Unstintingly: in a generous manner
Indent ¶ (new speakers)
Use quotation marks with direct quotations
Use comma with verb of speaking & direct quotation
Use lc to continue interrupted quotations
Homophone: you're/your
Exclamation marks may follow intro. interjections
Her, not *him* (he's speaking to Dorinda)
Dress-ups: strong verbs; -ly adverb

Now, what Dorinda Maribella and King Morton did not divine was that Arthur was not truely a frog, but a prince! *You* may have **surmised** this all ready but they hadnt read any fairy tales lately.

[T] Now, what Dorinda, Maribella, and King Morton did not <u>divine</u> was that Arthur was not truly a frog, but a prince! *You* may have <u>surmised</u> this already, but they hadn't read any fairy tales lately.

Surmised: guessed
Indent ¶ (new topic)
[!] Transitional Opener [T]
Use commas with 3 or more items in a series
Spelling: *truly*
Usage: *all ready/already*
Compound sentence needs comma: MC, cc MC
Use apostrophes in contractions
Dress-ups: strong verbs

Week 13

When he was a teenager sad to say Arthur was a bit swollen-headed and **pretentious**. One humid afternoon in July young Arthur was riding through a forest in his fathers kingdom, seeking some shady relief from the sweltering sun.

[5] When he was a teenager, sad to say, Arthur was a bit <u>swollen-headed</u> and <u>pretentious</u>. [2] One <u>humid</u> afternoon in July, young Arthur was riding through a forest in his father's kingdom, seeking some <u>shady</u> relief from the <u>sweltering</u> sun.

Pretentious: showy; pompous; self-important
Indent ¶ (new topic)
Use commas after #5 Sentence Openers
[!] Use commas around nonessential phrases
Comma needed after disguised #2 SO of 5+ words
Use apostrophes to show possession
[!] Alliteration: seeking some shady…sweltering sun
Dress-ups: quality adjectives

About halfway through the forest his horse reared up, startled, a young boy stood in the path. "Please sir I've lost my way", the boy pleaded would you kindly give me a ride out of this **desolate** forest

[2] About halfway through the forest, his horse <u>reared</u> up, <u>startled</u>. A young boy stood in the path. "Please, sir, I've lost my way," the boy <u>pleaded</u>. "Would you <u>kindly</u> give me a ride out of this <u>desolate</u> forest?"

Desolate: uninhabited; dreary; gloomy; lonely
Comma needed after #2 SO of 5 or more words
[!] Comma splice: needs period, not comma (2 MC)
Set off NDAs with commas (sir)
Periods and commas go inside quotation marks
Fused: use a period to separate 2 main clauses
Use quotation marks with quotations; question at end
Dress-ups: strong verbs; quality adj's; -ly adverb

Out of my way peasant the prince retorted, **oblivious** that the boy was a magician in disguise, instantly the boys voice thundered For you're lack of compassion and courtesy, you must spend your days as a frog.

"Out of my way, peasant," the prince <u>retorted</u>, <u>oblivious</u> that the boy was a magician in disguise.
[3] Instantly the boy's voice <u>thundered</u>, "For your lack of compassion and courtesy, you must spend your days as a frog."

Oblivious: unaware
Indent ¶ (new speakers)
Use quotation marks with direct quotations
Commas: NDA (peasant)
[!] Comma splice: needs period, not comma (2 MC)
Use apostrophes to show possession
Use comma with verb of speaking & direct quotation
Homophone: you're/your
Dress-ups: strong verbs; quality adjective

He zapped the air and the prince found himself hoping off the saddle, and **plummeting** onto the ground. The magician continued "perhaps as a frog you will learn humility and gratitude for simple kindness's people might offer you
[quotation continues]

He <u>zapped</u> the air, and the prince found himself hopping off the saddle and <u>plummeting</u> onto the ground. The magician continued, "Perhaps as a frog you will learn humility and gratitude for simple kindnesses people might offer you.
[quotation continues]

Plummeting: falling straight down; plunging
Use comma before cc to link 2 main clauses
Spelling: *hopping*
No comma before *and* to join 2 compound verbs
Use comma with verb of speaking & direct quotation
Capitalize the first word of a quoted sentence
Kindnesses is plural, not possessive
Use a period at end of statements
No close quotation marks b/c quotation continues
Dress-ups: strong verbs

Week 14

You will remain in this form, until a princess **bestows** on you a kiss, in true kindheartedness. However if you should ever tell anyone which you really are you will be fated to frog-hood the remainder of your days".

You will remain in this form <u>until</u> a princess <u>bestows</u> on you a kiss in true kindheartedness. [T,5] However, if you should ever tell anyone <u>who</u> you really are, you will be fated to frog-hood the remainder of your days."

Bestows: presents as a gift or honor
Continue quotation where the last sentence left off (no opening quotation marks)
[!] No commas with essential clauses and phrases
Use commas after introductory transitions & #5 SOs
Use *who* for people, *which* for things
Periods and commas go inside quotation marks
[!] Alliteration: fated to frog-hood
Dress-ups: adverb clause; strong verb; who clause

The frog had born his secret for 6 long years. Having come to reside in King Mortons **sequestered** garden he hoped he might make friends one day with one of the princess's who frequently wandered into the garden.

The frog had <u>borne</u> his secret for six long years. [4] Having come to <u>reside</u> in King Morton's <u>sequestered</u> garden, he hoped to make friends one day with one of the princesses, <u>who</u> <u>frequently</u> <u>wandered</u> into the garden.

Sequestered: providing privacy
Indent ¶ (time has passed)
Usage: *born/borne* confusion
Spell out numbers written as one or two words
Use apostrophes to show possession
Use commas after #4 SO (-ing phrase)
Princesses is plural, not possessive
Use commas to set off most who/which clauses
Dress-ups: strong verbs & adj.; who clause; -ly adv.

Just his luck the one he met 1st was Dorinda instead of Maribella. And now at the table he **conjectured** how he might charm the Princess.

[T] Just his luck, the one he met first was Dorinda instead of Maribella. [T,2] Now at the table, he <u>conjectured</u> how he might <u>charm</u> the princess.

Conjectured: formed a theory; guessed
[!] Transitional Openers (mark as [T])
Use commas after introductory transitional phrases
Spell out ordinal numbers
[!] Avoid starting sentences with coord. conjunctions
Use lc for titles without a name
Dress-ups: strong verbs

Unwilling to touch the frog with her own precious fingers Dorinda held her napkin between her thumb and first finger, then **unceremoniously** grabbed 1 of Arthurs hind legs. Depositing him on the table beside her plate.

[4] Unwilling to touch the frog with her own <u>precious</u> fingers, Dorinda held her napkin between her thumb and first finger, then <u>unceremoniously</u> <u>grabbed</u> one of Arthur's hind legs, <u>depositing</u> him on the table beside her plate.

Unceremoniously: abruptly, without ceremony
Indent ¶ (new topic)
Use commas after #4 SO (-ing phrase)
Spell out numbers written as one or two words
Use apostrophes to show possession
Correct fragment by joining phrase to main clause
Dress-ups: quality adjectives; -ly adverb; strong verb (advanced: *depositing* functions as an adjective, modifying *Dorinda*)

Week 15

She scrunched back into her chair as far as she could since he had never lost his taste for princely, but appetizing fare Arthur politely declined the main course, sturgeon roe **fricassee**.

She <u>scrunched</u> back into her chair as far as she could. [5] Since he had never lost his taste for princely but <u>appetizing</u> fare, Arthur <u>politely</u> <u>declined</u> the main <u>course,</u> <u>sturgeon</u> roe fricassee.

Fricassee: meat served with a sauce (fish eggs only marginally count as meat, indicating poor cuisine)
Indent ¶, 2nd part (new topic)
Fused: use a period to separate 2 main clauses
No comma before but to join 2 items in a series
Use commas after #5 Sentence Openers
Dress-ups: strong verbs; quality adjective; -ly adverb
[!] Find the invisible w/w: "course, which was …"

I'll go for just deserts he requested, eying with glee the side cart piled high with **delectable** tarts scones pies cobblers and cheesecakes.

"I'll go for just desserts," he requested, <u>eying</u> with glee the side cart piled high with <u>delectable</u> tarts, scones, pies, cobblers, and cheesecakes.

Delectable: delicious
Use quotation marks with direct quotations
Note pun on title & spelling confusion: *just deserts = deserved reward; just desserts = only dessert*
Use comma with verb of speaking & direct quotation
Use commas with 3 or more items in a series
Dress-ups: quality adjectives (advanced: *eying* functions as an adjective, modifying *he*)

After supper, King Morton **peremptorily** ordered Dorinda too set up Arthur in the Golden Guestroom. Velvet carpeted the floor silk blanketed the bed. He could tell he was going too relish his palace stay

[2] After supper King Morton <u>peremptorily</u> ordered Dorinda to set up Arthur in the Golden Guestroom. Velvet <u>carpeted</u> the floor; silk <u>blanketed</u> the bed. Arthur could tell he was going to <u>relish</u> his palace stay.

Peremptorily: without room for refusal; imperiously
Indent ¶ (time has passed and new scene)
Comma not needed after #2 SO of 4 words or fewer
Homophones: *too/to*
Use semicolons to separate 2 main clauses
[!] Unclear antecedent: is *he* Arthur or the king?
Use a period at end of statements
Dress-ups: -ly adverb; strong verbs

The next a.m., during a **substantial** breakfast of sturgeon roe omelet King Morton graciously insists Arthur stay at least a week.

[2] The next morning during a <u>substantial</u> breakfast of sturgeon roe omelet, King Morton <u>graciously</u> insisted Arthur stay at least a week.

Substantial: of ample or considerable quantity
Indent ¶ (time has passed)
Usage: use words instead of casual abbreviations
[!] With several intro. phrases, comma after last only
Don't switch tenses
Dress-ups: quality adjective; -ly adverb

Week 16

Dorinda groaned and glancing down she noticed Arthurs hind leg **inadvertently** touching her omelet. "Eww", she cried, sweeping him from her plate, and accidentally hurling him against the wall.

[6] Dorinda <u>groaned</u>. [4] Glancing down, she noticed Arthur's hind leg <u>inadvertently</u> touching her omelet. "Eww," she cried, <u>sweeping</u> him from her plate and <u>accidentally</u> <u>hurling</u> him against the wall.

Inadvertently: not intentionally
[!] Poor choice of *and* to join clauses
Use commas after #4 SO (-ing phrase)
Use apostrophes to show possession
Periods and commas go inside quotation marks
No comma before *and* to join 2 items in a series (sweeping … and … hurling)
Dress-ups: strong verb; -ly adverbs; quality adj's (advanced: *sweeping* and *hurling* are adj's here)

Oww grunted Arthur. Oops I do believe I've broken your leg, I'm *so* sorry!, Dorinda fibbed, "wish I had broken more than just your leg, she muttered **inaudibly**.

[6] "Oww!" <u>grunted</u> Arthur.
"Oops! I do believe I've broken your leg. I'm *so* sorry!" Dorinda <u>fibbed</u>. "Wish I had broken more than just your leg," she <u>muttered</u> <u>inaudibly</u>.

Inaudibly: not audibly (not able to be heard)
Indent ¶ (new speakers)
Use quotation marks with direct quotations
Exclamation marks can follow intro. interjections (commas would also be correct)
[!] Comma splice: needs period, not comma (2 MC)
[!] Do not use comma w/ an end mark of punctuation
Dress-ups: strong verbs; -ly adverb

Fortunately for Arthur, the palace vet knew how to set broken frog legs. It looks like it'll be a lengthy **convalescence** however he informed King Morton and his daughter. Because frog's are slow healers he'll have to stay in the infirmary for at least a month

[3] Fortunately for Arthur, the palace vet knew how to set broken frog legs. "It looks <u>as if</u> it'll be a <u>lengthy</u> convalescence, however," he informed King Morton and his daughter. [5] "Because frogs are slow healers, he'll have to stay in the infirmary for at least a month."

Convalescence: the time of gradual return to health
Indent ¶ (new topic)
Use quotation marks with direct quotations
[!] Usage: *like* vs. *as/as if*
Use commas to set off transitional words
Use comma with verb of speaking & direct quotation
Frogs is plural, not possessive
Use commas after #5 Sentence Openers
Use a period at end of statements
Dress-ups: adverb clause; quality adjective

What rotten luck, Dorinda thought to herself. Not only was he going to stick around but her father insisted she bring too him all his meals. Do whatever you can to make him comfortable while hes **recumbent** King Morton ordered.

"What rotten luck," Dorinda thought to herself.
Not only was he going to stick around, but her father insisted she bring to him all his meals. "Do whatever you can to make him comfortable <u>while</u> he's <u>recumbent</u>," King Morton ordered.

Recumbent: lying down; inactive
Indent ¶ (new topic; new topic & speaker)
Use quotation marks with direct quotations
   (advanced: thoughts are usually enclosed in " ")
Use comma before cc to link 2 main clauses
Homophone: too/to
Use apostrophes in contractions
Use comma with verb of speaking & direct quotation
Dress-ups: adverb clause; quality adjective

Week 17

"Cool" she cooed while wondering how to escape **infirmary** duty she may have to treat this slime-ball royally but she knew how to make herself a royal pain.

"Cool," she <u>cooed</u>, <u>while</u> wondering how to escape infirmary duty. She may have to treat this slime-ball <u>royally</u>, but she knew how to make herself a <u>royal</u> pain.

Infirmary: a place that cares for the sick or injured
Indent ¶ (new speaker)
Use comma with verb of speaking & direct quotation
[!] Use commas to set off contrasting adv. clauses
Fused: use a period to separate 2 main clauses
Compound sentence needs comma: MC, cc MC
Dress-ups: strong verb & adj.; adv. clause; -ly adverb

Offer to read to him—stories of his choice from the palace library, the King added. Not wanting to miss a **propitious** opportunity Arthur first selected the story of Jephthahs daughter.

"Offer to read to him—stories of his choice from the palace library," the king added.
[4] Not wanting to miss a <u>propitious</u> opportunity, Arthur first selected the story of Jephthah's daughter.

Propitious: favorable
Indent ¶ (new speaker; new topic)
Use quotation marks with direct quotations
[!] Use em-dashes to indicate a break in thought
Use lc for titles without a name
Use commas after #4 SO (-ing phrase)
Use apostrophes to show possession
Dress-ups: quality adjective

Now you may already know this story from the 11th chapter of the book of Judges. Although the Princess did not it seemed to Arthur **apropos**.

[T] Now, you may already know this story from the eleventh chapter of the book of Judges. [5] Although the princess did not, it seemed to Arthur <u>apropos</u>.

Apropos: fitting the circumstances well; pertinent
Use commas after introductory transitions
Spell out ordinal numbers
Use lc for titles without a name
Use commas after #5 Sentence Openers
Dress-ups: quality adjective

Jephthah had made an **impetuous** promise to God, that if he would give him victory in battle he would sacrifice the first thing to come out of the door's of his house when he returned.

Jephthah had made an impetuous promise to God that if He would give him victory in battle, Jephthah would sacrifice the first thing to come out of the doors of his house when he returned.

Impetuous: rash; impulsive
Indent ¶ (new topic)
[!] No commas w/ essential adj. clauses (that …)
[!] Unclear antecedent: *he* (twice): God or Jephthah?
Use commas after introductory adverb clauses ("if")
Doors is plural, not possessive
Dress-ups: quality adjective; adverb clauses

Week 18

After the battle, sadly it was his daughter which ran to greet him not an animal as he had **complacently** assumed. Bound by his promise to God however he had to follow through with it.

[2] After the battle, sadly it was his daughter who ran to greet him, not an animal as he had complacently assumed. [7] Bound by his promise to God, however, he had to follow through with it.

Complacently: without any concern or worry
Note: comma optional after short #2 openers
Use *who* for people, *which* for things
[!] Use commas to set off nonessential phrases
[!] Since *bound* is a past participle, count it as a #7
Use commas to set off transitional words
Dress-ups: -ly adverbs; who clause; adverb clause

Dorinda squirmed as she read the **veracious** story to Arthur, isn't there anything a little you know happier to read, she asked hopefully?

Dorinda squirmed as she read the veracious story to Arthur. "Isn't there anything a little, you know, happier to read?" she asked hopefully.

Veracious: accurate; truthful
Indent ¶ (new topic)
[!] Comma splice: needs period, not comma (2 MC)
Use quotation marks with direct quotations
Use commas to set off interrupters (you know)
Place " ? " after question in quotation marks
Dress-ups: verb; adv. clause; quality adj.; -ly adverb

"Sure, I know. Theres an **enthralling** story about healing you might enjoy reading," he replied. "Find Luke 17,12. He tells about 10 lepers which Jesus instantly and miraculously healed!"

[T] "Sure, I know. There's an enthralling story about healing you might enjoy reading," he replied. "Find Luke 17:12. He tells about ten lepers whom Jesus instantly and miraculously healed!"

Enthralling: captivating interest
Indent ¶ (new speaker)
Use apostrophes in contractions
Use a colon between Bible chapter and verse(s)
[!] Write Bible verses as numerals
Spell out numbers written as one or two words
[!] Use *whom* for objective case (He healed *them*)
Dress-ups: quality adjective; who clause
[!] Advanced style: dual -ly adverbs

Good night Dorinda exclaimed in amazement. Its still daytime, Arthur **wryly** observed pretending not to understand her slang.

"Good night!" Dorinda exclaimed in amazement.
"It's still daytime," Arthur wryly observed, pretending not to understand her slang.

Wryly: with dry humor (with a hint of scorn)
Indent ¶ (new speakers)
Use quotation marks with direct quotations
Exclamation marks follow introductory interjections
It's = it is
[!] Use commas around nonessential phrases
Dress-ups: strong verb; -ly adverb

Week 19

With interest Dorinda read the story, as Arthur indicated Jesus healed 10 leper's. What Arthur failed to **disclose** was that only one demonstrated any gratitude for the kindness, only one returned to thank Jesus and glorify God.

[2] With interest Dorinda read the story. [5] As Arthur indicated, Jesus healed ten lepers. What Arthur failed to <u>disclose</u> was that only one demonstrated any gratitude for the kindness; only one returned to thank Jesus and <u>glorify</u> God.

Disclose: reveal; make known
Indent ¶ (new topic)
[!] Comma splice: needs period, not comma (2 MC)
Use commas after #5 Sentence Openers
Spell out numbers written as one or two words
Lepers is plural, not possessive
Use semicolons to separate 2 main clauses when they belong in the same sentence (are closely related)
Dress-ups: strong verbs

Getting the message the book was slammed shut by Dorinda and she **ignobly** escaped to the palace grounds. Wandering through the gardens she approached the fateful well. Surprised she noticed someone their an old woman attempting to draw water from the deep well.

[4] Getting the message, Dorinda <u>slammed</u> the book shut and <u>ignobly</u> <u>escaped</u> to the palace grounds.
[4] Wandering through the gardens, she approached the <u>fateful</u> well. [7] Surprised, she noticed someone there, an old woman attempting to draw water from the deep well.

Ignobly: shamefully; dishonorably
Indent ¶, 2nd part (new scene)
Use commas after #4 SO (-ing phrase), twice
[!] Illegal #4: word after " , " should do the *inging* (Note that this faulty construction is also passive)
Better to drop the 2nd subject (*she*) than to add " , " (compound sentences need comma + cc)
[!] Use commas after #7 Sentence Openers (-ed)
Homophone: their/there
[!] Use commas around nonessential phrases
Dress-ups: strong verbs; -ly adverb; quality adjective

The old woman **futilely** tryed to turn the crank which would not budge clearly her finger's ached and what slight strength she had in them gave way. When she heard steps the woman turned her attention to the curious princess

The old woman <u>futilely</u> tried to turn the crank, <u>which</u> would not budge. [3] Clearly her fingers <u>ached</u>, and what <u>slight</u> strength she had in them gave way. [5] When she heard steps, the woman turned her attention to the curious princess.

Futilely: uselessly; ineffectively
Spelling: *tried*
Use commas to set off most who/which clauses
Fused: use a period to separate 2 main clauses
Fingers is plural, not possessive
Compound sentence needs comma: MC, cc MC
Use commas after #5 Sentence Openers
Use a period at end of statements
Dress-ups: -ly adv.; which clause; quality adjectives

"Gentle Princess the woman began I've got rheumatism in my hands which makes it painful to draw up the **brimming** bucket; would you be so kind as to fetch me a cup of water?"

"Gentle Princess," the woman began, "I've got rheumatism in my hands, <u>which</u> makes it painful to draw up the <u>brimming</u> bucket. Would you be so kind as to <u>fetch</u> me a cup of water?"

Brimming: full to the brim; almost overflowing
Indent ¶ (new speaker)
Comma: NDA & after *began* (interrupted quotation)
Use quotation marks around speech only
Use commas to set off most who/which clauses
[!] Discuss when periods are better than semicolons
Dress-ups: which clause; quality adj.; strong verb

Week 20

Tossing her golden locks Dorinda quickly turned away, why does everyone think I ought to be considerate she mumbled **querulously**?

[4] Tossing her golden locks, Dorinda <u>quickly</u> turned away. "Why does everyone think I ought to be <u>considerate</u>?" she <u>mumbled</u> <u>querulously</u>.

Querulously: in a complaining manner
Indent ¶ (new speaker)
Use commas after #4 SO (-ing phrase)
[!] Comma splice: needs period, not comma (2 MC)
Use quotation marks with direct quotations
" ? " goes with question, not at end of statement
Dress-ups: -ly adverbs; quality adjective; strong verb

Now youve probably guessed it again, sure enough, the old lady was a fairy in disguise. **Brandishing** her wand, Princess Dorinda was instantly zapped into a toad.

[T] Now, you've probably guessed it again. [T] Sure enough, the old lady was a fairy in disguise. [4] Brandishing her wand, she instantly zapped Princess Dorinda into a toad.

Brandishing: waving or flourishing
Indent ¶ (new topic)
Use apostrophes in contractions
[!] Comma splice: needs period, not comma (2 MC)
Use commas after introductory transitional words
[!] Illegal #4: word after " , " should do the *inging*
Dress-ups: -ly adverbs; strong verb

All that remained of the lovely lady was her crown conveniently miniaturized two fit her diminished stature and her beauty spot **prominent** on her high cheekbone between all the other toady wart's.

All that remained of the lovely lady was her crown, conveniently miniaturized to fit her diminished stature, and her beauty spot, prominent on her high cheekbone among all the other toady warts.

Prominent: easily visible; standing out
[!] Use commas around nonessential phrases
[!] Find 2 invisible w/w: "crown, which was conveniently"; "spot, which was prominent"
Homophone: two/to
Warts is plural, not possessive
Usage: *between/among* confusion
Dress-ups: invisible which clauses; -ly adverb; quality adjectives

---

"That'll teach you some manners Miss High and Mighty" the fairy snapped. "Maybe youll learn a little **humbleness** in your altered state! If you can ever find an honorable prince which will give you a kiss in true love you *might* be restored to humanity

"That'll teach you some manners, Miss High and Mighty," the fairy snapped. "Maybe you'll learn a little humbleness in your altered state! [5] If you can ever find an honorable prince who will give you a kiss in true love, you *might* be restored to humanity."

Humbleness: a lack of false pride; a humble attitude
Indent ¶ (new speaker)
Comma: NDA (Miss High and Mighty)
Use comma with verb of speaking & direct quotation
Use apostrophes in contractions
Use *who* for people, *which* for things
[!] No commas with essential who clauses
Use commas after #5 Sentence Openers
Close quotations with quotation marks
Use a period at end of statements
Dress-ups: strong verbs; quality adj's; who clause

Week 21

Alas Princess Dorinda bewails her new lot in life at the palace she has **inherent** difficulties convincing any one of her true identity although the beauty spot and crown get her a foot in the door.

[T] "Alas!" Princess Dorinda bewailed her new lot in life. [2] At the palace she had inherent difficulties convincing anyone of her true identity, although the beauty spot and crown got her a foot in the door.

Inherent: built-in; occurring as a natural result
Indent ¶ (new topic)
Use commas or exclamations after intro. interjections
Don't switch tenses
Fused: use a period to separate 2 main clauses
Spelling: *anyone* is one word
[!] Use commas with adv. clauses of extreme contrast
Dress-ups: strong verb; quality adjective; adverb clause

Puzzling over the crown which did look familiar Lady Constance decided to put the toad to the test. "If you truly are the princess she began Tell me where you have a **bona fide** wart, not that counterfeit beauty spot.

[4] Puzzling over the crown, which did look familiar, Lady Constance decided to put the toad to the test. [5] "If you truly are the princess," she began, "tell me where you have a bona fide wart, not that counterfeit beauty spot."

Bona fide: genuine; real
Indent ¶ (new topic and speaker)
Use commas after #4 SO (-ing phrase)
Use commas to set off most who/which clauses
[!] Alliteration: toad to the test
Commas after #5 SO and before continued quotation
Use quotation marks around spoken parts only
Use lc to continue interrupted quotations
Dress-ups: which clause; -ly adverb; quality adj's

That one was easy. "On the back of my head hidden by all my hair" Dorinda croaked. The palace maids **snickered.** "so thats why she'd never let us part her hair into to braids in back they giggled, Dorinda glared a toady glare.

[6] That one was easy. [2] "On the back of my head, hidden by all my hair," Dorinda <u>croaked</u>.

[6] The palace maids <u>snickered</u>. "So that's why she'd never let us part her hair into two braids in back," they <u>giggled</u>. [6] Dorinda <u>glared</u> a <u>toady</u> glare.

Snickered: uttered a partly stifled laugh
Indent ¶ (new speakers)
Use comma with verb of speaking & direct quotation
Capitalize the first word of a quoted sentence
Use apostrophes in contractions
Homophone: to/two
Close quotations with quotation marks
[!] Comma splice: needs period, not comma (2 MC)
Dress-ups: strong verbs; quality adjective

"What was your nickname, as a toddler Constance continued? Dorinda sighed **testily**, and rolled her eyes.

"What was your nickname as a toddler?" Constance continued.
Dorinda <u>sighed</u> <u>testily</u> and <u>rolled</u> her eyes.

Testily: impatiently; with irritation
Indent ¶ (new speakers)
[!] No commas with essential phrases (as a toddler)
Place " ? " immediately after question & close "
No comma before *and* to join 2 compound verbs
Dress-ups: strong verbs; -ly adverb

Week 22

"When I was really little friends called me "Toady" because I had a wart on the back of my head but then they dropped it when we were older because they realized I wasn't a **toady** *at all*" she snapped, "is that *enough*"?, she grouched.

[5] "When I was really little, friends called me 'Toady' <u>because</u> I had a wart on the back of my head, but then they dropped it <u>when</u> we were older <u>because</u> they realized I wasn't a toady *at all*," she <u>snapped</u>. "Is that *enough*?" she <u>grouched</u>.

Toady: a "yes" man or woman; flatterer (to excess)
Use commas after #5 Sentence Openers
Note pun on *toady*
Use single ' ' for quotes within quotes
Use comma before cc to link 2 main clauses
Use comma with verb of speaking & direct quotation
[!] Comma splice: needs period, not comma (2 MC)
Question inside " " if part of quoted material
[!] Do not use comma w/ an end mark of punctuation
Dress-ups: adv. clauses; verbs. Italics for emphasis

Dorindas final answer confirmed her status, when her cell phone had mysteriously disappeared some weeks ago she had confessed the truth to her longtime companion Lady Constance who now played her **trump card**: "What *really* happened to your cell phone

Dorinda's final answer <u>confirmed</u> her status. [5] When her cell phone had <u>mysteriously</u> disappeared some weeks ago, she had confessed the truth to her <u>longtime</u> companion, Lady Constance, <u>who</u> now played her trump card: "What *really* happened to your cell phone?"

Trump card: something giving one person an advantage over another
Indent ¶ (new topic)
Use apostrophes to show possession
[!] Comma splice: needs period, not comma (2 MC)
Use commas after #5 Sentence Openers
[!] Use commas w/ nonessential phrases and clauses (the appositive and the *who* clause)
Use a question mark after a question
Close quotations with quotation marks
Dress-ups: verb; -ly adv.; quality adj.; who clause

Properly, Dorinda had the good grace to blush. By mistake I dropped it in the commode she owned up. (Hmm seems like a **conspicuous** pattern of dropping things in water!

[3] Properly, Dorinda had the good grace to blush. [2] "By mistake I dropped it in the commode," she <u>owned up</u>. (Hmm, seems like a <u>conspicuous</u> pattern of dropping things in water!)

Conspicuous: easily observable
Indent ¶ (new speaker)
Use quotation marks with direct quotations
Use comma with verb of speaking & direct quotation
Use commas after introductory interjections
Close parentheses
Dress-ups: strong verb; quality adjective

The palace took her in but no one not even faithful Constance wanted to touch her, after all her skin was rough warty and **repulsive**.

    The palace took her in, but no one, not even <u>faithful</u> Constance, wanted to touch her. [T] After all, her skin was <u>rough</u>, <u>warty</u>, and <u>repulsive</u>.

Repulsive: causing deep dislike or aversion
Indent ¶ (new topic)
Use comma before cc to link 2 main clauses
[!] Use commas around nonessential phrases
[!] Comma splice: needs period, not comma (2 MC)
Use commas after introductory transitional phrases
Use commas with 3 or more items in a series
Dress-ups: quality adjectives

Week 23

Two weeks past; true, Dorindas basic needs were attended to but the luster had gone out of life. Accept with **revulsion**, no one noticed her, even all the footman who once toadied to her looked down on her.

    [6] Two weeks passed. [T] True, Dorinda's basic needs were attended to, but the luster had gone out of life. [2] Except with revulsion, no one noticed her. Even all the footmen, <u>who</u> once <u>toadied</u> to her, looked down on her.

Revulsion: strong feeling of distaste or dislike
Indent ¶ (time has passed)
Usage: *past/passed; accept/except; footmen* plural
Separate only closely-related MCs with semicolons
Use apostrophes to show possession
Use comma before cc to link two main clauses
[!] Comma splice: needs period, not comma (2 MC)
Note meaning of *toady* as a verb plus pun on word
Dress-ups: *who* clause (needs commas); strong verb

Involuntarily Maribella shuddered, whenever Dorinda pattered into the room. I know your my sister and all but you give me the creeps, especially when you sneak up on me like that

    [3] Involuntarily Maribella <u>shuddered</u> <u>whenever</u> Dorinda <u>pattered</u> into the room. "I know you're my sister and all, but you give me the creeps, <u>especially</u> <u>when</u> you <u>sneak</u> up on me like that."

Involuntarily: not by one's own choice
Indent ¶ (new topic)
[!] No commas with mid-sentence adv. clauses
Use quotation marks with direct quotations
Homophone: your/you're
Use comma before cc to link two main clauses
Use a period at end of statements
Dress-ups: strong verbs; adverb clauses; -ly adv.

Even King Morton has nothing hopeful too offer his daughter, although, he volunteers two **requisition** designs for a princess pond from the palace architect Dorinda miserably shakes her head

    Even King Morton had nothing hopeful to offer his daughter. [5] Although he <u>volunteered</u> to <u>requisition</u> designs for a princess pond from the palace architect, Dorinda <u>miserably</u> shook her head.

Requisition: to write an order for something
Indent ¶ (new topic)
Don't switch tenses
Homophone: too/two/to
[!] Comma splice: needs period, not comma (2 MC)
Use commas after #5 Sentence Openers. Note: the
    comma follows the whole clause, not the adverb
Use a period at end of statements
Dress-ups: strong verbs; -ly adverb

---

a few days later, feeling dejected and **forlorn** she wandered into the infirmary mending rapidly Arthur was in a mood to shower a little compassion on his fellow amphibian sufferer.

    [2] A few days later feeling <u>dejected</u> and <u>forlorn</u>, she <u>wandered</u> into the infirmary. [4] Mending <u>rapidly</u>, Arthur was in a mood to <u>shower</u> a little compassion on his fellow <u>amphibian</u> sufferer.

Forlorn: dreary; miserable
Indent ¶ (time has passed and new scene)
Capitalize the first word of sentences
Use comma after two or more introductory phrases
Fused: use a period to separate 2 main clauses
Use commas after #4 SO (-ing phrase)
Dress-ups: quality adjectives; strong verbs,
    -ly adverb

Week 24

Its not so dreadful being a toad he assured her while people aren't always **humane** your free to live as you please in the bounty's of nature.

"It's not so <u>dreadful</u> being a toad," he <u>assured</u> her. [5] "While people aren't always <u>humane</u>, you're free to live <u>as</u> you please in the bounties of nature."

Humane: showing compassion for people & animals
Use quotation marks with direct quotations
It's = it is; *you're = you are*; *bounties* is plural
Use comma with verb of speaking & direct quotation
Fused: use a period to separate 2 main clauses
Use commas after #5 Sentence Openers
Dress-ups: quality adj's; strong verb; adverb clause

Trying to cheer Dorinda Arthur oferred to read to *her* a few stories, he **regaled** her with humorous, fairy tales and wild adventures from the book the Arabian nights. Day after day, Arthur entertained Dorinda.

    [4] Trying to cheer Dorinda, Arthur offered to read to *her* a few stories. He <u>regaled</u> her with <u>humorous</u> fairy tales and <u>wild</u> adventures from the book *The Arabian Nights*. [2] Day after day, Arthur entertained Dorinda.

Regaled: entertained agreeably
Indent ¶ (new topic)
Use commas after #4 SO (-ing phrase)
Spelling: *offered*
[!] Comma splice: needs period, not comma (2 MC)
[!] No commas with cumulative adjectives
Titles of long works: UC and italicize (or underline)
Comma optional after #2 SO of 4 words or fewer
Dress-ups: strong verb; quality adjectives

Gradually, she grew to appreciate his sympathy toward her, and to respect his positive attitude when the infirmary **orderly** brought him meals with hardly a glance in his direction he didnt protest.

    [3] Gradually, she grew to appreciate his sympathy toward her and to <u>respect</u> his positive attitude. [5] When the infirmary orderly brought him meals with hardly a glance in his direction, he didn't <u>protest</u>.

Orderly: a hospital attendant w/ non-medical duties
Indent ¶ (new topic)
No comma before *and* to join 2 items in a series
Fused: use a period to separate 2 sentences
Use commas after #5 Sentence Openers
Use apostrophes in contractions
Dress-ups: strong verbs

When he nearly choked on learning that the palace cook had whipped up fly soup for him he didnt grumble even when Dorinda accidentally stumbled over his hurt leg he didnt **chastise** her for being clumsy, but readily forgave her

[5] When he nearly <u>choked</u> on learning that the palace cook had <u>whipped up</u> fly soup for him, he didn't <u>grumble</u>. [5] Even when Dorinda <u>accidentally</u> <u>stumbled</u> over his hurt leg, he didn't <u>chastise</u> her for being <u>clumsy</u> but <u>readily</u> forgave her.

Chastise: criticize severely
Use commas after #5 Sentence Openers (twice)
Use apostrophes in contractions
Fused: use a period to separate 2 sentences
No comma before *but* to join 2 compound verbs
Use a period at end of statements
Dress-ups: strong verbs; -ly adverbs; quality adjective

Week 25

How is it you stay so upbeat all the time Dorinda inquired of Arthur one day, although unpleasant things happen you manage to have **empathy** for others.

    "How is it you stay so <u>upbeat</u> all the time?" Dorinda <u>inquired</u> of Arthur one day. [5] "Although <u>unpleasant</u> things happen, you manage to have empathy for others."

Empathy: identifying with others' feelings, thoughts
Indent ¶ (new speaker)
Use quotation marks with direct quotations
Use a question mark after a question
[!] Comma splice: needs period, not comma (2 MC)
Use commas after #5 Sentence Openers
Dress-ups: quality adjectives; strong verb

Oh I learned the hard way. When I loose my temper folks just steer clear of me, when I give a bit of kindness it comes back to me. Besides whats there to be discontented about I have my health plenty of food—**albeit** not always to my taste—everything a lowly frog could need.

[T] "Oh, I learned the hard way. [5] When I lose my temper, folks just <u>steer</u> clear of me. [5] When I give a bit of kindness, it comes back to me. [T] Besides, what's there to be <u>discontented</u> about? I have my health, plenty of food—albeit not always to my taste—everything a <u>lowly</u> frog could need."

Albeit: even though; even if
Indent ¶ (new speaker)
Use quotation marks with direct quotations
Use commas after intro. transitions (*Oh; Besides*)
Spelling: *loose/lose* confusion
Use commas after #5 Sentence Openers
[!] Comma splice: needs period, not comma (2 MC)
Use apostrophes in contractions (*what's = what is*)
Fused: use " ? " to end question before 2nd MC
Use commas with 3 or more items in a series
Dress-ups: verb; quality adj's (*lowly* = imposter *-ly*)

The next day, Arthur **rummaged** through the books Dorinda has supplied to find an apt story to read to her he has something very particular in mind, at last he finds the precise tale that he desires.

[2] The next day Arthur <u>rummaged</u> through the books Dorinda had supplied to find an <u>apt</u> story to read to her. He had something very particular in mind. [T] At last he found the precise tale <u>that</u> he desired.

Rummaged: searched actively through
Indent ¶ (time has passed)
Comma optional after #2 SO of 4 words or fewer
Don't switch tenses
Fused: use a period to separate 2 main clauses
[!] Comma splice: needs period, not comma (2 MC)
Dress-ups: strong verb; quality adjective; [!] which
    clause using *that* (see Appendix)

"The celebrated king of the arthurian tales" he began "was out riding one day with his nephew Robert who enjoyed the kings special favor as the elder of his sisters three boys. Regrettably, the lad was **mute** from birth. *[quotation continues]*

"The <u>celebrated</u> king of the Arthurian tales," he began, "was out riding one day with his nephew Robert, <u>who</u> enjoyed the king's special favor as the <u>eldest</u> of his sister's three boys. [3] Regrettably, the lad was <u>mute</u> from birth. *[quotation continues]*

Mute: incapable of speech
Indent ¶ (new topic)
Capitalize proper nouns
Use commas with verb of speaking & direct quote
Use commas to set off *who* clauses
Use apostrophes to show possession (twice)
[!] Discuss why this *as* doesn't count as an adverb
[!] Use the superlative adj. to compare 3+ *(eldest)*
No close quotation marks b/c quotation continues
Dress-ups: quality adjectives; who clause

Week 26

Quick-witted and agile, Robert **compensated** for his limitation by an eagerness to please and to learn ever watchful of the king he had sought out opportunity's to serve or aid his uncle. *[quotation continues]*

<u>Quick-witted</u> and <u>agile</u>, Robert <u>compensated</u> for his limitation by an eagerness to please and to learn. Ever <u>watchful</u> of the king, he had sought out opportunities to serve or aid his uncle. *[quotation continues]*

Compensated: offset; counterbalanced
[!] Arthur is telling this story within a story, so it's a
    continuous quotation (no " " here)
[!] Both sentences can be seen as disguised #4s, with
    "Being" a hidden participle before the adj. phrases
Use commas after introductory adjective phrases
Fused: use a period to separate 2 main clauses
Opportunities is plural, not possessive
Dress-ups: quality adjectives; strong verb

"Now they were riding threw the royal forest with Roberts beloved hound Hrothgar by his side the lad had raised Hrothgar as a puppy, and trained him well. As the group passed through a cedar **grove** Hrothgar bounded ahead and out of site *[quotation continues]*

    [T] "Now they were riding through the royal forest with Robert's beloved hound Hrothgar by his side. The lad had raised Hrothgar as a puppy and trained him well. [5] As the group passed through a cedar grove, Hrothgar <u>bounded</u> ahead and out of sight. *[quotation continues]*

Grove: a small wood or forested area
Indent ¶ (new topic)
[!] New paragraphs in a continued quotation start but do not end with quotation marks
Homophone: threw/through; site/sight
Use apostrophes to show possession
Fused: use a period to separate 2 main clauses
No comma before *and* to join 2 compound verbs
Use commas after #5 Sentence Openers
Use a period at end of statements
Dress-ups: strong verb

Robert could here him barking wildly in the distance which surprised him sense his hound never barked without a **commendable** reason *[quotation continues]*

Robert could hear him barking <u>wildly</u> in the distance, <u>which</u> surprised him <u>since</u> his hound never barked without a <u>commendable</u> reason. *[quotation continues]*

Commendable: praiseworthy
No quotation marks b/c continued quotation
Homophone: here/hear; sense/since
Use commas to set off most who/which clauses
Use a period at end of statements
Dress-ups: -ly adverb; which clause; adverb clause; quality adjective

---

Although he did not know what was troubling Hrothgar he recognized the sound as a warning, his uncle seemed **undaunted**, or perhaps oblivious two the noise. *[quotation continues]*

[5] Although he did not know what was troubling Hrothgar, he recognized the sound as a warning. His uncle seemed <u>undaunted</u> or perhaps <u>oblivious</u> to the noise. *[quotation continues]*

Undaunted: not forced to abandon effort or purpose
No quotation marks b/c continued quotation
Use commas after #5 Sentence Openers
[!] Comma splice: needs period, not comma (2 MC)
No comma before *or* to join 2 items in a series
Homophone: two/to
Dress-ups: quality adjectives

Week 27

"Kneeling at the foot of a cliff where tiny drops of water trickled down king Arthur had cupped his hands for a drink, it was a mere dribble of water and the king had developed a **potent** thirst. *[quotation continues]*

    [4] "Kneeling at the foot of a cliff <u>where</u> tiny drops of water <u>trickled</u> down, King Arthur had <u>cupped</u> his hands for a drink. It was a <u>mere</u> dribble of water, and the king had developed a <u>potent</u> thirst. *[quotation continues]*

Potent: powerful; mighty
Indent ¶ (new topic)
[!] Start new par. in continued quotation with "
Use commas after several introductory elements
Capitalize titles used with names
[!] Note use of past perfect tense ("had cupped")
[!] Comma splice: needs period, not comma (2 MC)
Use comma before cc to link two main clauses
Dress-ups: adv. clause; strong verbs; quality adj's

Impatiently the king waited until his hands were full of water with anxious **foreboding**, Robert watched, and listened while Hrothgar continued too bark madly *[quotation continues]*

[3] Impatiently the king waited <u>until</u> his hands were full of water. [2] With <u>anxious</u> foreboding, Robert watched and listened <u>while</u> Hrothgar continued to bark <u>madly</u>. *[quotation continues]*

Foreboding: a sense of coming evil or misfortune
No quotation marks b/c continued quotation
Fused: use a period to separate 2 main clauses
No comma before *and* to join 2 compound verbs
Homophone: too/to
Use a period at end of statements
Dress-ups: adverb clauses; quality adjective; -ly adverb

Although he feared that something in the water might be **hazardous** being mute Robert was unable to warn his uncle, he took the only coarse of action he could envision too accomplish his objective swiftly *[quotation continues]*

[5] Although he feared that something in the water might be <u>hazardous</u>, being mute, Robert was unable to warn his uncle. He took the only course of action he could <u>envision</u> to accomplish his objective <u>swiftly</u>. *[quotation continues]*

Hazardous: unsafe; dangerous
No quotation marks b/c continued quotation
Use commas after #5 Sentence Openers
Use commas after introductory -ing phrases
[!] Comma splice: needs period, not comma (2 MC)
Homophone: coarse/course; too/to
Use a period at end of statements
Dress-ups: quality adjective; strong verb; -ly adverb

Rushing to his uncles side Robert knocked the water from his hands **Irately** King Arthur shouted at the boy telling him he was parched and needed water. *[quotation ends]*

[4] Rushing to his uncle's side, Robert <u>knocked</u> the water from his hands. [3] Irately King Arthur shouted at the boy, telling him he was <u>parched</u> and needed water."

Irately: angrily
Use apostrophes to show possession
Use commas after #4 SO (-ing phrase)
Fused: use a period to separate 2 main clauses
[!] Use commas to set off nonessential phrases
Close quotation with quotation marks
Dress-ups: strong verb; quality adjective

Week 28

Well that seems a **flimsy** excuse to bother his uncle Dorinda interrupted the poor man just wanted a drink of water why did Robert trust his dog over his uncle

[T] "Well, that seems a <u>flimsy</u> excuse to bother his uncle," Dorinda interrupted. "The poor man just wanted a drink of water! Why did Robert trust his dog over his uncle?"

Flimsy: weak; inadequate; not convincing
Indent ¶ (new speaker)
Use quotation marks with direct quotations
Use commas after introductory transitions
Use comma with verb of speaking & direct quotation
Fused: use a period to separate 2 main clauses
Use " ! " after exclamations; " ? " after questions
Dress-ups: quality adjective

Hounds, and other nonhuman creatures sometimes have a **tad** of wisdom Arthur commented try and see what happens and you'll understand. Dorinda waited more patiently.

"Hounds and other nonhuman creatures sometimes have a tad of wisdom," Arthur commented. "Try to see what happens and you'll understand." [6] Dorinda waited more <u>patiently</u>.

Tad: a small amount; a bit
Indent ¶ (new speaker)
Use " " w/ direct quotations & comma (speaking vb)
No comma before *and* to join 2 items in a series
Fused: use a period to separate 2 main clauses
Usage: try *to* do something, not try *and* do something
Dress-ups: -ly adverb

Cupping his hands again the king started to collect more of the precious liquid again Robert **jiggled** his uncles hands signaling that they should check the source before drinking *[quotation continues]*

[4] "Cupping his hands again, the king started to collect more of the <u>precious</u> liquid. [T] Again Robert <u>jiggled</u> his uncle's hands, signaling that they should check the source before drinking. *[quotation continues]*

Jiggled: moved with short, quick jerks
Indent ¶ (new topic)
Begin, but don't end, par. in cont. quotation with "
Use commas after #4 SO (-ing phrase)
Fused: use a period to separate 2 main clauses
Use apostrophes to show possession
[!] Use commas to set off nonessential phrases
Use a period at end of statements
Dress-ups: quality adjective; strong verb

Again Arthur ignored his nephew **callously** pushing him away the 3rd time Hrothgar came to his rescue jumping up against the king, and spilling the water. *[quotation continues]*

[T] Again Arthur ignored his nephew, <u>callously</u> pushing him away.
    [2] "The third time Hrothgar came to his rescue, jumping up against the king and spilling the water. *[quotation continues]*

Callously: unfeelingly; insensitively
Indent ¶, 2nd part (new topic)
[!] Use commas around nonessential phrases (twice)
Fused: use a period to separate 2 main clauses
[!] Start new par. in continued quotation with "
Spell out ordinal numbers
No comma before *and* to join 2 items in a series
Dress-ups: -ly adverb

Week 29

King Arthur lost all patients that hound dog is forever banished from my kingdom he snapped at his nephew. And you must quit Camelot and return to your home for such **insubordination.** *[Arthur's story continues but not the king's words]*

[6] King Arthur lost all patience. 'That hound dog is forever <u>banished</u> from my kingdom,' he <u>snapped</u> at his nephew, 'and you must <u>quit</u> Camelot and return to your home for such insubordination.' *[quotation continues]*

Insubordination: defiance of authority
No double quotation marks b/c continued quotation
Homophone: patients/patience
Fused: use a period to separate 2 main clauses
[!] Use single ' ' for quotations within quotations
Capitalize the first word of a quoted sentence
Use comma with verb of speaking & direct quotation
Use lc to continue interrupted quotations, and use
    comma before cc to link two main clauses
Dress-ups: strong verbs

Grievingly Robert turned away signaling Hrothgar to his side, and through the woods he wound his way back to the castle anxious in his heart for his uncles safety yet **discerning** their was nothing he could do. *[quotation ends]*

    [3] "Grievingly Robert turned away, signaling Hrothgar to his side. [2] Through the woods he <u>wound</u> his way back to the castle, <u>anxious</u> in his heart for his uncle's safety yet <u>discerning</u> there was nothing he could do."

Discerning: recognizing; perceiving
Indent ¶ (new topic)
[!] Start new par. in continued quotation with "
[!] Use commas around nonessential phrases (twice)
[!] Poor choice of *and* to join main clauses
Use apostrophes to show possession
Homophone: their/there
Close quotation with quotation marks
Dress-ups: strong verb; quality adjectives

Well I would have made that King listen to me Dorinda exclaimed! How would you have accomplished that **queried** Arthur? Kings are all powerful plus Robert couldn't speak I guess your write Dorinda realized Go on. Tell me the rest of the story

    [T] "Well, I would have made that king listen to me!" Dorinda exclaimed.
    "How would you have accomplished that?" <u>queried</u> Arthur. [6] "Kings are all powerful. [T] Plus, Robert couldn't speak."
    "I guess you're right," Dorinda realized. "Go on. Tell me the rest of the story."

Queried: asked; inquired about
Indent ¶ (new speakers)
Use quotation marks with direct quotations
Use commas after introductory transitional words
Use lc for titles without a name
Use " ! " after exclamation, not at end of statement
Use " ? " after question, not at end of statement
Fused (2): use a period to separate 2 main clauses
Homophone: your/you're; write; right
Use comma with verb of speaking & direct quotation
Use a period at end of statements
Dress-ups: strong verb

Frustrated king Arthur decided to climb to the top of the cliff where he could drink from the pool of water collected above hand over hand he made the **laborious** climb *[quotation continues]*

    [7] "Frustrated, King Arthur decided to climb to the top of the cliff <u>where</u> he could drink from the pool of water collected above. [2] Hand over hand he made the <u>laborious</u> climb. *[quotation continues]*

Laborious: requiring much work and effort
Indent ¶ (new topic)
[!] Begin, but don't end, par. in cont. quotation with "
[!] Use commas after #7 Sentence Openers (-ed)
Capitalize titles used with names
Fused: use a period to separate 2 main clauses
[!] Disguised #2 ("With hand over hand...")
Dress-ups: adverb clause; quality adjective

Week 30

When he reached the top of the cliff he stood **aghast** their in the pool of water lied a enormous poisonous snake—dead. *[quotation continues]*

[5] When he reached the top of the cliff, he stood <u>aghast</u>. There in the pool of water lay an enormous poisonous snake—dead. *[quotation continues]*

Aghast: struck with horror or shock (quality adj.)
Use commas after #5 Sentence Openers
Fused: use a period to separate 2 main clauses
Usage: *their/there; lay* = past of *lie; a/an*
[!] Use em-dash to draw attention
Dress-ups: quality adjective

The poison had **contaminated** the water Hrothgar and Robert had been trying to save his life all along whereas he had been to foolish to listen to they *[quotation continues]*

The poison had <u>contaminated</u> the water. Hrothgar and Robert had been trying to save his life all along, <u>whereas</u> he had been too <u>foolish</u> to listen to them. *[quotation continues]*

Contaminated: made impure or polluted
No quotation marks b/c continued quotation
Fused: use a period to separate 2 main clauses
[!] Use commas with adv. clauses of extreme contrast
Homophone: to/too
Usage: *them* → objective pronoun (object of prep.)
Dress-ups: strong verb; adverb clause; quality adj.

"When the king returned to the castle he sought out his nephew without delay finding Robert in his room with his servant packing to return home Arthur humbled himself **contritely** *[quotation continues]*

    [5] "When the king returned to the castle, he sought out his nephew without delay. [4] Finding Robert in his room with his servant packing to return home, Arthur <u>humbled</u> himself <u>contritely</u>. *[quotation continues]*

Contritely: with genuine regret or sorrow
Indent ¶ (new scene)
[!] Start new par. in continued quotation with "
Use commas after #5 Sentence Openers
Fused: use a period to separate 2 main clauses
Use commas after #4 SO (-ing phrase)
Use a period at end of statements
Dress-ups: strong verb; -ly adverb

Can you forgive me nephew he began? You were write all along and wise to act on your instincts, you **astutely** trusted your beloved Hrothgar while I depended on no one but myself. *[quotation continues]*

'Can you forgive me, nephew?' he began. 'You were right all along and wise to act on your instincts. You <u>astutely</u> trusted your <u>beloved</u> Hrothgar, <u>while</u> I depended on no one but myself. *[quotation continues]*

Astutely: wisely; perceptively
No double quotation marks b/c continued quotation
[!] Use single ' ' for quotations within quotations
Set off NDAs with commas ("nephew")
Use " ? " after question, not at end of statement
Homophone: write/right
[!] Comma splice: needs period, not comma (2 MC)
[!] Comma w/ adv. clause of extreme contrast (while)
Dress-ups: -ly adverb; quality adjective; adv. clause

Week 31

I must reward you for your loyalty I shall elevate you to the **coveted** position of arm bearer to the king and Hrothgar shall dine on steak every day *[Arthur's story continues but not the king's words]*

I must reward you for your loyalty. I shall <u>elevate</u> you to the <u>coveted</u> position of Arm Bearer to the King, and Hrothgar shall <u>dine</u> on steak every day.' *[quotation continues]*

Coveted: greatly desired
No double quotation marks b/c continued quotation
Fused: use a period to separate 2 main clauses
Capitalize titles except for little words
Use comma before cc to link two main clauses
Use a period at end of statements
[!] Use single ' to close quotation within quotation
Dress-ups: strong verbs; quality adjective

Modestly Robert signed a reply to his servant who translated his words to the king: you're safety is all that matters I am content to be of service to my **liege** lord and I shall do everything I can to be worthy of this position entrusted to me *[quotation ends]*

[3] "Modestly Robert signed a reply to his servant, who translated his words to the king: 'Your safety is all that matters. I am content to be of service to my liege lord, and I shall do everything I can to be worthy of this position entrusted to me.'"

Liege: entitled to the loyalty and services of subjects
Indent ¶ (new speaker)
[!] Start new par. in continued quotation with "
Use commas to set off most who/which clauses
[!] Use single ' ' for quotations within quotations
Capitalize the first word of a quoted sentence
Homophone: you're/your
Fused: use a period to separate 2 main clauses
Use comma before cc to link two main clauses
Close quotation with period & ' " (single and double)
Dress-ups: who clause; quality adj's; strong verb

Dorinda realized at once the message of this simple story, deeply she felt the injury committed yet **poignantly** forgiven Struck by the boys kindness she examined her own heart.

Dorinda realized at once the message of this simple story. [3] Deeply she felt the injury committed yet poignantly forgiven. [7] Struck by the boy's kindness, she examined her own heart.

Poignantly: touchingly; in a profoundly moving way
Indent ¶ (new topic)
[!] Comma splice: needs period, not comma (2 MC)
Fused: use a period to separate 2 main clauses
Use apostrophes to show possession
[!] Disguised #7 (irregular past participle)
[!] Use commas after #7 Sentence Openers
Dress-ups: -ly adverb

Why had she not recognized how **abhorrent** her own behavior to Arthur had been a mere promise to befreind him was all he had asked. In truth she had treated him as dreadfully as the King had treated his faithful nephew

Why had she not recognized how abhorrent her own behavior to Arthur had been? A mere promise to befriend him was all he had asked. [2] In truth, she had treated him as dreadfully as the king had treated his faithful nephew.

Abhorrent: hateful; loathsome; detestable
Use a question mark after a question and also to fix the fused sentence (two main clauses)
Spelling: *befriend* ("i before e")
Use commas after introductory transitional phrases
Use lc for titles without a name
Use a period at end of statements
Dress-ups: quality adjectives; strong verb; -ly adv.; adverb clause

---

Week 32

With heartfelt tears and **remorse** for her appalling behavior to him Princess Dorinda kissed him on his cheek, she knew now that kindness to others was far more rewarding then nurturing ones selfish interests

[2] With heartfelt tears and remorse for her appalling behavior to him, Princess Dorinda kissed him on his cheek. She knew now that kindness to others was far more rewarding than nurturing one's selfish interests.

Remorse: deep regret for wrongdoing
Comma needed after #2 SO of 5 or more words
[!] With several intro. phrases, comma after last only
[!] Comma splice: needs period, not comma (2 MC)
Usage: *then/than* confusion
Use apostrophes to show possession
Use a period at end of statements
Dress-ups: quality adjectives

Now what do you think Arthur did after that kiss, he kissed her back of course—the only **sensible** action for a self-respecting frog which secretly had grown rather fond of the princess.

[T] Now what do you think Arthur did after that kiss? He kissed her back, of course—the only sensible action for a self-respecting frog who secretly had grown rather fond of the princess.

Sensible: showing good sense or sound judgment
Indent ¶ (new topic)
[!] Comma splice: needs " ? " not comma (2 MC)
Use commas to set off transitional expressions
[!] Invisible who/which clause: "course, which was"
Use em-dashes to draw attention
Use *who* for people and animals treated like people
[!] No commas with essential *who* clauses
Dress-ups: quality adj's; *who* clause; -ly adverb

Then what occured you guessed it. Poof instantly both transformed into the prince and princess they were meant to be. Both breathed a **colossal** sigh of relief delighting in there transformation.

    [6] Then what occurred? [6] You guessed it. Poof! [3] Instantly both transformed into the prince and princess they were meant to be. Both <u>breathed</u> a <u>colossal</u> sigh of relief, delighting in their transformation.

Colossal: huge; gigantic
Indent ¶ (new topic)
Spelling: *occurred*
Fused: use a " ? " to separate these 2 main clauses
Exclamation marks follow introductory interjections
[!] Use commas to set off nonessential phrases
Homophone: there/their
Dress-ups: strong verb; quality adjective

The only noticeable change, was that Dorinda had **fortuitously** lost her beauty mark, along with all the other wart's, free at last of the magicians spell Arthur revealed to Dorinda the truth about his past.

The only <u>noticeable</u> change was that Dorinda had <u>fortuitously</u> lost her beauty mark, along with all the other warts.
    [4] Free at last of the magician's spell, Arthur revealed to Dorinda the truth about his past.

Fortuitously: luckily; fortunately, though by chance
Indent ¶, 2nd part (new topic)
No need for comma between subject and verb
Warts is plural, not possessive
[!] Comma splice: needs period, not comma (2 MC)
[!] Disguised #4 ("Being free …")
Use commas after #4 Sentence Openers
Use apostrophes to show possession
Dress-ups: quality adjective; -ly adverb

Week 33

He told her the real secret to his kindness, was learning humility in the guise of a frog, Dorinda nodded her head in **fervent** agreement

He told her the real secret to his kindness was learning humility in the guise of a frog. Dorinda nodded her head in <u>fervent</u> agreement.

Fervent: intensely felt; showing great emotion
No need for comma between subject and verb
[!] Comma splice: needs period, not comma (2 MC)
Use a period at end of statements
Dress-ups: quality adjective

When asked if he would permit them to marry King Morton uncharacteristically replied sweet with joy he gave them his blessing **indebted** to Arthur and the fairy for restoring Dorinda too her lovable self.

    [5] When asked <u>if</u> he would permit them to marry, King Morton <u>uncharacteristically</u> replied, "Sweet!" [2] With joy he gave them his blessing, <u>indebted</u> to Arthur and the fairy for restoring Dorinda to her <u>lovable</u> self.

Indebted: obligated for kindness or favors received
Indent ¶ (new topic)
Use commas after #5 Sentence Openers
Use comma with verb of speaking & direct quotation
Use quotation marks with direct quotations
Fused: use " ! " here to separate 2 MC (inside " ")
[!] Use commas to set off nonessential phrases
Homophone: too/to
Dress-ups: adverb clause; -ly adverb; quality adj's

Epilogue: The wedding was a smashing success despite the fact that Dorinda true to form tripped, and dropped her crown in the new sturgeon pond it simply gave Arthur a chance to fish it out gallantly—a little **dejà vu**?

    Epilogue: The wedding was a <u>smashing</u> success, despite the fact that Dorinda, true to form, tripped and dropped her crown in the new sturgeon pond. It simply gave Arthur a chance to fish it out <u>gallantly</u>—a little dejà vu?

Dejà vu: the feeling that a new situation had happened before
Indent ¶ (new scene)
[!] Use commas to set off nonessential phrases (2)
No comma before *and* to join 2 compound verbs
Fused: use a period to separate 2 main clauses
[!] Discuss not splitting infinitives (see Appendix)
[!] Use em-dashes to indicate a break in thought
Dress-ups: quality adjective; -ly adverb

Atop the wedding cake, the Iron Chef fashioned a frog and toad, anticipating joyous matrimony while at the wedding feast the **erstwhile** Frog and Toad skipped the main course of sturgeon roe soufflé, and enjoyed just desserts.

[2] Atop the wedding cake the Iron Chef <u>fashioned</u> a frog and toad <u>anticipating joyous</u> matrimony, <u>while</u> at the wedding feast the <u>erstwhile</u> Frog and Toad <u>skipped</u> the main course of sturgeon roe soufflé and enjoyed just desserts.

Erstwhile: former; of times past
Indent ¶ (new topic)
Comma optional after #2 SO of 4 words or fewer
[!] No commas w/ essential phrases (anticipating…)
[!] Use commas w/ contrasting adv. clauses (while…)
No comma before *and* to join 2 compound verbs
Note pun on title & spelling confusion: *just deserts = deserved reward; just desserts = only dessert*
Dress-ups: strong verbs; quality adj's; adverb clause

The Little Mermaid

Introduction

Far superior to Disney's movie by the same title, Hans Christian Andersen's classic short story "The Little Mermaid" has captivated readers for years. This Fix-It version has been abridged and edited for modern grammar while attempting to be faithful to the original.

Recommended for grades six through nine, the Little Mermaid Fix-Its are divided into thirty-three weeks, with four passages to rewrite and correct each week. See the Introduction under Teaching Procedure for instructions for students and teachers.

In the notes beside the Fix-Its, exclamations in brackets [!] will alert you to advanced concepts you may wish to explain to your students, depending on their ability. These often have corresponding errors for students to locate, but do not necessarily expect students to find them. In the Appendix you will find a fuller discussion of the Dress-ups and Sentence Openers as well as most grammar issues. Starting with Week 5, I stop marking #1 Subject Openers. If your students are having trouble recognizing them, however, you may wish to continue marking these.

Because the Fix-It stories are usually taught over the course of a school year, students may sometimes have trouble following the storyline. When you introduce them to the Fix-It exercises, you may wish to tell them a little about the story and author. As you discuss the sentences each week, I recommend you check students' reading comprehension first, discussing the events leading up to and including that week's reading.

Background to Hans Christian Andersen (1805–1875)

Author and poet Hans Christian Andersen was Denmark's most beloved storyteller of the nineteenth century, best known today for his children's fairy tales. He endured great poverty and sadness in his early life. Writing more than 350 children's stories, he wanted to bring children joy, which he missed in his own childhood. Often his rich tales have deep themes, exploring such ideas as sacrificial love ("The Little Mermaid") and the follies of vanity ("The Emperor's New Clothes").

Andersen first published "The Little Mermaid" in 1836 in a collection of fairy tales. In the 1989 animated adaptation by the same title, Walt Disney Company dramatically altered the ending, characters, and theme of the original tale. Most notably, in Andersen's story the mermaid's desire to gain an eternal soul is at least as strong as her desire to win the love of the prince. The tale has a bittersweet ending, unlike Disney's happy ending, which also avoids the spiritual import of the original.

The Little Mermaid

Fix-Its and Corrections

Grammar, Skills, and Vocabulary

Week 1

Far out in the ocean where the water is as blue as the most stunning cornflower and as clear as crystal it is very deep—so deep indeed that no cable could **fathom** it.

[2] Far out in the ocean <u>where</u> the water is as blue as the most <u>stunning</u> cornflower and as clear as crystal, it is very deep—so deep, indeed, that no cable could <u>fathom</u> it.

Fathom: measure the depths of
Indent ¶ (new topic)
[!] SO #2 is preceded by an adverb (Far)
Similes: water is *like* cornflower, crystal
Use commas after 2 or more introductory elements
Note use of em-dash to draw attention
Use commas to set off transitional words (*indeed*)
Dress-ups: adverb clause; quality adj.; strong verb

Many, church steeples, piled one upon another, would not reach from the ground beneath too the surface of the water above, in that place, dwells the Sea King, and his **aquatic** subjects.

[1] Many church steeples <u>piled</u> one upon another would not reach from the ground beneath to the surface of the water above. [2] In that place <u>dwell</u> the Sea King and his <u>aquatic</u> subjects.

Aquatic: living or growing in water
[!] No commas with cumulative adjectives
[!] No commas with essential phrases
Homophone: too/to
Comma splice: needs period, not comma (2 MC)
Comma not needed after #2 SO of 4 words or fewer
Agreement: Sea King *and* subjects *dwell*
No comma before *and* to join 2 items in a series
Dress-ups: strong verbs; quality adjective

We must not imagine that there is nothing at the bottom of the sea but bare, yellow sand no indeed the most remarkable plants grow their. The leaves and stems of which are so **pliant** that the most slight agitation of the water causes them to stir like they had life

[1] We must not imagine that there is nothing at the bottom of the sea but <u>bare</u> yellow sand. [T] No, indeed, the most <u>remarkable</u> plants grow there, the leaves and stems of <u>which</u> are so <u>pliant</u> that the <u>slightest</u> agitation of the water causes them to stir <u>as if</u> they had life.

Pliant: easily bending; flexible
[!] No commas with cumulative adjectives
Fused: use a period to separate 2 main clauses
Use commas to set off transitional words
Homophone: their/there
Correct fragment by joining clause to main clause
Usage: *slightest* (use *most* with 3+ syllables)
Usage: *like/as if* confusion
Use a period at end of statements
Dress-ups: quality adjectives; *which* clause; adverb
    clause

Fish both large and small glide between the branches, as birds fly between the trees here upon land. In the most deepest spot of all stands the castle of the sea king, and it's walls are built of coral and the long gothic windows are of the clearest **amber**.

[1] Fish, both large and small, <u>glide</u> among the branches, <u>as</u> birds fly among the trees here upon land. [2] In the deepest spot of all, stands the castle of the Sea King. [1] Its walls are built of coral, and the long <u>gothic</u> windows are of the clearest amber.

Amber: a pale reddish-yellow fossil resin
[!] Use commas around nonessential phrases
Use *between* to compare 2 items; *among*, 3 or more
Simile: fishes are *like* birds
Usage: don't use *most* with *-est* in superlatives
Comma needed after #2 SO of 5 or more words
Capitalize proper nouns (*Sea King*)
Poor choice of *and* to join main clauses
It's = it is; Its = possessive of *it*
Compound sentence needs comma: MC, cc MC
Dress-ups: strong verb; adv. clause; quality adjective

Week 2

Splendidly the roof is formed of shells which open and close as the water flows over them, there appearance is magnificent because in each lays a glittering pearl fit for the **diadem** of a queen.

[3] Splendidly the roof is formed of shells, <u>which</u> open and close <u>as</u> the water flows over them. [1] Their appearance is magnificent <u>because</u> in each lies a <u>glittering pearl fit</u> for the diadem of a queen.

Diadem: crown; cloth headband adorned w/ jewels
Use commas to set off most who/which clauses
Comma splice: needs period, not comma (2 MC)
Homophone: there/their
Usage: *lies*, not *lays* (the pearl lies itself)
[!] Invisible *which* clause: "pearl which is fit..."
Dress-ups: *which* clause; adverb clauses; quality adjective

For many years the sea king had been a widower so his aged mother kept house for him she deserved very great praise especially for her **nurturance** of the little sea-princess's her granddaughters.

[2] For many years the Sea King had been a widower, so his <u>aged</u> mother kept house for him. [1] She deserved very great praise, especially for her nurturance of the little <u>sea-princesses, her</u> granddaughters.

Nurturance: warm physical and emotional care
Indent ¶ (new topic)
Capitalize proper nouns (*Sea King*)
Compound sentence needs comma: MC, cc MC
Fused: use a period to separate 2 main clauses
[!] Use commas to set off nonessential phrases
Sea-princesses is plural, not possessive
Invisible *who* clause + comma: "princesses, who"
Dress-ups: quality adjective

Although, all six were **comely** children the younger were the most striking of them all her skin was as delicate as a rose leaf, and her eyes as blue as the deepest sea, like all the others she had no feet and her body ended in a fish's tail.

[5] Although all six were <u>comely</u> children, the youngest was the most <u>striking</u> of them all. [1] Her skin was as <u>delicate</u> as a rose leaf and her eyes as blue as the deepest sea. [2] Like all the others she had no feet, and her body ended in a fish's tail.

Comely: pleasing in appearance; attractive
Use commas after #5 SO (not after the adverb)
Use superlatives for 3 or more
Subject/Verb agreement: "the youngest was"
Fused: use a period to separate 2 main clauses
Simile: skin is *like* rose leaf; eyes *like* sea
No comma before *and* to join 2 items in a series
Comma splice: needs period, not comma (2 MC)
Compound sentence needs comma: MC, cc MC
Dress-ups: quality adjectives

throughout the day they frolicked in the **palatial** halls of the castle, fish swam in threw the large amber windows right up to the princess's where they nibbled from the mermaids hands, and allowed themselves to be stroked.

[2] Throughout the day they <u>frolicked</u> in the <u>palatial</u> halls of the castle. [1] Fish swam in through the large <u>amber</u> windows right up to the princesses, <u>where</u> they <u>nibbled</u> from the mermaids' hands and allowed themselves to be <u>stroked</u>.

Palatial: suitable for a palace; magnificent
Capitalize first word of sentences
Comma splice: needs period, not comma (2 MC)
Homophone: threw/through
Princesses is plural, not possessive
[!] Use commas w/ nonessential adj. clauses (where)
Use apostrophe after "s" for plural possession
No comma before *and* to join 2 compound verbs
Dress-ups: strong verbs; quality adj's; adv. clause

Week 3

to each of the young princesses the sea king **bequeathed** a little garden plot where they might dig and plant as they pleased, one princess arranged her flowerbed as a whale, another as a mermaid, that of the youngest contained flowers as red as the suns ray's at sunset.

[2] To each of the young princesses, the Sea King <u>bequeathed</u> a little garden plot <u>where</u> she might dig and plant <u>as</u> she pleased. [1] One princess arranged her flowerbed like a whale, another like a mermaid. [1] That of the youngest contained flowers as red as the sun's rays at sunset.

Bequeathed: passed on to another; handed down
Indent ¶ (new topic)
Capitalize first word of sentences
Use commas after 2+ intro prep. phrases (to … of …)
Capitalize proper nouns (*Sea King*)
Agreement: "each (one) … she"
Comma splices: need period, not comma (2 MC)
Usage: *like/as* confusion
Sun's rays is possessive, then plural (*rays of the sun*)
Simile: flowers are *like* sun's rays at sunset
Dress-ups: strong verb; adverb clauses

She was a **singular** child quiet and thoughtful, whereas her sisters would be thrilled with the marvelous things they obtained from the wrecks of vessels' the younger princess cherished nothing, but her lovely flowers—except one thing a marble statue

[1] She was a <u>singular</u> child, quiet and thoughtful. [5] Whereas her sisters would be <u>thrilled</u> with the <u>marvelous</u> things they obtained from the wrecks of vessels, the youngest princess <u>cherished</u> nothing but her lovely flowers—except one thing, a marble statue.

Singular: distinctive; unique; unusual
[!] Use commas to set off nonessential phrases, twice
Comma splice: needs period, not comma (2 MC)
Use commas after #5 Sentence Openers
Vessels is plural, not plural possessive
Use superlatives for 3 or more
No comma before cc to join 2 items in a series
Note use of em-dash to draw attention
Use a period at end of statements
Dress-ups: quality adjectives; strong verb

Carved out of pure white stone the statue was the **rendering** of a handsome boy which had fallen to the bottom of the sea from a wreck, beside the statue, the youngest mermaid had planted a rose-colored, weeping willow

[7] Carved out of <u>pure</u> white stone, the statue was the rendering of a handsome boy, <u>which</u> had fallen to the bottom of the sea from a wreck. [2] Beside the statue the youngest mermaid had planted a <u>rose-colored</u> weeping willow.

Rendering: an artistic depiction or representation
Use commas after #7 Sentence Openers (-ed)
Use commas to set off most who/which clauses
Comma splice: needs period, not comma (2 MC)
Comma not needed after #2 SO of 4 words or fewer
[!] No commas with cumulative adjectives
Use a period at end of statements
Dress-ups: quality adjectives; *which* clause

Splendidly it had grown, and soon hanged it's fresh branches over the statue, enchanted by any information she might gain about the world above the sea the little mermaid made her **venerable** grandmother tell her all she new of the ships and towns.

[3] Splendidly it had grown and soon hung its fresh branches over the statue.
[7] Enchanted by any information she might gain about the world above the sea, the little mermaid made her <u>venerable</u> grandmother tell her all she knew of the ships and towns.

Venerable: worthy of respect b/c of age & dignity
Indent ¶, 2nd part (new topic)
No comma before *and* to join 2 compound verbs
Usage: *hung* is preferred, but *hanged* is also correct
It's = *it is; Its* = possessive of *it*
Comma splice: needs period, not comma (2 MC)
Use commas after #7 Sentence Openers (-ed)
Homophone: new/knew
Dress-ups: quality adjective

Week 4

To her, it seemed most amazing that flowers of the land should have fragrance, and that fish among the tree's could sing so sweetly, when you have reached your 15th year said the grandmother. You will have our **sanction** to rise up out of the sea. *[quotation continues]*

[2] To her it seemed most amazing that flowers of the land should have fragrance and that fish among the trees could sing so <u>sweetly</u>.
    [5] "When you have reached your fifteenth year," said the grandmother, "you will have our sanction to rise up out of the sea. *[quotation continues]*

Sanction: authoritative permission
Indent ¶, 2nd part (new speaker)
Comma not needed after #2 SO of 4 words or fewer
No comma before *and* to join 2 items in a series (2 *that* clauses)
Trees is plural, not possessive
Comma splice: needs period, not comma (2 MC)
Use quotation marks with direct quotations
Spell out ordinal numbers
Use comma with verb of speaking & direct quotation
Use comma + lc for 2nd part of interrupted quotation
Dress-ups: -ly adverb

---

you may sit on the rocks in the **luminous** moonlight while the great ships are sailing by in the following year, one of the sister's would be 15 since each mermaid was a year younger then the next the youngest would have to endure 5 years before her turn came.

[1] You may sit on the rocks in the <u>luminous</u> moonlight <u>while</u> the great ships are sailing by."
    [2] In the following year one of the sisters would be fifteen. [5] Since each mermaid was a year younger than the next, the youngest would have to <u>endure</u> five years <u>before</u> her turn came.

Luminous: bright; shining
Indent ¶, 2nd part (new topic)
No starting quotation marks b/c continued quotation
Capitalize first word of sentences
Close quotations with quotation marks
Fused: use a period to separate 2 main clauses (twice)
Comma optional after #2 SO of 4 words or fewer
Sisters is plural, not possessive
Spell out numbers written as one or two words
Usage: *then/than* confusion
Use commas after #5 Sentence Openers
Dress-ups: strong adj, verb; adv clauses (incl. *before*)

However each promised to tell the others' what they discovered on their **impending** visit, and what they thought the most pleasing, because there grandmother could not tell them as much as they wanted to know.

[T] However, each promised to tell the others what she discovered on her <u>impending</u> visit and what she thought the most pleasing, <u>because</u> their grandmother could not tell them as much <u>as</u> they wanted to know.

Impending: about to occur
Use commas after introductory transitions
Others is plural, not plural possessive
Agreement: "each (one) … she … her"
No comma before *and* to join 2 items in a series (here, two clauses starting with *what*)
Homophone: there/their
Dress-ups: quality adjective; adverb clauses

None of them **yearned** so much for their turn to come as the younger. She who had the longest time to wait, and who was so quiet and thoughtful

[1] None of them <u>yearned</u> so much for her turn to come as the youngest, she <u>who</u> had the longest time to wait and <u>who</u> was so quiet and thoughtful.

Yearned: had a strong but sorrowful desire
Agreement: "None … her"
Correct fragment by joining clause to main clause
No comma before *and* to join 2 items in a series (two *who* clauses)
Use a period at end of statements
Dress-ups: strong verb; *who* clauses

Week 5

As soon as the eldest were 15 she was allowed to rise to the surface of the ocean, and when she returned she had 100s of things to wondrously **recount** to her sisters.

　　[5] As soon as the eldest was fifteen, she was allowed to rise to the surface of the ocean. [5] When she returned, she had hundreds of things wondrously to recount to her sisters.

Recount: to relate or narrate; tell in detail
Indent ¶ (time has passed)
Agreement: "the eldest" is singular, so "was"
Spell out numbers written as one or two words
Use commas after #5 Sentence Openers (twice)
Poor choice of *and* to join main clauses
[!] Discuss not splitting infinitives (see Appendix)
Dress-ups: -ly adverb; strong verb

The exquisitest experience she told her sisters was to lay in the moonlight and gaze on a town where the lights were twinkling like 100s of stars, having heard the voices, and the merry bells pealing out from the churches I **pine** for them.

"The most exquisite experience," she told her sisters, "was to lie in the moonlight and gaze on a town where the lights were twinkling like hundreds of stars. [4] Having heard the voices and the merry bells pealing out from the churches, I pine for them."

Pine: long for deeply
Use quotation marks with direct quotations
Form the superlative with *most* if adj. is 3+ syllables
Use comma with verb of speaking & direct quotation
Usage: *lay/lie* confusion
Simile: lights are *like* stars
Spell out numbers written as one or two words
Comma splice: needs period, not comma (2 MC)
No comma before *and* to join 2 items (voices, bells)
Use commas after #4 SO (-ing phrase)
SO note: #1 no longer marked; continue if needed
Dress-ups: quality adj's; strong verbs; adverb clause

Listening eagerly to all these descriptions the littlest mermaid fancies she can here the **hustle and bustle** all the way down in the depths of the sea

[4] Listening eagerly to all these descriptions, the littlest mermaid fancied she could hear the hustle and bustle all the way down in the depths of the sea.

Hustle and bustle: energetic commotion; noisy and rapid activity
Use commas after #4 SO (-ing phrase)
Don't switch tenses
Homophone: here/hear
Use a period at end of statements
Dress-ups: -ly adverb; strong verb

In another year the 2ⁿᵈ sister was permitted too rise two the surface and too swim about, where she pleased, rising just as the sun was setting she murmured upon her return that was the most **pictorial** site of all because the hole sky resembled gold.

　　[2] In another year the second sister was permitted to rise to the surface and to swim about where she pleased. [4] Rising just as the sun was setting, she murmured upon her return, "That was the most pictorial sight of all because the whole sky resembled gold."

Pictorial: suggesting the visual appeal of a picture
Indent ¶ (time has passed)
Spell out ordinal numbers
Homophone: too/two/to; site/sight; hole/whole
[!] No commas w/ mid-sentence adv. clause (where)
Comma splice: needs period, not comma (2 MC)
Use commas after #4 SO (-ing phrase)
Use comma with verb of speaking & direct quotation
Use quotation marks with direct quotations
Dress-ups: adverb clauses; strong verbs; quality adj.

Week 6

The 3ʳᵈ sisters turn followed, the boldest of them all, she **brazenly** swam up a broad river that emptied itself into the sea on the banks she saw hills covered with beautiful vines while castles peeped out from amid the proud trees of the forest.

　　[6] The third sister's turn followed. [4] The boldest of them all, she brazenly swam up a broad river that emptied itself into the sea. [2] On the banks she saw hills covered with beautiful vines, while castles peeped out from amid the proud trees of the forest.

Brazenly: boldly; with great self-confidence
Indent ¶ (time has passed)
Spell out ordinal numbers
Use apostrophes to show possession
Comma splice: needs period, not comma (2 MC)
Disguised #4 ("*Being* the boldest of them all")
[!] *which* clause using *that* (see Appendix)
Fused: use a period to separate 2 main clauses
[!] Use commas to set off contrasting adv. clauses
Dress-ups: quality adj's & verb; -ly adv.; adv clause

In a narrow creek, she found a whole troop of human children **cavorting** in the water, she wanted to play with them but they fled in great fright. Then a little black animal jumped into the water, and barked at her so terribly she became frightened

[2] In a <u>narrow</u> creek she found a whole troop of human children <u>cavorting</u> in the water. She wanted to play with them, but they <u>fled</u> in great fright. [T] Then a little black animal jumped into the water and barked at her so <u>terribly</u> she became <u>frightened</u>.

Cavorting: having lively fun
Comma optional after #2 SO of 4 words or fewer
Comma splice: needs period, not comma (2 MC)
Compound sentence needs comma: MC, cc MC
No comma before *and* to join 2 compound verbs
    (What is different about these 2 sentences? One
    repeats a subject after the cc; the other doesn't.)
Use a period at end of statements
Dress-ups: quality adjectives; strong verb; -ly adverb

More **timorous** the forth sister remained in the sea; she reported that the sky above looked like a bell of glass the dolphins sported in the waves and the grate whales spouted water from its nostrils till it seemed like a hundred fountains were gushing.

[4] More <u>timorous</u>, the fourth sister remained in the sea. She reported that the sky above looked like a bell of glass, the dolphins <u>sported</u> in the waves, and the great whales <u>spouted</u> water from their nostrils <u>till</u> it seemed <u>as if</u> a hundred fountains were <u>gushing</u>.

Timorous: fearful; timid
Indent ¶ (time has passed)
[!] Disguised #4 ("Being more timorous …")
Use commas after #4 SO (-ing phrase)
Homophone: forth/fourth; grate/great
Separate only closely-related MCs with semicolons
Simile: sky is *like* glass bell
Use commas with 3 or more items in a series
Agreement: "whales … their"
Usage: *like/as if* confusion
Dress-ups: quality adj.; strong verbs; adverb clauses

Since the 5th sisters birthday occurred in the winter she saw what the others had not seen the first time they went up, immense icebergs were floating about, each like a pearl she said but larger and **loftier** than the churches built by men.

[5] Since the fifth sister's birthday occurred in the winter, she saw what the others had not seen the first time they went up. "<u>Immense</u> icebergs were floating about, each like a pearl," she said, "but larger and <u>loftier</u> than the churches built by men."

Loftier: extending higher in the air
Indent ¶ (time has passed)
Spell out ordinal numbers
Use apostrophes to show possession
Use commas after #5 Sentence Openers
Comma splice: needs period, not comma (2 MC)
Use quotation marks with direct quotations
Use comma with verb of speaking & direct quotation
Simile: icebergs are *like* pearl, church
Dress-ups: quality adjectives

Week 7

when at first the sisters had permission to **ascend** to the surface they were each delighted, now as grown-up girls however they could go when they pleased, and had grown indifferent to it.

[5] When at first the sisters had permission to <u>ascend</u> to the surface, they were each delighted. [T] Now as grown-up girls, however, they could go <u>when</u> they pleased and had <u>grown</u> <u>indifferent</u> to it.

Ascend: go upward; rise
Indent ¶ (new topic)
Capitalize first word of sentences
Use commas after #5 Sentence Openers
Comma splice: needs period, not comma (2 MC)
Use commas to set off transitional words
No comma before *and* to join 2 compound verbs
Dress-ups: strong verbs; adverb clause; quality adj.

They wished themselves back again in the water, and after a month had past they said it was much more **picturesque** down below, and often pleasanter to be at home.

They wished themselves back again in the water. [5] After a month had passed, they said it was much more <u>picturesque</u> down below and often <u>pleasanter</u> to be at home.

Picturesque: striking, attractive, and vivid
Poor choice of *and* to join main clauses
Homophone: past/passed
[!] Tricky #5: *after* is a conjunction here, not prep.
Use commas after #5 Sentence Openers
No comma before *and* to join 2 items in a series
    (2 adjectives: "more picturesque and pleasanter")
Dress-ups: quality adjectives

Having still to wait her turn the youngest sister felt quite **forlorn**. Oh were I but fifteen years old spoke she I know that I should love the world up there, and all the people which live in it.

[4] Having still to wait her turn, the youngest sister felt quite <u>forlorn</u>. [T] "Oh, were I but fifteen years old," spoke she, "I know that I should love the world up there and all the people <u>who</u> live in it."

Forlorn: miserable; dreary (quality adjective)
Indent ¶ (new topic & speaker)
Use commas after #4 SO (-ing phrase)
Use quotation marks with direct quotations
Use commas after introductory interjections
[!] "Were I" correct—subjunctive (she's *not* fifteen)
Use comma with verb of speaking & direct quotation
No comma before *and* to join 2 items (*world, people*)
Use *who* for people, *which* for things (who clause)

At last the little mermaid reached her 15th year well now you are grown up said the old **dowager** her grandmother let me adorn you like your sisters lovingly she placed a wreath of white lilys in her hair.

[T] At last the little mermaid reached her fifteenth year.
[T] "Well, now, you are grown up," said the old <u>dowager, her</u> grandmother. "Let me <u>adorn</u> you like your sisters."
[3] Lovingly she placed a wreath of white lilies in her hair.

Dowager: an elderly woman of social importance
Indent ¶ (time has passed; new speaker)
Spell out ordinal numbers
Fused (3): use a period to separate 2 main clauses
Use quotation marks with direct quotations
Use commas to set off transitions & quotations
Invisible *who* + comma: "dowager, who was her …"
Spelling: *lilies*
Dress-ups: strong verb

Week 8

Her grandmother ordered 8 great oysters to attach themself to the tail of the princess to properly **betoken** her high rank. But they hurt me so protested the little mermaid pride must suffer pain replied the old lady

Her grandmother ordered eight great oysters to attach themselves to the tail of the princess to <u>betoken</u> her high rank <u>properly</u>.
"But they hurt me so," <u>protested</u> the little mermaid.
"Pride must <u>suffer</u> pain," replied the old lady.

Betoken: gave evidence of; was a sign of
Indent ¶, 2nd part (new speakers)
Spell out numbers written as one or two words
Spelling: *themselves*
[!] Discuss not splitting infinitives (see Appendix)
Use quotation marks with direct quotations
Use comma with verb of speaking & direct quotation
Fused: use a period to separate 2 main clauses
Use a period at end of statements
Dress-ups: strong verbs; -ly adverb

Oh how gladly she would have shaken off all this **pomp** and lain aside the heavy wreath, the red flowers in her own garden would have suited her much better but she could not altar her circumstances.

[T] Oh, how <u>gladly</u> she would have shaken off all this pomp and laid aside the heavy wreath! The red flowers in her own garden would have suited her much better, but she could not <u>alter</u> her circumstances.

Pomp: stately or ceremonial display
Indent ¶ (new topic)
Use commas to set off transitional words
Laid = past of lay (lay, laid, laid)
Fix this comma splice with exclamation rather than period in place of the comma
Compound sentence needs comma: MC, cc MC
Homophone: altar/alter
Dress-ups: -ly adverb; strong verb

Saying farewell she raised as lightly as a bubble to the surface of the water, the sun had just set as she rose her head above the waves and through the glimmering twilight beamed the evening star in all it's beauty and the clouds were **tinted** with crimson and gold.

[4] Saying farewell, she rose as lightly as a bubble to the surface of the water. The sun had just set <u>as</u> she raised her head above the waves. [2] Through the <u>glimmering</u> twilight <u>beamed</u> the evening star in all its beauty, and the clouds were <u>tinted</u> with <u>crimson</u> and <u>gold</u>.

Tinted: given a shade of a color
Indent ¶ (new scene)
Use commas after #4 SO (-ing phrase)
Usage: *raise/rise* confusion (twice). You raise an object; rise oneself. *Rose*=past of *rise*
Simile: the little mermaid is *like* a bubble
Comma splice: needs period, not comma (2 MC)
Poor choice of *and* to join main clauses
Its = possessive of *it*
Compound sentence needs comma: MC, cc MC
Dress-ups: adverb clause; quality adj's; strong verbs

Looming nearby, she beheld a large ship which lied **becalmed** on the water for not a breeze stirred; the sailors sat idly on deck or among the rigging. She heard music and song on board, as darkness drew near one hundred colored lanterns were lighted.

[4] Looming nearby, a large ship lay <u>becalmed</u> on the water, for not a breeze <u>stirred</u>. The sailors sat <u>idly</u> on deck or among the rigging. She heard music and song on board. [5] As darkness drew near, one hundred colored lanterns were lighted.

Becalmed: motionless because no wind
Illegal #4: word after " , " should do the *inging*
Lay = past of *lie (lie, lay, lain)*
Compound sent. needs comma: MC, cc MC (cc = *for*)
Separate only closely-related MCs with semicolons
Comma splice: needs period, not comma (2 MC)
Use commas after #5 Sentence Openers
Usage: *lighted* and *lit* are both correct past tense
Dress-ups: quality adjective; strong verb; -ly adverb

Week 9

The little mermaid swimmed close to the cabin windows, as the waves lifted her up now and then she could peer in through clear, glass windowpanes, and glimpse a number of **well-attired** people within.

The little mermaid swam close to the cabin windows. [5] As the waves lifted her up, now and then she could <u>peer</u> in through clear glass windowpanes and <u>glimpse</u> a number of <u>well-attired</u> people within.

Well-attired: well-dressed
Spelling: *swam* is the past of *swim*
Comma splice: needs period, not comma (2 MC)
Use commas after #5 Sentence Openers (confusing w/o comma: does "now and then" go w/ the waves lifting her up or with her looking in the window?)
[!] No commas with cumulative adjectives
No comma before *and* to join 2 compound verbs
Dress-ups: strong verbs; quality adjective

---

among them was a young Prince with large black eyes who was sixteen years of age and his birthday was being **commemorated** with much rejoicing

[2] Among them was a young prince with large black eyes <u>who</u> was sixteen years of age. His birthday was being <u>commemorated</u> with much rejoicing.

Commemorated: honored by ceremony, observance
Capitalize first word of sentences
Use lc for common nouns
[!] No commas with essential *who* clauses
Poor choice of *and* to join main clauses
Use a period at end of statements
Dress-ups: *who* clause; strong verb

When the **vibrant** prince came out of the cabin more than 100 rockets raised in the air, making it as dazzling as day, the ship was so brightly lit that the mermaid could gaze at all the people distinctly and plainly

[5] When the <u>vibrant</u> prince came out of the cabin, more than a hundred rockets rose in the air, making it as <u>dazzling</u> as day. The ship was so <u>brightly</u> lit that the mermaid could <u>gaze</u> at all the people <u>distinctly and plainly</u>.

Vibrant: vigorous; energetic; exciting
Use commas after #5 Sentence Openers
Spell out numbers written as one or two words
Usage: *raise/rise* confusion (*rose* = past tense)
Comma splice: needs period, not comma (2 MC)
Use a period at end of statements
Dress-ups: quality adjectives; -ly adverb; strong verb
Advanced Dress-up: dual -ly adverbs

Never having observed such fireworks before they so startled the little mermaid that she dived under water, when she again stretched out her hand it appeared like all the **celestial** stars were falling from the sky

[4] Never having observed such fireworks before, the little mermaid was so startled that she dived under water. [5] When she again stretched out her hand, it appeared <u>as if</u> all the <u>celestial</u> stars were falling from the sky.

Celestial: pertaining to the visible heaven
Use commas after #4 SO (-ing phrase)
Illegal #4: word after " , " should do the *inging*
Usage: *dove* is also correct
Comma splice: needs period, not comma (2 MC)
Use commas after #5 Sentence Openers
Usage: *like/as if* confusion
Use a period at end of statements
Dress-ups: adverb clause; quality adjective

Week 10

Dreamily the young prince appeared very handsome. As he pressed the hands of all present, and smiled at them while the music **resounded** through the clear, night air

[3] Dreamily the young prince appeared very handsome <u>as</u> he <u>pressed</u> the hands of all present and smiled at them, <u>while</u> the music <u>resounded</u> through the clear night air.

Resounded: filled with sound; sounded loudly
Correct fragment by joining clause to main clause
No comma before *and* to join 2 compound verbs
[!] Comma w/ adv. clause of extreme contrast (while)
[!] No commas with cumulative adjectives
Use a period at end of statements
Dress-ups: adverb clauses; strong verbs

---

although it was late the little mermaid could not take his eyes from the striking prince, the colored lanterns had been extinguished no more rockets **illuminated** the air and the cannon had ceased firing.

[5] Although it was late, the little mermaid could not take her eyes from the <u>striking</u> prince. The <u>colored</u> lanterns had been <u>extinguished</u>, no more rockets <u>illuminated</u> the air, and the cannon had <u>ceased</u> firing.

Illuminated: brightened with light
Capitalize first word of sentences
Use commas after #5 Sentence Openers
Her, referring to the mermaid, not *his*
Comma splice: needs period, not comma (2 MC)
Use commas with 3 or more items in a series
[!] Note use of past perfect tense (*had been; had ceased*)
Dress-ups: quality adjectives, strong verbs

Suddenly the sea became restless and a moaning grumbling sound could be heard beneath the waves; rocking up and down on the **unquiet** water the little mermaid remained buy the cabin window

[3] Suddenly the sea became <u>restless</u>, and a <u>moaning</u>, <u>grumbling</u> sound could be heard beneath the waves. [4] Rocking up and down on the <u>unquiet</u> water, the little mermaid remained by the cabin window.

Unquiet: agitated or disturbed; not quiet
Indent ¶ (new topic)
Compound sentence needs comma: MC, cc MC
Use commas with coordinate adjectives
Separate only closely-related MCs with semicolons
Use commas after #4 SO (-ing phrase)
Homophone: buy/by
Use a period at end of statements
Dress-ups: quality adjectives

The sales were quickly **unfurled** and the noble ship continued her passage but soon the waves rose higher heavy clouds darkened the sky and lightning appeared in the distance.

The sails were <u>quickly</u> unfurled and the <u>noble</u> ship continued her passage, but soon the waves rose higher. Heavy clouds <u>darkened</u> the sky, and lightning appeared in the distance.

Unfurled: spread open or out
Homophone: sales/sails
[!] 1st sentence: b/c of *two* "MC, cc MC," placing a comma before *and* makes the sentence too choppy
Fused: use a period to separate 2 main clauses
2nd sentence needs comma: MC, cc MC
Dress-ups: -ly adverb; strong verbs; quality adjective

Week 11

A dreadful storm was approaching, the great ship pursued her flying course over the **tempestuous** sea the waves rose mountains high as if they would have overtopped the mast but the ship dived like a swan between them.

[6] A <u>dreadful</u> storm was approaching. The great ship <u>pursued</u> her <u>flying</u> course over the <u>tempestuous</u> sea. The waves rose mountains high <u>as if</u> they would have <u>overtopped</u> the mast, but the ship dived like a swan between them.

Tempestuous: violent; stormy
Comma splice: needs period, not comma (2 MC)
Fused: use a period to separate 2 main clauses
Metaphor: waves = mountains
Compound sentence needs comma: MC, cc MC
Usage: *dived* and *dove* are both correct past tense
Simile: ship is *like* swan
Dress-ups: quality adj's; strong verbs; adverb clause

---

at length the ship groaned the thick planks gave way under the lashing of the sea as it broke over the deck and the mainmast snapped **asunder** like a reed the ship lied over on her side and the water rushed in

[T] At length the ship <u>groaned</u>, the thick planks gave way under the lashing of the sea <u>as</u> it broke over the deck, and the mainmast <u>snapped</u> asunder like a reed. The ship lay over on her side, and the water <u>rushed</u> in.

Asunder: into pieces
Capitalize first word of sentences
Use commas with 3 or more items in a series
Simile: mainmast is *like* reed
Fused: use a period to separate 2 main clauses
Lay = past of *lie (lie, lay, lain)*
Compound sentence needs comma: MC, cc MC
Use a period at end of statements
Dress-ups: strong verbs; adverb clause

The little mermaid now percieved that the crew were in **imminent** danger, and when a flash of lightning revealed the hole seen she could see every one who had been on bored accepting the prince.

    The little mermaid now <u>perceived</u> that the crew were in <u>imminent</u> danger. [5] When a flash of lightning revealed the whole scene, she could see everyone <u>who</u> had been on board excepting the prince.

Imminent: likely to occur at any moment
Indent ¶ (new topic)
Spelling: *perceived* ("*i* before *e*" rule)
Poor choice of *and* to join main clauses
Homophones: hole/whole; seen/scene; bored/board
Use commas after #5 Sentence Openers
Spelling: *everyone* is one word
Usage: *accept/except* confusion
Dress-ups: strong verb; quality adjective; who clause

When the ship parted she saw the prince sink **exhaustedly** into the deep waves, at first, she was glad because she thought he would now be with her but then she remembered that human beings could not live in the water he must not die

[5] When the ship <u>parted</u>, she saw the prince sink <u>exhaustedly</u> into the deep waves. [T] At first she was glad <u>because</u> she thought he would now be with her, but then she remembered that human beings could not live in the water. [6] He must not die!

Exhaustedly: completely worn out or drained
Use commas after #5 Sentence Openers
Comma splice: needs period, not comma (2 MC)
Comma not needed after #2 SO of 4 words or fewer
Compound sentence needs comma: MC, cc MC
Fused: use a period to separate 2 main clauses
Use an end mark at end of sentences (here, an
    exclamation mark)
Dress-ups: strong verb; -ly adverb; adverb clause

Week 12

With beams and planks **strewn** about the sea heaved as she swam between the peaces forgetting that the wood could crush her then she dived under the dark waters until at length she managed to reach the prince.

[2] With beams and planks strewn about, the sea heaved <u>as</u> she swam among the pieces, forgetting that the wood could <u>crush</u> her. [T] Then she dived under the dark waters <u>until</u> at length she managed to reach the prince.

Strewn: scattered or sprinkled over
Use commas after long #2 Sentence Openers
Usage: *between/among* confusion
Use commas to set off nonessential phrases
Homophone: peaces/pieces
Fused: use a period to separate 2 main clauses
Usage: *dived* and *dove* are both correct past tense
Dress-ups: adverb clauses; strong verbs

Loosing the power of swimming in that stormy sea the prince would have **precipitately** perished had not the little mermaid come too his assistance, his limbs were failing him, his beautiful eyes were closed.

[4] Losing the power of swimming in that <u>stormy</u> sea, the prince would have <u>precipitately</u> perished had not the little mermaid come to his assistance. His limbs were <u>failing</u> him; his beautiful eyes were closed.

Precipitately: suddenly; unexpectedly; prematurely
Spelling: *losing/loosing* confusion
Use commas after #4 SO (-ing phrase)
Alliteration: stormy sea; precipitately perished
Homophone: too/to
Comma splice: needs period, not comma (2 MC)
Use semicolons to separate closely-related MCs
Dress-ups: quality adjective; -ly adverb; strong verbs

She held his head above the water, and let the waves drift them where they would, in the morning, the storm had ceased but she could not percieve a single fragment of the **vanished** ship.

She held his head above the water and let the waves <u>drift</u> them <u>where</u> they would.
    [2] In the morning the storm had <u>ceased</u>, but she could not <u>perceive</u> a single fragment of the <u>vanished</u> ship.

Vanished: gone from sight; disappeared
Indent ¶, 2nd part (time has passed)
No comma before *and* to join 2 compound verbs
Comma splice: needs period, not comma (2 MC)
Comma optional after #2 SO of 4 words or fewer
Compound sentence needs comma: MC, cc MC
Spelling: *perceive* ("*i* before *e*" rule)
Dress-ups: strong verbs; adverb clause; quality adj.

Although, the sun restored the **hue** of health to the princes cheeks his eyes remained closed the mermaid kissed his high smooth brow, and stroked back his wet hair.

[5] Although the sun <u>restored</u> the hue of health to the prince's cheeks, his eyes remained closed. The mermaid kissed his high, <u>smooth</u> brow and <u>stroked</u> back his wet hair.

Hue: appearance; aspect; color
Use commas after #5 SO (not after the adverb)
Use apostrophes to show possession
Fused: use a period to separate 2 main clauses
Use commas with coordinate adjectives
No comma before *and* to join 2 compound verbs
Dress-ups: strong verbs; quality adjective

Week 13

He seemed to her as the marble statue in her little garden and she wished that he might live. Presently they came in site of land, near the coast stood a well-built **convent**.

He seemed to her like the marble statue in her little garden, and she wished that he might live.
    [3] Presently they came in sight of land. [2] Near the coast <u>stood</u> a <u>well-built</u> convent.

Convent: a community of nuns
Indent ¶, 2nd part (new scene)
Usage: *like/as* confusion
Compound sentence needs comma: MC, cc MC
Homophone: site/sight
Comma splice: needs period, not comma (2 MC)
Dress-ups: strong verb; quality adjective

She swam with the prince to the beach which was covered with fine white sand and their she lay him in the warm **vital** sunshine, taking care to rise his head higher than his body.

She swam with the prince to the beach, <u>which</u> was covered with <u>fine</u> white sand, and there she laid him in the warm, <u>vital</u> sunshine, taking care to raise his head higher than his body.

Vital: necessary to life or well-being
Use commas to set off most who/which clauses
Compound sentence needs comma: MC, cc MC
Homophone: their/there
Usage: *Laid* = past of *lay; raise/rise* confusion
Use commas with coordinate adjectives
Dress-ups: which clause; quality adjectives

When bells **pealed** in the large, white building several young girls came into the garden, and the little mermaid swam out further from the shore, and hid herself among 2 high rocks covering herself with sea foam so that her face might not be scene.

[5] When bells <u>pealed</u> in the large white building, several young girls came into the garden. The little mermaid swam out farther from the shore and hid herself between two high rocks, covering herself with sea foam so that her face might not be seen.

Pealed: rang or chimed
[!] No commas with cumulative adjectives
Use commas after #5 Sentence Openers
Poor choice of *and* to join main clauses
Usage: use *farther* for distance
No comma before *and* to join 2 compound verbs
Use *between* to compare 2 items
Spell out numbers written as one or two words
[!] Use commas to set off nonessential phrases
Homophone: scene/seen
Dress-ups: strong verb

Timidly, a young girl approached the spot where the prince laid and then she fetched others to help, and when the prince came to life again he smiled upon those which stood **confounded** around him

[3] Timidly a young girl <u>approached</u> the spot <u>where</u> the prince lay, and then she <u>fetched</u> others to help. [5] When the prince came to life again, he smiled upon those <u>who</u> stood <u>confounded</u> around him.

Confounded: confused; bewildered; perplexed
Comma optional after #3 Sentence Opener
Lay = past of *lie (lie, lay, lain)*
Compound sentence needs comma: MC, cc MC
Poor choice of *and* to join main clauses
Use commas after #5 Sentence Openers
Use *who* for people, *which* for things
Use a period at end of statements
Dress-ups: strong verbs, adj; adv. clause; *who* clause

Week 14

To the little mermaid, he sent no smile since he new not that she had saved him, **disheartened** she dived down into the water and sorrowfully retreated to her fathers castle.

[2] To the little mermaid he sent no smile <u>since</u> he knew not that she had saved him. [7] Disheartened, she dived down into the water and <u>sorrowfully</u> <u>retreated</u> to her father's castle.

Disheartened: discouraged; less hopeful
Comma optional after #2 SO of 4 words or fewer
Homophone: new/knew
Comma splice: needs period, not comma (2 MC)
Use commas after #7 Sentence Openers (-ed)
Use apostrophes to show possession
Dress-ups: adverb clause; -ly adverb; strong verb

Initially, the youngest mermaid **divulged** nothing about what she had seen during her first visit to the surface of the water; many an evening and morning did she raise to the place where she had left the prince

    [3] Initially the youngest mermaid <u>divulged</u> nothing about what she had seen during her first visit to the surface of the water. [2] Many an evening and morning did she rise to the place <u>where</u> she had left the prince.

Divulged: made known; revealed
Indent ¶ (time has passed)
Comma optional after #3 Sentence Opener
Separate only closely-related MCs with semicolons
[!] Disguised #2 (*During, In, On, At* that time period)
Usage: *raise/rise* confusion
Use a period at end of statements
Dress-ups: strong verb; adverb clause

---

she beholded the fruits in the garden ripen and the snow on the tops of the mountains melt away but she never saw the prince, and therefore she returned home always more **despondent** then before.

She <u>beheld</u> the fruits in the garden <u>ripen</u> and the snow on the tops of the mountains melt away, but she never saw the prince. [T] Therefore, she returned home always more <u>despondent</u> than before.

Despondent: discouraged; gloomy; hopeless
Capitalize first word of sentences
Spelling: *beheld* is the past of *behold*
Use commas before cc (*but*) in MC, cc MC
Avoid stringing together sentences with *and*
Use commas after introductory transitions
Usage: *then/than* confusion
Dress-ups: strong verbs; quality adjective

At length when she could bare it no longer she told her sister's everything, an intimate friend of one, who happened to no who the prince was, told them where he came from, and where his **opulent** palace stood.

    [2] At length <u>when</u> she could bear it no longer, she told her sisters everything. An <u>intimate</u> friend of one, <u>who</u> happened to know <u>who</u> the prince was, told them <u>where</u> he came from and <u>where</u> his <u>opulent</u> palace stood.

Opulent: wealthy; luxurious
Indent ¶ (new topic)
Homophones: bare/bear; no/know
Use commas after two or more introductory elements
Sisters is plural, not possessive
Comma splice: needs period, not comma (2 MC)
No comma before *and* to join 2 items (*where* clauses)
Dress-ups: adv. clauses; quality adj's; *who* clauses

Week 15

"Come little sister", said the other princesses. Eagerly they **entwined** their arms and rose up close to the princes palace bright with shining yellow stone long flights of marble steps and gilded cupolas.

 "Come, little sister," said the other princesses.
 [3] Eagerly they <u>entwined</u> their arms and rose up close to the prince's <u>palace, bright</u> with shining yellow stone, long flights of marble steps, and <u>gilded</u> cupolas.

Entwined: interlaced; clasped or enfolded together
Cupola: a dome, or a small rounded, domed structure
Indent ¶ (new speaker; new topic)
Set off NDAs with commas ("little sister")
Periods & commas go inside quotation marks
Use apostrophes to show possession
[!] Use commas to set off nonessential phrases
Use commas with 3 or more items in a series
Dress-ups: strong verb; invisible which; quality adj.

Knowing where her prince lived the little mermaid spent many an evening in the water near the palace she would swim much nearer the shore then any of the other's **ventured** two do.

[4] Knowing <u>where</u> her prince lived, the little mermaid spent many an evening in the water near the palace. She would swim much nearer the shore than any of the others <u>ventured</u> to do.

Ventured: dared; risked
Use commas after #4 SO (-ing phrase)
Fused: use a period to separate 2 main clauses
Usage: *then/than* confusion
Others is plural, not possessive
Homophone: two/to
Dress-ups: adverb clause; strong verb

Indeed once she swam **unflaggingly** up the narrow channel under the marble balcony which through a broad shadow on the water, and in this spot she would sit and watch the young prince which thought himself quite alone in the bright moonlight

[T] Indeed, once she swam <u>unflaggingly</u> up the narrow channel under the marble balcony, <u>which</u> threw a <u>broad</u> shadow on the water. [2] In this spot she would sit and watch the young prince, <u>who</u> thought himself quite alone in the bright moonlight.

Unflaggingly: without tiring
Use commas after introductory transitions
Use commas with most who/which clauses (twice)
Homophone: through/threw
Poor choice of *and* to join main clauses
Use *who* for people, *which* for things
Use a period at end of statements
Dress-ups: -ly adverb; *which* clause; quality
 adjective; *who* clause

On many a night two when the fisherman with there torch's were out at sea she heard them relate so many wonderful things about the **exemplary** doings of the young prince, that she was thankful she had saved his life.

[2] On many a night, too, <u>when</u> the fishermen with their torches were out at sea, she heard them <u>relate</u> so many wonderful things about the <u>exemplary</u> doings of the young prince that she was thankful she had saved his life.

Exemplary: worthy of imitation; serving as a model
Homophone: two/too; there/their
Use commas to set off transitional words
Agreement: fishermen … their
Torches is plural, not possessive
Use commas after introductory adverb clauses
[!] No commas around noun clauses ("that …")
Dress-ups: adverb clause; strong verb; quality
 adjective

Week 16

remembering how she had saved him he knew nothing of that and could not even dream of her, she realized **ruefully** increasingly, she marveled at human beings, and longed to be able to wander with those who's world seemed so much larger then her own.

[4] Remembering how she had saved him, she realized <u>ruefully</u> that he knew nothing of that and could not even dream of her.
 [3] Increasingly she <u>marveled</u> at human beings and <u>longed</u> to be able to <u>wander</u> with those <u>whose</u> world seemed so much larger than her own.

Ruefully: with sorrow or regret
Indent ¶, 2nd part (new topic)
Capitalize first word of sentences
Use commas after #4 SO (-ing phrase)
Illegal #4: word after " , " should do the *inging*
Fused: use a period to separate 2 main clauses
Comma optional after #3 Sentence Opener
No comma before *and* to join 2 compound verbs
Whose = possessive form of *who*
Usage: *then/than* confusion
Dress-ups: -ly adv.; strong verbs; [!] who (whose)

Because their was so much she wished to know she finally **applied** to her old grandmother who knew all about the upper world which she rightly called the lands above the sea

[5] Because there was so much she wished to know, she finally <u>applied</u> to her old grandmother, <u>who</u> knew all about the upper world, <u>which</u> she rightly called the lands above the sea.

Applied: made a request
Homophone: their/there
Use commas after #5 Sentence Openers
Use commas to set off most who/which clauses
[!] Note: this is true only when they are nonessential
Use a period at end of statements
Dress-ups: strong verb; *who* clause; *which* clause

If human beings are not drowned asked the little mermaid Can they live forever, do they never die as we do here in the sea no they must also die replied the old lady and their **term** of life is even shorter than ours. *[quotation continues]*

[5] "If human beings are not drowned," asked the little mermaid, "can they live forever? Do they never die <u>as</u> we do here in the sea?"
[T] "No, they must also die," replied the old lady, "and their term of life is even shorter than ours. *[quotation continues]*

Term: a period of time with set limits
Indent ¶ (new speakers)
Use quotation marks with direct quotations
Use comma with verb of speaking & direct quotation
Use lc to continue interrupted quotations
Comma splice: needs question mark, not comma
[!] No commas needed with adv. clause (as…)
Fused: use " ? " to separate these 2 main clauses
Use commas after introductory interjections
Dress-ups: adverb clause

We sometimes live 300 years but when we cease too exist here we become only the foam on the surface of the water, down here we have not even a **watery** grave of those who we love. *[quotation continues]*

We sometimes live three hundred years, but <u>when</u> we <u>cease</u> to exist here, we become only the foam on the surface of the water. [2] Down here we have not even a <u>watery</u> grave of those <u>whom</u> we love. *[quotation continues]*

Watery: consisting of water
No quotation marks b/c continued quotation
Spell out numbers written as one or two words
Compound sentence needs comma: MC, cc MC
Homophone: too/to
Use commas after introductory adverb clauses
Comma splice: needs period, not comma (2 MC)
Use *whom* for the objective case (we love *them*)
Dress-ups: adv. clause; verb; adjective; *who* clause

Week 17

We have not immortal souls but as the green seaweed when once it has been cut off we can never flourish more, by contrast human beings have a soul, that lives **eternally**. *[quotation continues]*

We have not <u>immortal</u> souls, but, like the green seaweed <u>when</u> once it has been cut off, we can never <u>flourish</u> more.
[T] "By contrast, human beings have a soul <u>that</u> lives eternally. *[quotation continues]*

Eternally: without end
Indent ¶, 2nd (new topic); continued quotation, so "
Compound sentence needs comma: MC, cc MC
[!] Use commas to set off nonessential phrases
Usage: *like/as* confusion
Comma splice: needs period, not comma (2 MC)
Use commas after introductory transitional phrases
[!] Essential *which* clause using *that*; no comma
Dress-ups: quality adj. & verb; adv. clause; -ly adv.

There soles raise up through the clear pure air beyond the **remote** glittering stars. As we raise out of the water and behold all the land of the earth so do they raise to unknown glorious regions which we shall never witness *[quotation ends]*

Their souls rise up through the clear, <u>pure</u> air beyond the <u>remote</u>, glittering stars. [5] As we rise out of the water and <u>behold</u> all the land of the earth, so do they rise to <u>unknown</u>, glorious regions, <u>which</u> we shall never <u>witness</u>."

Remote: far distant in space
No opening quotation marks b/c continued quotation
Homophones: there/their; soles/souls
Usage: *raise/rise* confusion
Use commas with coordinate adjectives
Use commas after #5 Sentence Openers
Use commas to set off most who/which clauses
Use a period at end of statements
Close quotation with quotation mark
Dress-ups: quality adj's; strong verbs; *which* clause

"I would give all the 100s of years that I have to live to be a human being for only 1 day cried the little mermaid **mournfully** and to have the hope of knowing the happiness of that splendid world above the stars."

"I would give all the hundreds of years <u>that</u> I have to live to be a human being for only one day," cried the little mermaid <u>mournfully</u>, "and to have the hope of knowing the happiness of that <u>splendid</u> world above the stars."

Mournfully: with sorrow or grief
Indent ¶ (new speaker)
Spell out numbers written as one or two words
[!] Essential *which* clause using *that*; no commas
[!] Note: The 2nd *that* is a demonstrative pronoun, which functions as an adjective ("that world")
Use quotation marks around spoken parts only
Use comma with verb of speaking & direct quotation
Dress-ups: w/w clause; -ly adverb; quality adjective

You must not think of that shuddered the old woman. So I shall die and be driven about as sea foam said the little mermaid. Can I do any thing to win a **immortal** sole.

"You must not think of that," <u>shuddered</u> the old woman.
"So I shall die and be <u>driven</u> about as sea foam," said the little mermaid. "Can I do anything to <u>win</u> an <u>immortal</u> soul?"

Immortal: not subject to death; not mortal
Indent ¶ (new speakers)
Use quotation marks with direct quotations
Use comma with verb of speaking & direct quotation
Usage: *anything*, not *any thing*; *an immortal*, not *a*
Homophone: sole/soul.   Close with question mark
Dress-ups: strong verbs; quality adjective

Week 18

No said the old woman unless a man were to love you so much that he promised to be true to you and the priest placed your hands together. Then his soul would **glide** into your body, and you and him both would have a soul. *[quotation continues]*

[T] "No," said the old woman, "<u>unless</u> a man were to love you so much that he promised to be true to you and the priest placed your hands together. [T] Then his soul would <u>glide</u> into your body, and you and he both would have a soul. *[quotation continues]*

Glide: flow or pass smoothly or easily
Indent ¶ (new speaker)
Use quotation marks with direct quotations
Use commas after introductory interjections
Use comma with verb of speaking & direct quotation
[!] No comma before *and* in 1st sentence b/c it joins 2 dependent clauses, the 2nd implied (unless…)
Usage: *he*, not *him* ("you and he would have …")
No close quotation marks b/c quotation continues
Dress-ups: adverb clause; strong verb

Since you have a fishes tale. This can never happen. Sorrowfully the little mermaid sighed, and looked at her fishes tail to distract her, the old lady told her of that evenings **gala** let us be content because this evening we are going to have a court ball.

[5] Since you have a fish's tail, this can never happen."
[3] Sorrowfully the little mermaid <u>sighed</u> and looked at her fish's tail.
To <u>distract</u> her, the old lady told her of that evening's gala. "Let us be <u>content</u> <u>because</u> this evening we are going to have a court ball."

Gala: festive occasion; special celebration
Indent ¶ (new topic; new speaker)
Fish's is possessive, not plural
Homophone: tale/tail
Correct fragment by joining dependent clause to MC
No comma before *and* to join 2 compound verbs
Fused (2): use a period to separate 2 main clauses
Use apostrophes to show possession
Use quotation marks with direct quotations
Capitalize the first word of a quoted sentence
Dress-ups: strong verbs; quality adj.; adverb clause

The crystal ballroom was illuminated by 100s of colossal shells which burned with **iridescent** fire, and through it all, a broad stream of mermen and mermaids danced to the music of there own sweet singing.

The <u>crystal</u> ballroom was <u>illuminated</u> by hundreds of <u>colossal</u> shells, <u>which</u> burned with <u>iridescent</u> fire. [2] Through it all a <u>broad</u> stream of mermen and mermaids danced to the music of their own sweet singing.

Iridescent: varying in rainbow-like colors
Indent ¶ (new scene)
Spell out numbers written as one or two words
Use commas to set off most who/which clauses
Poor choice of *and* to join main clauses
Comma not needed after #2 SO of 4 words or fewer
Homophone: there/their
Dress-ups: quality adjectives; strong verb; *which* clause

The little mermaid sang more sweetly then them all, **fervently**, the whole court applauded her with hands and tails and for a moment the little mermaids heart felt gay because she knew she had the most loveliest voice of any on earth, or in the sea.

The little mermaid sang more sweetly than them all. [3] Fervently the whole court applauded her with hands and tails, and for a moment the little mermaid's heart felt gay because she knew she had the loveliest voice of any on earth or in the sea.

Fervently: showing great warmth and enthusiasm
Usage: *then/than* confusion
Comma splice: needs period, not comma (2 MC)
Comma optional after #3 Sentence Opener
Compound sentence needs comma: MC, cc MC
Use apostrophes to show possession
Superlative error: *most + -est* is redundant
No comma before cc to join 2 items in a series
Dress-ups: -ly adverb; strong verb; adverb clause

Week 19

Despite the **acclamation**, she soon recalled the world above her for she could not forget the charming prince, or her regret that she had not a immortal soul like his.

[2] Despite the acclamation, she soon recalled the world above her, for she could not forget the charming prince or her regret that she had not an immortal soul like his.

Acclamation: demonstration of approval
Compound sentence needs comma: MC, cc MC
No comma before *or* to join 2 items in a series
   (here, both nouns: "the prince or her regret")
Usage: *an* before a vowel
Dress-ups: strong verb; quality adjectives

Silently the young mermaid crept away from her fathers palace, and withdrew to her garden where she sat **melancholy** and alone. He is certainly sailing above she thought to herself he in who's hands I should like to place the happiness of my life. *[quotation continues]*

[3] Silently the young mermaid crept away from her father's palace and withdrew to her garden, where she sat melancholy and alone. "He is certainly sailing above," she thought to herself, "he in whose hands I should like to place the happiness of my life. *[quotation continues]*

Melancholy: mournful; depressed
Indent ¶ (new scene and speaker)
Use apostrophes to show possession
No comma before *and* to join 2 compound verbs
[!] Use commas w/ nonessential adj. clauses (where)
[!] Treat thoughts like speech
Use quotation marks with direct quotations
Use comma with verb of speaking & direct quotation
Whose = possessive form of *who*
No close quotation marks b/c quotation continues
Dress-ups: verbs; adv. clause; adj.; -ly adverb; who

I will venture all to win him, and an immortal soul, while my sisters are dancing in my fathers palace I will go to the sea which by whom I have always been **intimidated** but she can provide me advise and assistance.

I will venture all to win him and an immortal soul. [5] While my sisters are dancing in my father's palace, I will go to the Sea Witch, by whom I have always been intimidated, but she can provide me advice and assistance."

Intimidated: filled with fear
No comma before *and* to join 2 items in a series
Comma splice: needs period, not comma (2 MC)
Use apostrophes to show possession
Use commas after #5 Sentence Openers
Capitalize proper nouns
Usage: *which/witch* and *advise/advice* confusion
[!] Use commas around nonessential clauses
Close quotation with quotation marks
Dress-ups: strong verbs; *who* clause; quality adj.

To reach the **dominions** of the Sea Witch, the little mermaid was obliged to pass through crushing whirlpools, and across warm bubbling mire; next came the forest, where polypi half animals and half plants attempted to grab any thing passing through.

To reach the dominions of the Sea Witch, the little mermaid was obliged to pass through crushing whirlpools and across warm, bubbling mire. [T] Next came the forest, where polypi, half animals and half plants, attempted to grab anything passing through.

Dominions: territories under someone's control
Indent ¶ (new scene)
[!] SO = infinitive phrase functioning as adjective
No comma before *and* to join 2 items in a series
   (here, 2 prepositional phrases: *through & across*)
Use commas with coordinate adjectives
Separate only closely-related MCs with semicolons
[!] Use commas to set off nonessential phrases
Spelling: *anything* is one word
Dress-ups: strong verbs; quality adjectives; adverb
   clause

Week 20

Darting through the polypi the little mermaid narrowly managed too escape from there clutches, and at last she reached the **barren** marshy clearing around the Sea Witches house built with the bones of shipwrecked human beings.

[4] Darting through the polypi, the little mermaid <u>narrowly</u> managed to escape from their clutches. [T] At last she reached the <u>barren</u>, <u>marshy</u> clearing around the Sea Witch's <u>house</u>, <u>built</u> with the bones of <u>shipwrecked</u> human beings.

Barren: not fruitful; lacking vegetation
Use commas after #4 SO (-ing phrase)
Homophones: too/to; there/their
Avoid stringing together sentences with *and*
Use commas with coordinate adjectives
Use apostrophes to show possession + sp. change
Invisible which clause: "house, which was built"
Use commas to set off invisible who/which clauses
Dress-ups: -ly adverb; quality adjectives; w/w clause

There sat the Sea Witch allowing a toad to eat from her mouth just like people sometimes feed a canary with a peice of sugar; calling the hideous water-snakes her little chickens she allowed them to **repugnantly** crawl all over her bosom

There sat the Sea Witch, allowing a toad to eat from her mouth <u>just as</u> people sometimes feed a canary with a piece of sugar. [4] Calling the <u>hideous</u> water-snakes her little chickens, she allowed them to <u>crawl</u> <u>repugnantly</u> all over her bosom.

Repugnantly: disgustingly; distastefully; repulsively
[!] Use commas to set off nonessential phrases
Usage: *like/as* confusion
Spelling: *piece* ("*i* before *e*" rule)
Separate only closely-related MCs with semicolons
Use commas after #4 SO (-ing phrase)
[!] Discuss not splitting infinitives (see Appendix)
Use a period at end of statements
Dress-ups: adv. clause; quality adj. & verb; -ly adv.

I know what you want the sea which **chortled** you want to get rid of your fish's tail, and two have too supports instead of it like human beings so that the young prince may fall in love with you and you may have an immortal soul. *[quotation continues]*

"I know what you want," the Sea Witch <u>chortled</u>. "You want to get rid of your fish's tail and to have two supports instead of it, like human beings, so that the young prince may fall in love with you and you may have an immortal soul. *[quotation continues]*

Chortled: to chuckle or laugh gleefully
Indent ¶ (new speaker)
Use quotation marks with direct quotations
Use comma with verb of speaking & direct quotation
Homophone & capitalization: *Sea Witch; too/two/to*
Fused: use a period to separate 2 main clauses
No comma before *and* to join 2 compound verbs
[!] Use commas to set off nonessential phrases
No close quotation marks b/c quotation continues
Dress-ups: strong verb

Its very foolish of you the Sea Witch sneered although you shall have your way it will bring you sorrow then she **cackled** so loudly and disgustingly the toad and the snakes fell to the ground and lied there wriggling about.

It's very <u>foolish</u> of you," the Sea Witch <u>sneered</u>. [5] "Although you shall have your way, it will bring you sorrow." [T] Then she <u>cackled</u> so <u>loudly and disgustingly</u> the toad and the snakes fell to the ground and lay there <u>wriggling</u> about.

Cackled: uttered a shrill, broken sound
No starting quotation marks b/c continued quotation
It's = *it is; Its* = possessive of *it*
Stop and start quotation marks with interruption
Use comma with verb of speaking & direct quotation
Fused: use a period to separate 2 main clauses (twice)
Use commas after #5 Sentence Openers
Lay = past of *lie (lie, lay, lain)*
Dress-ups: quality adjective; strong verbs; dual -lys

Week 21

I will prepare a **potent** draught for you witch you must carry to land tomorrow before sunrise and drink said the sea which, your tail will then disappear, and shrink up into what mankind calls legs and you will feel great pain. *[quotation continues]*

"I will prepare a <u>potent</u> draught for you, <u>which</u> you must carry to land tomorrow before sunrise and drink," said the Sea Witch. "Your tail will then disappear and <u>shrink</u> up into what mankind calls legs, and you will feel great pain. *[quotation continues]*

Potent: powerful; mighty
Indent ¶ (new topic)
Use quotation marks with direct quotations
Use commas to set off most who/which clauses
Homophone: which/witch; UC: Witch
Use comma with verb of speaking & direct quotation
Comma splice: needs period, not comma (2 MC)
Use comma before *and* when it connects 2 MC
No close quotation marks b/c quotation continues
Dress-ups: quality adj.; *which* clause; strong verb

All which observe you will declare you the most prettiest human, and the most **nimble** dancer ever seen, however every step you take will feel like you were treading upon sharp knives, if you will bear all this I will help you." *[end quotation]*

All <u>who</u> <u>observe</u> you will declare you the prettiest human and the most <u>nimble</u> dancer ever seen. [T] However, every step you take will feel <u>as if</u> you were <u>treading</u> upon sharp knives. [5] If you will bear all this, I will help you."

Nimble: quick and light in movement
Use *who* for people, *which* for things
Usage: don't use *most* with *-est* in superlatives
No comma before *and* to join 2 items (human,dancer)
Comma splices: needs period, not comma (2 MC)
Use commas after introductory transitions
Usage: *like/as if* confusion
Use commas after #5 Sentence Openers
Dress-ups: *who* clause; verbs; adjective; adv. clause

Trembling with yearning for the prince and an immortal soul the young princess replied yes I will. Think again said the sea witch. For you will never again return through the water to your sisters or to your fathers **imperial** palace. *[quotation continues]*

[4] Trembling with yearning for the prince and an immortal soul, the young princess replied, "Yes, I will."
"Think again," said the Sea Witch, "for you will never again return through the water to your sisters or to your father's <u>imperial</u> palace. *[quotation continues]*

Imperial: befitting an emperor or supreme ruler
Indent ¶ (new speakers)
Use commas after #4 SO (-ing phrase)
Use comma with verb of speaking & direct quotation
Use quotation marks with direct quotations + UC
Use commas after introductory transitional words
Capitalize proper nouns
Use comma + lc to continue interrupted quotations
Use apostrophes to show possession
No close quotation marks b/c quotation continues
Dress-ups: quality adjective

Unless you win the **absolute** love of the prince you will never have an immortal soul, the 1st morning after he marries another your heart will brake, and you will become foam on the crest of the waves. *[quotation ends]*

[5] Unless you win the <u>absolute</u> love of the prince, you will never have an immortal soul. [2] The first morning <u>after</u> he marries another, your heart will break, and you will become foam on the crest of the waves."

Absolute: complete and perfect
Use commas after #5 Sentence Openers
Comma splice: needs period, not comma (2 MC)
[!] Disguised #2 (*During, In, On, At* that time period)
Spell out ordinal numbers
Use commas after 2+ introductory elements
Homophone: brake/break
Close quotations with quotation marks
Dress-ups: quality adj.; tricky adv. clause ("after …")

Week 22

I will do it uttered the little mermaid pale as death. Wait I must also be paid said the Sea Witch and it is not a **trifle** that I exact, you have the sweetest voice of any which dwell here in the depths of the sea. *[quotation continues]*

    "I will do it," <u>uttered</u> the little <u>mermaid, pale</u> as death.
    "Wait! I must also be paid," said the Sea Witch, "and it is not a trifle <u>that</u> I <u>exact</u>. You have the sweetest voice of any <u>who</u> <u>dwell</u> here in the depths of the sea. *[quotation continues]*

Trifle: something of little value
Indent ¶ (new speakers)
Use quotation marks with direct quotations
Use comma with verb of speaking & direct quotation
Invisible *who* needs comma: "mermaid, who was ..."
Exclamation marks can follow intro. interjections [!] *Which* clause using *that* (see Appendix)
Comma splice: needs period, not comma (2 MC)
Use *who* for people, *which* for things
Dress-ups: strong verbs; *who* clauses

You believe that you will be able to charm the prince with your voice but this voice you must relinquish to me coaxed the Sea Witch, I will gain you're most cherished gift as the price of my **draught**".

You believe that you will be able to <u>charm</u> the prince with your voice, but this voice you must <u>relinquish</u> to me," <u>coaxed</u> the Sea Witch. "I will gain your most <u>cherished</u> gift as the price of my draught."

Draught: a drink
No starting quotation marks b/c continued quotation
Compound sentence needs comma: MC, cc MC
Use comma with verb of speaking & direct quotation
Stop and start quotation marks with interruption
Comma splice: needs period, not comma (2 MC)
Homophone: you're/your
Period goes inside closing quotation marks
Dress-ups: strong verbs; quality adjective

If you take away my voice implored the mermaid what is left for me. Your beautiful form your floating gracefulness of movement and your expressive eyes, surely, with these you can **enchain** a mans heart.

    [5] "If you take away my voice," <u>implored</u> the mermaid, "what is left for me?"
    "Your beautiful form, your <u>floating</u> gracefulness of movement, and your <u>expressive</u> eyes. [3] Surely with these you can <u>enchain</u> a man's heart."

Enchain: hold fast, or bind as if in chains
Indent ¶ (new speakers)
Use quotation marks with direct quotations
Use comma with verb of speaking & direct quotation
Use question mark after questions (inside quotations)
Use commas with 3 or more items in a series
Comma splice: needs period, not comma (2 MC)
Comma optional after #3 Sentence Opener
Man's is possessive
Dress-ups: strong verbs; quality adjectives

It shall be, spoke the little mermaid. When at last the magic draught was ready the Sea Witch said there it is for you, then she cut off the mermaids tongue so that she became **dumb**, and would never again speak or sing.

    "It shall be," spoke the little mermaid.
    [5] When at last the magic draught was ready, the Sea Witch said, "There it is for you." [T] Then she cut off the mermaid's tongue so that she became dumb and would never again speak or sing.

Dumb: lacking the power of speech (currently has negative connotations not intended by Andersen)
Indent ¶ (new speakers)
Use quotation marks with direct quotations
Use commas after #5 Sentence Openers
Use comma with verb of speaking & direct quotation
Capitalize the first word of a quoted sentence
Comma splice: needs period, not comma (2 MC)
Mermaid's is possessive, not plural
No comma before *and* to join 2 compound verbs

Week 23

Hastily the little mermaid escaped the enchanted wood of the Sea Witch stopping to steel a blossom from each of her sisters gardens. Since she was now **mute** and going to leave them forever she felt like her heart would brake.

[3] Hastily the little mermaid escaped the <u>enchanted</u> wood of the Sea Witch, stopping to steal a blossom from each of her sisters' gardens. [5] Since she was now <u>mute</u> and going to leave them forever, she felt <u>as if</u> her heart would break.

Mute: incapable of speech; dumb (but with no negative connotations)
Indent ¶ (new scene)
[!] Use commas to set off nonessential phrases
Homophone: steel/steal; brake/break
Sisters' = plural possessive (gardens of her sisters)
Use commas after #5 Sentence Openers
Usage: *like/as if* confusion
Dress-ups: quality adjectives; adverb clause

After kissing her hand 1000 times toward the palace she then rose up through the **translucent**, blue waters, and the moon shown clear and bright. As she approached the beautiful marble steps of the princes palace.

[2] After kissing her hand a thousand times toward the palace, she then rose up through the <u>translucent</u> blue waters. The moon shone clear and bright <u>as</u> she approached the beautiful marble steps of the prince's palace.

Translucent: clear; transparent
Spell out numbers written as one or two words
Comma needed after #2 SO of 5 or more words
[!] No commas with cumulative adjectives
Poor choice of *and* to join main clauses
Homophone: shown/shone
Correct fragment by joining clause to main clause
Use apostrophes to show possession
Dress-ups: quality adjective; adverb clause

On the steps, the little mermaid drank the magic draught; it seemed like a two-edged sword peirced her delicate body and she fell into a **swoon** and lied as one dead. When the sun arose she recovered.

[2] On the steps the little mermaid drank the magic draught. It seemed <u>as if</u> a <u>two-edged</u> sword <u>pierced</u> her <u>delicate</u> body, and she fell into a swoon and lay like one dead.
[5] When the sun arose, she recovered.

Swoon: a faint
Indent ¶, 2nd part (time has passed)
Comma not needed after #2 SO of 4 words or fewer
Separate only closely-related MCs with semicolons
Usage: *like/as/as if* confusion (twice); *lay* =past of *lie*
Spelling: *pierced* ("*i* before *e*" rule)
Compound sentence needs comma: MC, cc MC
Use commas after #5 Sentence Openers
Dress-ups: adv. clause; quality adjectives; strong verb

Before her stood the young prince who fixed his coal-black eyes upon her so earnestly that she cast down her own marveling she became aware that her fishes tale was gone, and that she had as lovely a pear of white legs and **petite** feet like any maiden could have.

[2] Before her stood the young prince, <u>who</u> <u>fixed</u> his <u>coal-black</u> eyes upon her so <u>earnestly</u> that she <u>cast</u> down her own. [4] Marveling, she became aware that her fish's tail was gone and that she had as lovely a pair of white legs and <u>petite</u> feet <u>as</u> any maiden could have.

Petite: tiny and slim
Use commas to set off most who/which clauses
Fused: use a period to separate 2 main clauses
Use commas after #4 SO (-ing word or phrase)
Use apostrophes to show possession *(fish's)*
Homophone: tale/tail; pear/pair
No comma before *and* to join 2 items in a series (here, 2 dependent clauses starting with *that*)
Usage: *like/as* confusion
Dress-ups: *who* clause; strong verbs; quality adjectives; -ly adverb; adverb clause

---

Week 24

the prince asked her who she was and where she came from, and while she looked at him mildly and sorrowfully with her deep, blue eyes she could make no **utterance**.

The prince asked her <u>who</u> she was and <u>where</u> she came from. [5] While she looked at him <u>mildly and sorrowfully</u> with her <u>deep</u> blue eyes, she could make no utterance.

Utterance: sound; vocal expression
Capitalize first word of sentences
Avoid stringing together sentences with *and*
[!] No commas with cumulative adjectives
Use commas after #5 Sentence Openers
Dress-ups: *who* clause; adverb clause; dual -ly adverbs; quality adjective

Every step she took was like the Sea Witch had **presaged** she felt like she was treading upon the points of needles, however she bore it willingly, and stepped as lightly by the princes side as a floating bubble, so that all who beheld her wondered at her graceful swaying movements.

Every step she took was <u>as</u> the Sea Witch had <u>presaged</u>. She felt <u>as if</u> she was <u>treading</u> upon the points of needles. [T] However, she bore it <u>willingly</u> and stepped as <u>lightly</u> by the prince's side as a <u>floating</u> bubble, so that all <u>who</u> <u>beheld</u> her <u>wondered</u> at her <u>graceful</u>, <u>swaying</u> movements.

Presaged: predicted
Usage: *like/as/as if* confusion (twice)
Fused: use a period to separate 2 main clauses
Comma splice: needs period, not comma (2 MC)
Use commas after introductory transitional words
No comma before *and* to join 2 compound verbs
Use apostrophes to show possession
Simile: mermaid is *like* a floating bubble
Use commas with coordinate adjectives
Dress-ups: adverb clauses; strong verbs; -ly adverbs; quality adjectives; *who* clause

---

When she arrived at the palace she was soon **arrayed** in costly robes of silk, and was thought a most beautiful creature being mute however she could neither speak or sing.

[5] When she arrived at the palace, she was soon <u>arrayed</u> in <u>costly</u> robes of silk and was thought a most beautiful creature. [4] Being <u>mute</u>, however, she could neither speak nor sing.

Arrayed: adorned; dressed in finery
Indent ¶ (new scene)
Use commas after #5 Sentence Openers
No comma before *and* to join 2 compound verbs
Fused: use a period to separate 2 main clauses
Commas after #4 SO & around transition (*however*)
Usage: *neither* takes *nor*, not *or*
Dress-ups: strong verb; quality adj's (1 imposter -ly)

---

exotic female slaves clothed in silk and gold stepped forward to sing and dance before the prince and his royal parent's, in her turn, the little mermaid glided over the floor, and danced enchantingly

<u>Exotic</u> female slaves clothed in silk and gold stepped forward to sing and dance before the prince and his royal parents. [2] In her turn the little mermaid <u>glided</u> over the floor and danced <u>enchantingly</u>.

Exotic: foreign & strikingly unusual in appearance
Capitalize the first word of a quoted sentence
Parents is plural, not possessive
Comma splice: needs period, not comma (2 MC)
Comma optional after #2 SO of 4 words or fewer
No comma before *and* to join 2 compound verbs
Use a period at end of statements
Dress-ups: quality adjective; strong verb; -ly adverb

Week 25

As she danced her **ethereal** beauty revealed itself more and more the prince decreed she must remain with him always sleep at his door and accompany him where ever he went.

[5] As she danced, her <u>ethereal</u> beauty revealed itself more and more. The prince <u>decreed</u> she must remain with him always, sleep at his door, and <u>accompany</u> him <u>wherever</u> he went.

Ethereal: extremely delicate or refined
Use commas after #5 Sentence Openers
Fused: use a period to separate 2 main clauses
Use commas with 3 or more items in a series
Wherever is one word, not two
Dress-ups: quality adjective; strong verbs; adverb clause

Jauntily, she climbed with the prince to the very tops of high mountains, although her tender feet bled so that even her steps were marked she only laughed, and followed him

[3] Jauntily she climbed with the prince to the very tops of high mountains. [5] Although her <u>tender</u> feet bled so that even her steps were <u>marked</u>, she only laughed and followed him.

Jauntily: in an easy, brisk manner
Comma optional after #3 Sentence Opener
Comma splice: needs period, not comma (2 MC)
Use commas after #5 Sentence Openers
No comma before *and* to join 2 compound verbs
Use a period at end of statements
Dress-ups: quality adjectives

---

when all the household was asleep she would sit on the broad marble steps because it eased her burning feet to bathe them in the cold seawater; then she thought of all those below in the **boundless** deep.

[5] When all the household were asleep, she would sit on the <u>broad</u> marble steps <u>because</u> it <u>eased</u> her <u>burning</u> feet to bathe them in the cold seawater. [T] Then she thought of all those below in the <u>boundless</u> deep.

Boundless: unlimited; having no bounds
Indent ¶ (new scene)
Capitalize first word of sentences
Agreement: "all" works better as a plural subject here
Use commas after #5 Sentence Openers
Separate only closely-related MCs with semicolons
Dress-ups: quality adjectives; adverb clause; strong verb

During the night her sisters once came up arm in arm singing sorrowfully; when she **beckoned** to them they spoke of how she had greived them; after that they came to the palace every night.

[2] During the night her sisters once came up arm-in-arm, singing <u>sorrowfully</u>. [5] When she <u>beckoned</u> to them, they spoke of how she had <u>grieved</u> them. [2] After that they came to the palace every night.

Beckoned: signaled or summoned, as by waving
Join words w/ a hyphen that function as a single adj.
[!] Use commas to set off nonessential phrases
Separate only closely-related MCs with semicolons
Use commas after #5 Sentence Openers
Spelling: *grieved* ("*i* before *e*" rule)
Separate only closely-related MCs with semicolons
Dress-ups: -ly adverb; strong verbs

Week 26

One time the aged sea king her father appeared in the distance stretching out his arms toward her although he would not venture so near the land as her sister's did, as the days **elapsed** she loved the prince more and more fondly.

[2] One time the aged Sea <u>King, her</u> father, appeared in the distance stretching out his arms toward her, <u>although</u> he would not <u>venture</u> so near the land <u>as</u> her sisters did. [5] As the days <u>elapsed</u>, she loved the prince more and more <u>fondly</u>.

Elapsed: slipped or passed by
Indent ¶, 2nd part (time has passed)
[!] Disguised #2 (*During, In, On, At* that time period)
Capitalize proper nouns
Invisible *who*: "Sea King, who was" (takes commas)
[!] Use commas w/ contrasting adv. clause (although)
Sisters is plural, not possessive
Comma splice: needs period, not comma (2 MC)
Use commas after #5 Sentence Openers
Dress-ups: adverb clauses; strong verbs; -ly adverb

Gently, he loved her as hed cherish a little child, the thought never entered his head to make her his wife. Do you not love me the best of them all the eyes of the little mermaid seemed to **beseech**.

[3] Gently, he loved her <u>as</u> he'd <u>cherish</u> a little child. The thought never entered his head to make her his wife.
"Do you not love me the best of them all?" the eyes of the little mermaid seemed to <u>beseech</u>.

Beseech: beg for earnestly
Indent ¶, 2nd part (new speaker)
Use apostrophes in contractions
Comma splice: needs period, not comma (2 MC)
    (a semicolon would also work here)
Use quotation marks with direct quotations
Use question mark after questions
Dress-ups: adverb clause; strong verbs

The prince replied yes your dear to me for you have the best heart. Devoted to me you are like a young maiden who I once saw but who I shall never **encounter** again. My ship wrecked. *[quotation continues]*

The prince replied, "Yes, you're dear to me, for you have the best heart. [7] Devoted to me, you are like a young maiden <u>whom</u> I once saw but <u>whom</u> I shall never <u>encounter</u> again.
[6] "My ship wrecked. *[quotation continues]*

Encounter: come upon or meet with
Indent ¶ (new speaker; new topic)
Use comma with verb of speaking & direct quotation
Use quotation marks with direct quotations
Use commas after introductory interjections
Homophone: your/you're
Compound sentence needs comma: MC, cc (*for*) MC
Use commas after #7 Sentence Openers (-ed)
Use *whom* for the objective case
[!] Start new par. in continued quotation with "
Dress-ups: *who* clauses; strong verb

The **turbulent** waves cast me ashore near a sacred temple, where a radiant maiden found me, and saved my life; although I beheld her but twice shes the only one in the world which I could love. Because she belongs to the convent however she will never be mine.

The turbulent waves cast me ashore near a sacred temple, where a radiant maiden found me and saved my life. [5] Although I beheld her but twice, she's the only one in the world whom I could love. [5] Because she belongs to the convent, however, she will never be mine."

Turbulent: agitated; disturbed
No starting quotation marks b/c quotation continues
No comma before *and* to join 2 compound verbs
Separate only closely-related MCs with semicolons
Use commas after #5 Sentence Openers (twice)
Use apostrophes in contractions
Use *who* for people, *which* for things
[!] Use *whom* for the objective case
Use commas to set off transitional words
Close quotations with quotation marks
Dress-ups: quality adj's & verb; adv. & who clauses

Week 27

Sighing, with grief the little mermaid thought ah he knows not that it was me who lovingly saved his life. While I am by his side, I will take care of him love him and **forfeit** my life for his sake.

[4] Sighing with grief, the little mermaid thought, "Ah, he knows not that it was I who lovingly saved his life. [5] While I am by his side, I will take care of him, love him, and forfeit my life for his sake."

Forfeit: lose, as in a breach of contract
Indent ¶ (new speaker)
Comma comes after whole -ing phrase, not the word
Use comma with verb of speaking & direct quotation
[!] Treat thoughts like speech w/ quotation marks
Capitalize the first word of a quoted sentence
Use commas after introductory interjection
[!] Nominative case: predicate nominative *(was I)*
Use commas with 3 or more items in a series
Dress-ups: *who* clause; -ly adverb; strong verb

Very soon it was reported that the prince must wed, and that the noble **virtuous** daughter of a neighboring king would be his bride a fine ship was being fitted out for the journey.

Very soon it was reported that the prince must wed and that the noble, virtuous daughter of a neighboring king would be his bride. A fine ship was being fitted out for the journey.

Virtuous: morally excellent
Indent ¶ (time has passed)
Acceptable passives: we don't care who reported it or who fitted out the ship
No comma before *and* to join two items in a series (two "that" clauses)
Use commas with coordinate adjectives
Fused: use a period to separate two main clauses
Dress-ups: quality adjectives

"Since my parents desire it I must travel to meet this beautiful princess he told his little **foundling** But they will not obligate me to bring her home as my bride".

[5] "Since my parents desire it, I must travel to meet this beautiful princess," he told his little foundling, "but they will not obligate me to bring her home as my bride."

Foundling: an abandoned child w/o known parents
Indent ¶ (new speaker)
Use commas after #5 Sentence Openers
Stop and start quotation marks with interruption
Use comma with verb of speaking & direct quotation
Use lc to cont. interrupted quotations (MC, cc MC)
Periods & commas go inside quotation marks

The next morning they sailed into the harbor wear church bells **reverberated** and trumpets sounded with a flourish; everyday was a festival, balls and entertainments followed one another.

[2] The next morning they sailed into the harbor, where church bells reverberated and trumpets sounded with a flourish. [6] Every day was a festival. Balls and entertainments followed one another.

Reverberated: echoed back
Indent ¶ (time has passed)
[!] Disguised #2 (*During, In, On, At* that time period)
[!] Use commas w/ nonessential adj. clauses (where)
Homophone: wear/where
Separate only closely-related MCs with semicolons
Usage: *every day* 2 words here (each day)
Comma splice: needs period, not comma (2 MC)
Dress-ups: adverb clause; strong verbs

Week 28

When the princess arrived the little mermaid was **obliged** to acknowledge that she had never scene a more perfect vision of beauty for the laughing, blue eyes of the princess shown with truth and purity.

[5] When the princess arrived, the little mermaid was <u>obliged</u> to <u>acknowledge</u> that she had never seen a more perfect vision of beauty, for the <u>laughing</u> blue eyes of the princess <u>shone</u> with truth and purity.

Obliged: bound by conscience
Indent ¶ (new topic)
Use commas after #5 Sentence Openers
Homophone: scene/seen; shown/shone
Compound sentence needs comma: MC, cc MC
[!] No commas with cumulative adjectives
Dress-ups: strong verbs; adverb clause;
    quality adjective

It was you! exclaimed the prince which saved my life when I lied all but dead on the beach. He folded his blushing bride in his arms. Oh I am to blissful he confided to the little mermaid. My most **ardent** hopes are all fulfilled. *[quotation continues]*

"It was you," <u>exclaimed</u> the prince, "<u>who</u> saved my life <u>when</u> I lay all but dead on the beach!" He <u>folded</u> his <u>blushing</u> bride in his arms.
[T] "Oh, I am too <u>blissful</u>," he <u>confided</u> to the little mermaid. "My most <u>ardent</u> hopes are all <u>fulfilled</u>. *[quotation continues]*

Ardent: characterized by intense feeling
Indent ¶ (new speaker; new scene)
Use quotation marks with direct quotations
Use exclamation mark at end of exclamation
Use comma with verb of speaking & direct quotation
Use *who* for people, *which* for things
Lay = past of *lie (lie, lay, lain)*
Use commas after introductory interjections
Homophone: to/too
No close quotation marks b/c quotation continues
Dress-ups: verbs & adj's; who clause; adverb clause

You will rejoice at my delight for your **unobtrusive** devotion to me has been absolute and sincere, kissing his hand the little mermaid felt like her heart were already broken.

You will rejoice at my delight, for your <u>unobtrusive</u> devotion to me has been <u>absolute</u> and sincere."
[4] Kissing his hand, the little mermaid felt <u>as if</u> her heart were already broken.

Unobtrusive: quiet; not putting herself forward
No starting " but closing " b/c continued quotation
Indent ¶ (new topic)
Compound sentence needs comma: MC, cc MC
Comma splice: needs period, not comma (2 MC)
Use commas after #4 SO (-ing phrase)
Usage: *like/as if* confusion
[!] Note subjunctive (*heart were*); see Appendix
Dress-ups: quality adjectives; adverb clause

His **nuptials** would bring death to her and she would transform into the foam of the sea. Heralds proclaimed the betrothal, the church bells joyously rang while the bride and bridegroom recieved the wholly sacrament from the bishop

His nuptials would bring death to her, and she would <u>transform</u> into the foam of the sea.
[6] Heralds proclaimed the betrothal. The church bells <u>joyously</u> rang <u>while</u> the bride and bridegroom received the holy sacrament from the bishop.

Nuptials: wedding or marriage
Indent ¶, 2nd part (time has passed)
Compound sentence needs comma: MC, cc MC
Comma splice: needs period, not comma (2 MC)
Spelling: *received* ("*i* before *e*, except after *c*")
Homophone: wholly/holy
Use a period at end of statements
Dress-ups: strong verb; -ly adverb; adverb clause

Week 29

Thinking of all she had lost in the world the little mermaid saw not the **lavish**, wedding ceremony, and she thought only of the night of death, that was coming to her

[4] Thinking of all she had lost in the world, the little mermaid saw not the <u>lavish</u> wedding ceremony. She thought only of the night of death <u>that</u> was coming to her.

Lavish: generous; rich and extravagant
Use commas after #4 SO (-ing phrase)
[!] No commas with cumulative adjectives
Poor choice of *and* to join main clauses
[!] Essential *which* clause using *that*; no comma
Use a period at end of statements
Dress-ups: quality adjective

On the same evening, the bride and bridegroom boarded the ship. While cannons roared, and flags waved. With swelling sails and a favorable wind the ship glided away smoothly and lightly over the **tranquil** sea.

[2] On the same evening the bride and bridegroom boarded the ship while cannons roared and flags waved. [2] With swelling sails and a favorable wind, the ship glided away smoothly and lightly over the tranquil sea.

Tranquil: peaceful; quiet; calm
Indent ¶ (new scene)
Comma optional after #2 SO of 4 words or fewer
Correct fragment by joining clause to main clause
No comma before *and* to join 2 compound verbs
Comma needed after #2 SO of 5 or more words
Dress-ups: strong verbs; adv. clause; quality adjectives; dual -ly adverbs

---

All was joy and **jubilation** on board ship, the mermaid laughed and danced with the rest while thoughts of death pierced her heart; she had no soul and now she could never win one

All was joy and jubilation on board ship. The mermaid laughed and danced with the rest while thoughts of death pierced her heart. She had no soul, and now she could never win one.

Jubilation: expression of rejoicing, festivity
Alliteration: "joy and jubilation"
Comma splice: needs period, not comma (2 MC)
Separate only closely-related MCs with semicolons
Compound sentence needs comma: MC, cc MC
Use a period at end of statements
Dress-ups: adverb clause; strong verb

When all became still on bored the little mermaid leaned her trembling arms on the edge of the vessel, and peered toward the east, for the first **blush** of dawn which would bring her certain death.

[5] When all became still on board, the little mermaid leaned her trembling arms on the edge of the vessel and peered toward the east for the first blush of dawn, which would bring her certain death.

Blush: rosy or pinkish tinge
Indent ¶ (time has passed)
Homophone: bored/board
Use commas after #5 Sentence Openers
No comma before *and* to join 2 compound verbs
For = preposition here, not cc
[!] No commas with essential phrases ("for …")
Use commas to set off nonessential *which* clauses
Dress-ups: strong verbs; quality adj's; which clause

Week 30

Palely rising out of the sea her sisters approached. We have given our beautiful flowing **tresses** to the Sea Witch they said to obtain help for you that you may not die tonight. *[quotation continues]*

[3,4] Palely rising out of the sea, her sisters approached. "We have given our beautiful, flowing tresses to the Sea Witch," they said, "to obtain help for you that you may not die tonight. *[quotation continues]*

Tresses: long locks or curls of hair
Indent ¶ (new speaker)
Use commas after #4 SO (-ing phrase)
Use quotation marks with direct quotations
Use commas with coordinate adjectives
Use comma with verb of speaking & direct quotation
No close quotation marks b/c quotation continues
Dress-ups: quality adjective; strong verb

Our old grandmother so moans for you that her **hoary** hair is falling off from sorrow like ours fell under the Sea Witches scissors. The Sea Witch has given us a knife. *[quotation continues]*

Our old grandmother so moans for you that her hoary hair is falling off from sorrow, as ours fell under the Sea Witch's scissors.
  "The Sea Witch has given us a knife. *[quotation continues]*

Hoary: white with age
Indent ¶, 2nd part (new topic)
No starting quotation marks b/c continued quotation
[!] Use commas w/ contrasting adv. clauses ("as…")
Usage: *like/as* confusion
Use apostrophes to show possession *(Witch's)*
[!] Start new par. in continued quotation with "
Dress-ups: strong verb; quality adjective; adv. clause

Before the sun raises you must **plunge** it into the heart of the prince; when the warm blood falls upon your feet it will form back into a fish's tail. *[quotation continues]*

[5] Before the sun rises, you must <u>plunge</u> it into the heart of the prince. [5] When the warm blood falls upon your feet, they will form back into a fish's tail. *[quotation continues]*

Plunge: thrust forcibly into something
Usage: *raise/rise* confusion
[!] Tricky #5: *before* is a conjunction here, not prep.
Use commas after #5 Sentence Openers (twice)
Separate only closely-related MCs with semicolons
Agreement: "feet, they"
Dress-ups: strong verb

You or he must die before sunrise, **hasten** then, do you not see the first red streaks in the sky they asked? Sighing deeply and mournfully they sank down beneath the waves.

You or he must die before sunrise. [6] Hasten, then. Do you not see the first red streaks in the sky?" they asked. [4] Sighing <u>deeply and mournfully</u>, they sank down beneath the waves.

Hasten: hurry
No starting " but closing " b/c continued quotation
Comma splices: need periods, not commas (2 MC)
Use commas to set off transitional words
Use " ? " after question, not at end of statement
Use commas after #4 SO (-ing phrase)
Dress-ups: dual -ly adverbs

Week 31

Quietly, the little mermaid drew back the crimson curtain of the tent, and lovingly **beheld** the sleeping prince and his fair bride, kissing his brow she then looked at the sky in which the rosy dawn glimmered more and more bright.

　　[3] Quietly the little mermaid drew back the <u>crimson</u> curtain of the tent and <u>lovingly</u> beheld the sleeping prince and his fair bride. [4] Kissing his brow, she then looked at the sky, in <u>which</u> the <u>rosy</u> dawn <u>glimmered</u> more and more <u>brightly</u>.

Beheld: saw; observed
Indent ¶ (new scene)
Comma optional after #3 Sentence Opener
No comma before *and* to join 2 compound verbs
　　("drew back … and … beheld")
Comma splice: needs period, not comma (2 MC)
Use commas after #4 SO (-ing phrase)
[!] Use commas to set off nonessential elements
Use adverb *brightly* to modify verb *glimmered*
Dress-ups: quality adj's; -ly adv's; w/w; strong verb

The knife trembled in her hand gazing at the prince once more the knife was flung far away from her into the waves where the water turned red, and the drops that **spurted** up looked like blood.

The knife <u>trembled</u> in her hand. [4] Gazing at the prince once more, she <u>flung</u> the knife far away from her into the waves, <u>where</u> the water turned red and the drops that <u>spurted</u> up looked like blood.

Spurted: gushed forth or up
Fused: use a period to separate 2 main clauses
Use commas after #4 SO (-ing phrase)
Illegal #4: word after " , " should do the *inging*
[!] Use commas to set off nonessential adj. clauses
[!] No comma before *and* to join 2 items in a series
　　(here, 2 *where* clauses, w/ the 2nd *where* implied)
Simile: water is *like* blood
Dress-ups: strong verbs; adverb clause

Casting one more **lingering** half-fainting glance at the prince she then through herself from the ship into the sea, regretfully she thought her body was dissolving into sea foam but she did not feel like she were dying.

[4] Casting one more <u>lingering</u>, <u>half-fainting</u> glance at the prince, she then threw herself from the ship into the sea. [3] Regretfully she thought her body was <u>dissolving</u> into sea foam, but she did not feel <u>as if</u> she were dying.

Lingering: slow in leaving
Use commas with coordinate adjectives
Use commas after #4 SO (-ing phrase)
Homophone: through/threw
Comma splice: needs period, not comma (2 MC)
Compound sentence needs comma: MC, cc MC
Usage: *like/as if* confusion
[!] "Were dying" is correct—subjunctive mood
Dress-ups: quality adjectives; strong verb; adv. clause

The suns warm rays fell on the cold foam of the sea, around the little mermaid floated 100s of **transparent** beautiful beings, through which she could distinguish the white sails of the ship, and the red clouds in the brilliant sky.

The sun's warm rays fell on the cold foam of the sea.
[2] Around the little mermaid <u>floated</u> hundreds of <u>transparent</u>, beautiful beings, through <u>whom</u> she could <u>distinguish</u> the white sails of the ship and the red clouds in the <u>brilliant</u> sky.

Transparent: so sheer that light passes through
Indent ¶, 2nd part (new topic)
Use apostrophes to show possession
Comma splice: needs period, not comma (2 MC)
Spell out numbers written as one or two words
Use commas with coordinate adjectives
Use *who* for people, *which* for things
[!] Use *whom* for objective case
No comma before *and* to join 2 items in a series
Dress-ups: strong verbs; quality adj's; who clause

Week 32

As **melodious** as a celestial choir there speech nevertheless was to ethereal two be heard by mortal ears as the beings also were unseen by mortal eyes, and perceiving she had a body like there's she continued to raise more higher and higher out of the foam.

[4] As <u>melodious</u> as a <u>celestial</u> choir, their speech nevertheless was too <u>ethereal</u> to be heard by <u>mortal</u> ears, <u>as</u> the beings also were <u>unseen</u> by mortal eyes. [4] Perceiving she had a body like theirs, she continued to rise higher and higher out of the foam.

Melodious: sweet-sounding; musical
Disguised #4 ("Being as melodious as …")
Use commas after #4 SOs
Homophone: there/their; to/too/two; there's/theirs
[!] Use commas w/ contrasting adv. clause ("as…")
Avoid stringing together sentences with *and*
Usage: *raise/rise* confusion
Usage: don't use *more* with *-er* in comparatives
Dress-ups: quality adjectives; adverb clause;
    strong verb

Where am I she asked and her voice sounded as **otherworldly** as the voices of those which were with her; no earthly music could imitate it. Among the daughters of the air one of them responded.

"Where am I?" she asked, and her voice sounded as <u>otherworldly</u> as the voices of those <u>who</u> were with her. No <u>earthly</u> music could <u>imitate</u> it.
[2] Among the daughters of the air, one of them <u>responded</u>.

Otherworldly: pertaining to another world
Indent ¶ (new speaker; new topic)
Use quotation marks with direct quotations
Use question mark after questions
Compound sentence needs comma: MC, cc MC
Use *who* for people, *which* for things
[!] Essential *who* clause, so keep no commas
Separate only closely-related MCs with semicolons
Comma needed after #2 SO of 5 or more words
Dress-ups: adj's (w/ an imposter -ly); who; verbs

No mermaid has an immortal soul nor can they obtain one unless they win the love of a human being; on the power of another hangs their eternal **destiny**. *[quotation continues]*

"No mermaid has an immortal soul, nor can she <u>obtain</u> one <u>unless</u> she wins the love of a human being. [2] On the power of another <u>hangs</u> her <u>eternal</u> destiny. *[quotation continues]*

Destiny: a predetermined, inevitable course of events
Use quotation marks with direct quotations
Compound sentence needs comma: MC, cc MC
Agreement: "mermaid … she … she wins … her"
Separate only closely-related MCs with semicolons
No close quotation marks b/c quotation continues
Dress-ups: strong verbs; adverb clause; quality adj.

While the daughters of the air can, by their good deeds, **procure** a immortal soul for theirselves. After we have striven for 300 years to do all the good in our power we recieve a immortal soul, and take part in the happiness of mankind. *[quotation continues]*

[T] By contrast, the daughters of the air can, by their good deeds, <u>procure</u> an immortal soul for themselves. [5] After we have <u>striven</u> for three hundred years to do all the good in our power, we receive an immortal soul and take part in the <u>happiness</u> of mankind. *[quotation continues]*

Procure: obtain or get by effort
No quotation marks b/c continued quotation
Fragment: revise sentence construction to correct
Usage: "an immortal," not "a immortal"
Spelling: *themselves*
[!] Tricky #5: *after* is a conjunction here, not prep.
Spell out numbers written as one or two words
Use commas after #5 Sentence Openers
Spelling: *receive* ("i before e except after c")
No comma before *and* to join 2 compound verbs
Dress-ups: strong verbs

Week 33

Poor little mermaid you have tried with your whole heart to do as we are doing. And you have suffered and endured rising yourself to the spirit-world by your noble deeds, now by striving **diligently** for 300 years in the same way, you may obtain an immortal soul.

"Poor little mermaid, you have tried with your whole heart to do <u>as</u> we are doing. You have <u>suffered and endured</u>, raising yourself to the spirit-world by your noble deeds. [T] Now, by striving <u>diligently</u> for three hundred years in the same way, you may obtain an immortal soul."

Diligently: with persistence and tirelessness
Indent ¶ (new topic)
[!] Start new par. in continued quotation with "
Set off NDAs with commas
Avoid starting sentences with coord. conjunctions
[!] Use commas w/ nonessential phrases (raising…)
Usage: *rising/raising* confusion
Comma splice: needs period, not comma (2 MC)
Spell out numbers written as one or two words
Close quotations with quotation marks
Dress-ups: adverb clause; dual verbs; -ly adverb

Gratefully the little mermaid lifted his **glorified** eyes toward the sun, and felt them for the first time filling with tears on the ship on which she had left the prince there was life and noise, she saw the prince and his beautiful bride searching for she.

[3] Gratefully the little mermaid lifted her <u>glorified</u> eyes toward the sun and felt them for the first time filling with tears. [2] On the ship on <u>which</u> she had left the prince, there was life and noise. She saw the prince and his beautiful bride searching for her.

Glorified: made more splendid; invested with glory
Indent ¶ (new topic)
Pronoun error: *her*, not *his*
No comma before *and* to join 2 compound verbs
Fused: use a period to separate 2 main clauses
Use commas after 2+ introductory elements
Comma splice: needs period, not comma (2 MC)
Use objective case: "searching for *her*"
Dress-ups: quality adjective; *which* clause

They gazed **somberly** at the pearly foam, as if they new she had throne herself into the waves unseen; the little mermaid tenderly kissed the forehead of the bride, and fanned the prince

They gazed <u>somberly</u> at the <u>pearly</u> foam, <u>as if</u> they knew she had thrown herself into the waves <u>unseen</u>. The little mermaid <u>tenderly</u> kissed the forehead of the bride and <u>fanned</u> the prince.

Somberly: seriously; gravely
Homophone: new/knew; throne/thrown
Separate only closely-related MCs with semicolons
No comma before *and* to join 2 compound verbs
Use a period at end of statements
Dress-ups: strong verbs; -ly adverbs; quality adj's
    (incl. *pearly*, an imposter -ly); adverb clause

With a light heart, she then joyously mounted with the other children of the air to a rosy cloud, that floated through the **ether**, after 300 years thought the little mermaid thus shall we float into the kingdom of heaven.

[2] With a light heart she then <u>joyously</u> <u>mounted</u> with the other children of the air to a <u>rosy</u> cloud <u>that</u> floated through the ether. [2] "After three hundred years," thought the little mermaid, "thus shall we <u>float</u> into the kingdom of heaven."

Ether: the upper regions of space; the heavens
Indent ¶ (new topic)
Comma optional after #2 SO of 4 words or fewer
[!] Essential *which* clause using *that*; no comma
Comma splice: needs period, not comma (2 MC)
[!] Treat thoughts like speech
Spell out numbers written as one or two words
Use comma with verb of thinking & quotation
Dress-ups: -ly adverb; strong verbs; quality
    adjective; *which* clause ("that …")

The King and the Discommodious Pea

Introduction

Recommended for grades seven through ten, "The King and the Discommodious Pea" Fix-Its are divided into thirty-three weeks, with four passages to rewrite and correct each week. See the Introduction under Teaching Procedure for instructions for students and teachers.

In this Fix-It story, I have dropped the [!] advanced concepts. Do not, however, expect students to find all errors. I try to challenge them with grammar problems they will continue to learn through high school. Also, starting with Week 4, I stop marking #1 Subject Openers. If your students are having trouble recognizing them, however, you may wish to continue marking these. In the Appendix you will find a fuller discussion of the dress-ups and sentence openers as well as most grammar issues.

Because the Fix-It stories are usually taught over the course of a school year, students may sometimes have trouble following the storyline. As you discuss the sentences each week, I recommend you check students' reading comprehension first, discussing the events leading up to and including that week's reading.

Background

By way of introduction to this Fix-It story, you may wish to read to your students the tale on which my adaptation was based, "The Princess and the Pea," a fairy tale by the Danish master storyteller Hans Christian Andersen. Also known as "The Real Princess" or "How to Tell a True Princess," Andersen's "The Princess and the Pea" was first published in 1835 in *Fairy Tales, Told for Children*. The story has lent itself to numerous adaptations, mainly because of its central character: Do we admire her sensitivity or find her too fastidious? "The King and the Discommodious Pea" only loosely follows the original tale.

The Princess and the Pea

Once upon a time there was a prince who wanted to marry a princess, but he worried how he would find a *real* princess. He traveled all over the world looking, but nowhere could he get what he wanted. There were princesses enough, but it was difficult to discover whether they were real ones. There was always something about them that was not as it should be. So he came home again and was heartbroken, for he would have liked to have a real princess.

One evening a terrible storm arose. There was thunder and lightning, and rain poured down in torrents. Suddenly a knocking was heard at the city gate, and the old king went to open it. A girl who claimed to be a princess stood in front of the gate, but she certainly did not look like one. The water ran down from her hair and clothes; it ran down into the toes of her shoes and out again at the heels. Yet she insisted that she was a real princess.

"Well, we'll soon find that out," thought the old queen. She went into the guest bedroom, took all the bedding off the bedstead, and laid a pea on the bottom. She then took twenty mattresses and laid them on the pea, and then topped it off with twenty eiderdown beds on top of the mattresses. On this the princess had to lie all night.

In the morning they asked the princess how she had slept. "Oh, very poorly!" exclaimed she. "I have scarcely closed my eyes all night. Heaven only knows what was in the bed, but I was lying on something hard, so that my whole body is black and blue this morning."

Now they knew that she was a real princess because she had felt the pea right through the twenty mattresses and the twenty eiderdown beds. Nobody but a real princess could be as sensitive as that or could have such delicate skin. So the prince took her for his wife, for now he knew that he had a real princess, and the pea was put in the museum, where it may still be seen if no one has stolen it.

There, that is a true story.

The King and the Discommodious Pea

Fix-Its and Corrections

Grammar, Skills, and Vocabulary

Week 1

Once upon a time **nestled** between several vast mountains was a peaceful modern yet tiny country called flovenia surrounded by friendly neighboring countrys.

[2] Once upon a time <u>nestled</u> among several <u>vast</u> mountains was a peaceful, modern, yet tiny country called <u>Flovenia, surrounded</u> by friendly neighboring countries.

Nestled: lying in a sheltered area
Indent ¶ (new topic)
Use *between* to compare 2 items; *among*, 3 or more
Use commas with three or more items in a series
UC: *Flovenia.* Spelling: *countries*
Invisible *which* needs comma: "Flovenia, which was"
Dress-ups: strong verb; quality adj.; invisible which

Although the belief was occasionally yet **fanatically** debated in Parliament tradition held that the name derived from it's first queen Florence who preferred to be called Flo

[5] Although the belief was <u>occasionally yet fanatically</u> debated in Parliament, tradition held that the name <u>derived</u> from its first queen, Florence, <u>who</u> preferred to be called "Flo."

Fanatically: w/ extreme political enthusiasm or zeal
Use commas after #5 Sentence Openers
Decoration: noun clause w/ "that." See Appendix
Its = possessive of *it*
Use commas w/ nonessential appositives & clauses
Use quotation marks w/ words/names used as words
Closing period needed, inside quotation marks
Dress-ups: dual -lys; strong verb; who clause

Some however associated the name with another event—the springtime, water flow; snow melted rapid from the mountains each spring which caused **torrential** floods threw the town.

[1] Some, however, associated the name with another event— the springtime water flow. [1] Snow melted <u>rapidly</u> from the mountains each spring, <u>which</u> caused <u>torrential</u> floods through the town.

Torrential: flowing in rapid, violent streams/gushes
Use commas to set off transitional words
No commas with cumulative adjectives
Separate only closely-related MCs with semicolons
Usage: needs adverb *rapidly* instead of adjective
Use commas to set off nonessential *which* clauses
Homophone: threw/through
Dress-ups: -ly adverb; which clause; quality adj.

Three months before our story begins one such frightful **deluge** swept away worthy King William who had rained in Flovenia four forteen peaceful years.

[2] Three months <u>before</u> our story begins, one such frightful deluge swept away worthy King William, <u>who</u> had reigned in Flovenia for fourteen peaceful years.

Deluge: flood
Indent ¶ (flashback)
Disguised #2 (*During, In, On, At* that time period)
Comma needed after #2 SO of 5 or more words
Use commas to set off nonessential *who* clauses
Homophone: *rained/reigned; four/for.* Sp: *fourteen*
Note use of past perfect tense (see Appendix)
Dress-ups: adverb clause (with "before"); who clause

Week 2

Sadly his **amicable** wife Queen Mary who had conveniently born to her husband 4 healthy sons traveled with him at the time.

[3] Sadly, his <u>amicable</u> wife, Queen Mary, <u>who</u> had <u>conveniently</u> borne to her husband four healthy sons, traveled with him at the time.

Amicable: friendly; showing goodwill
Comma optional after #3 Sentence Opener
Use commas w/ nonessential appositives and clauses
Note use of past perfect tense
Spelling: borne; spell out *four*
Dress-ups: quality adjective; who clause; -ly adverb

Even more sadly crown prince Richard prince Edward and their brother Prince Philip out hunting in the royal forest met a **untimely demise** from this catastrophe.

[3] Even more sadly, Crown Prince Richard, Prince Edward, and their brother Prince <u>Philip, out</u> hunting in the royal forest, met an <u>untimely</u> demise from this catastrophe.

Untimely demise: death happening before expected
Comma after adverbs + #3 Sentence Opener
Capitalize titles used with names
Use commas with three or more items in a series
Invisible *who* needs commas: "Philip, who were …"
Usage: *an* before a vowel
Dress-ups: invisible who; quality adj. (imposter -ly)

Bored with the usual princely activities next in line Melvin was back at home **executing** flawless moves against his computer, chess opponent.

[7] Bored with the usual princely activities, next-in-line Melvin was back at home <u>executing</u> <u>flawless</u> moves against his computer chess opponent.

Executing: performing; making
Indent ¶ (back to the present)
Imposter -ly adverb: *princely* (adj.)
Use commas after #7 Sentence Openers (-ed)
Hyphenate words that function as a single adj.
No commas with cumulative adjectives
Dress-ups: strong verb; quality adjective

In prior years, Melvins tutor had **bemoaned** to court adviser's Big Lord Fauntleroy and Lord Ashton Mel just doesn't have what it takes to be a king.

[2] In prior years Melvin's tutor had <u>bemoaned</u> to court advisers Big Lord Fauntleroy and Lord Ashton, "Mel just doesn't have what it takes to be a king."

Bemoaned: expressed disapproval and regret for
Indent ¶ (flashback)
Comma not needed after #2 SO of 4 words or fewer
Note use of past perfect tense (next passage too)
Use apostrophes for possession, not for plurals
Use " " w/ direct quotations + comma (speaking vb)
Dress-ups: quality verb

Week 3

After a pause, his tutor had added he is of diminished princely **stature** and he doesn't care for polo hunting or courtly balls fortunately he's not likely to ever be king since he has three brothers ahead of him.

[2] After a pause his tutor had added, "He is of <u>diminished</u> princely stature, and he doesn't care for polo, hunting, or courtly balls. [3] Fortunately he's not <u>likely</u> ever to be king <u>since</u> he has three brothers ahead of him."

Stature: height (i.e., he's not particularly tall)
Comma not needed after #2 SO of 4 words or fewer
Use " " w/ quotations + comma (speaking vb) + UC
Imposter -lys: *princely*; *courtly*
Compound sentence needs comma: MC, cc MC
Use commas with 3 or more items in a series
Fused: use a period to separate 2 main clauses
Discuss not splitting infinitives (see Appendix)
Dress-ups: quality adj.; -ly adverb; adverb clause

Every thing had now changed. When Prince Mel was suddenly elevated to the position of King the flovenian advisers realized they had a **daunting** task.

[6] Everything had now changed. [5] When Prince Mel was <u>suddenly</u> <u>elevated</u> to the position of king, the Flovenian advisers realized they had a <u>daunting</u> task.

Daunting: discouraging; overwhelming
Indent ¶ (back to the present)
Spelling: *everything* is one word
Use lc for titles without a name
Use commas after #5 Sentence Openers
Capitalize proper nouns
Dress-ups: -ly adverb; strong verb; quality adjective

With the tutors assessment lurking in the back of there minds neither Big Lord Fauntleroy or Lord Ashton were **sanguine** about the outcome.

[2] With the tutor's assessment <u>lurking</u> in the back of their minds, neither Big Lord Fauntleroy nor Lord Ashton was <u>sanguine</u> about the outcome.

Sanguine: cheerfully optimistic or hopeful
Use apostrophes to show possession
Homophone: there/their
Comma needed after #2 SO of 5 or more words
Usage: *neither … nor*
Agreement: verb agrees w/ the noun following *nor*
Dress-ups: quality adjectives

At least one thing was unmistakable the most **indispensable** business at hand was the matter of the kings nuptials; searching throughout the castle for the king the to advisers found him at length in the computer room.

[2] At least one thing was <u>unmistakable</u>: the most <u>indispensable</u> business at hand was the matter of the king's nuptials.

    [4] Searching throughout the castle for the king, the two advisers found him, at length, in the computer room.

Indispensable: essential; cannot be neglected
Indent ¶, 2nd part (new scene)
Use colon after MC to give an explanation
Use apostrophes to show possession
Separate only closely-related MCs with semicolons
Use commas after #4 SO (-ing phrase)
Homophone: to/two
Use commas around transitional expressions
Dress-ups: quality adjectives

Week 4

Unplugging the computer Big Lord Fauntleroy **sonorously** cleared his throat, and began too advice. Ahem—sire it is my duty to remind you of the longstanding Flovenian tradition he awaited an answer.

[4] Unplugging the computer, Big Lord Fauntleroy <u>sonorously</u> cleared his throat and began to advise. "Ahem—Sire, it is my duty to remind you of the <u>longstanding</u> Flovenian tradition."
[6] He awaited an answer.

Sonorously: with a loud and deep sound
Use commas after #4 SO (-ing phrase)
No comma before *and* to join 2 compound verbs
Homophone: *too/to.* Usage: *advice/advise* confusion
Use quotation marks with direct quotations
Capitalize titles when used as NDAs
Set off NDAs with commas
Fused: use a period to separate 2 main clauses
Dress-ups: -ly adverb; quality adjective

When none was **forthcoming** he continued it's your obligation to ensure continuation of the royal line by marrying an appropriate true-blooded princess within one year.

    [5] When none was <u>forthcoming</u>, he continued. "It's your obligation to <u>ensure</u> continuation of the royal line by marrying an appropriate, <u>true-blooded</u> princess within one year."

Forthcoming: coming forth when expected
Indent ¶ (time has passed)
Use commas after #5 Sentence Openers
Fused: use a period to separate 2 main clauses
Use quotation marks with direct quotations
Use commas with coordinate adjectives
Dress-ups: quality adjectives; strong verb

How can one **differentiate** a true from a false Princess?, Mel wondered, don't they all appear about the same you know, two eyes a nose a mouth a couple arms and legs. Whats in them to make them the *real* thing

    "How can one <u>differentiate</u> a true from a false princess?" Mel wondered. "Don't they all appear about the same—you know, two eyes, a nose, a mouth, a couple arms and legs? What's in them to make them the *real* thing?"

Differentiate: distinguish (strong verb)
Indent ¶ (new speaker)
Use quotation marks with quotations
Do not use comma with an end mark of punctuation
Comma splice: needs period, not comma (2 MC)
Use em-dashes to indicate a break in thought
Use commas with 3 or more items in a series
Use question marks after questions (twice)
Use apostrophes in contractions ("What is")

According to state history Big Lord Fauntleroy replied. The only **indisputable** test for real princess blood is the mattress test a secret, that has been in the royal family for generations. *[quotation continues]*

    [2] "According to state history," Big Lord Fauntleroy replied, "the only <u>indisputable</u> test for real princess blood is the mattress test, a secret <u>that</u> has been in the royal family for generations. *[quotation continues]*

Indisputable: incontestable (won't be challenged)
Indent ¶ (new speaker)
Use quotation marks with parts quoted
Use commas with vb. of speaking & direct quotation
Use lc to continue interrupted quotations
Use commas w/ nonessential phrases ("a secret …")
Essential *which* clause using *that*; no comma
No closing quotation marks b/c continued quotation
Dress-ups: quality adjective; which clause (w/ *that*)

Week 5

With a single pea placed at the bottom of 20 King Mattresses and 20 eiderdown comforters only an authentic Princess will be sensitive enough to feel it's bump, and **indubitably**, she alone will be the next, royal spouse.

[2] With a single pea placed at the bottom of twenty King Mattresses and twenty eiderdown comforters, only an authentic princess will be sensitive enough to feel its bump. [3] Indubitably, she alone will be the next royal spouse."

Indubitably: unquestionably (won't be doubted)
No open " " b/c quotation continues, but close "
Spell out numbers written as one or two words
"King Mattresses" UC because it is a brand name
Comma needed after #2 SO of 5 or more words
Use lc for titles without a name
Its = possessive of *it*
Poor choice of *and* to join main clauses
No commas with cumulative adjectives

Why can't I just find somebody I love asked the **perturbed** and bewildered new king Somebody which can enjoy me for who I am Mel sighed heavily.

"Why can't I just find somebody I love," asked the perturbed and bewildered new king, "somebody who can enjoy me for who I am?" [6] Mel sighed heavily.

Perturbed: uneasy and anxious
Indent ¶ (new speaker)
Use " " w/ direct quotations + commas (speaking vb)
Use lc to continue interrupted quotations
Use *who* for people, *which* for things
Fused: use a question mark to separate these MCs
Dress-ups: dual adjectives; who clauses; -ly adverb

Throwing up they're hands in exasperation Lord Ashton and Big Lord Fauntleroy exited in a huff we certainly have our work cut out four us Lord Ashton grumbled **cantankerously**.

[4] Throwing up their hands in exasperation, Lord Ashton and Big Lord Fauntleroy exited in a huff. "We certainly have our work cut out for us," Lord Ashton grumbled cantankerously.

Cantankerously: in a disagreeable, ill-tempered way
Indent ¶ (new topic)
Homophones: they're/their; four/for
Use commas after #4 SO (-ing phrase)
Fused: use a period to separate 2 main clauses
Use quotation marks with direct quotations
Use comma with verb of speaking & direct quotation
Dress-ups: strong verbs; -ly adverbs

Realizing they would need to take matters into there own hands Lord Ashton and Big Lord Fauntleroy schemed and **connived**, and Big Lord Fauntleroy had the 1st inspiration.

[4] Realizing they would need to take matters into their own hands, Lord Ashton and Big Lord Fauntleroy schemed and connived. Big Lord Fauntleroy had the first inspiration.

Connived: cooperated secretly; conspired
Indent ¶ (new topic)
Homophones: there/their
Use commas after #4 SO (-ing phrase)
Avoid stringing together sentences with *and*
Spell out ordinal numbers
Dress-ups: dual verbs

Week 6

Ashton we must send out invitations at once to the fifty-seven local princesses asserted Big Lord Fauntleroy confident that his **capital** plan would succeed.

"Ashton, we must send out invitations at once to the fifty-seven local princesses," asserted Big Lord Fauntleroy, confident that his capital plan would succeed.

Capital: first-rate; excellent
Indent ¶ (new speaker)
Use quotation marks with direct quotations
Set off NDAs with commas
Use comma with verb of speaking & direct quotation
Invisible *who* needs comma: "Fauntleroy, who was"
Decoration: noun clause w/ "that." See Appendix
Dress-ups: strong verb, invisible who, quality adj.

Invitations for what inquired Lord Ashton? A courtly ball of course replied Big Lord Fauntleroy. All princesses fancy courtly balls especially when given by an **eligible** king. *[quotation continues]*

    "Invitations for what?" <u>inquired</u> Lord Ashton.
    "A courtly ball, of course," replied Big Lord Fauntleroy. "All princesses <u>fancy</u> courtly balls, especially <u>when</u> given by an <u>eligible</u> king. *[quotation continues]*

Eligible: fit or proper to be chosen; worthy of choice
Indent ¶ (new speakers)
Use quotation marks with direct quotations
Use " ? " after question, not at end of statement
Use commas to set off transitional expressions
Use comma with verb of speaking & direct quotation
Use commas to set off nonessential phrases
No closing quotation marks b/c continued quotation
Dress-ups: strong verbs; adverb clause; quality adj.

They recieve new gowns can practice thier dance steps and may **coyly** flirt with the gentleman. But king mel loathes courtly balls Lord Ashton protested.

They receive new gowns, can practice their dance steps, and may <u>coyly</u> flirt with the gentlemen."
    "But King Mel loathes courtly balls," Lord Ashton protested.

Coyly: artfully or flirtatiously shy, modest (-ly adv.)
Indent ¶, 2nd part (new speaker)
No opening quotes (cont.); use " " w/ quotations
Spelling: *receive; their; gentlemen;* UC: *King Mel*
Use commas with 3 or more items in a series
Avoid starting sentences with cc *(but),* but okay in
    fiction, especially dialogue
Use comma with verb of speaking & direct quotation

He once told me he hates to make **insufferable** mind numbing small talk with all the woman he despises eating finger sandwiches especially cucumber ones and all those princess's step on his toes

"He once told me he hates to make <u>insufferable</u>, <u>mind-numbing</u> small talk with all the women; he <u>despises</u> eating finger sandwiches, especially cucumber ones; and all those princesses step on his toes."

Insufferable: unbearable; not to be endured
Use commas w/ coordinate adj's but not cumulative
Hyphenate words that function as a single adjective
Use semicolons with items in a series when the items
    have internal commas
Use commas to set off nonessential phrases ("esp…")
Spelling: *women. Princesses* is plural, not possessive
Use a period at end of statements
Dress-ups: quality adjectives; strong verb

Week 7

After a pause, Lord Ashton summed it up. Truth be told Fauntleroy if it was up to Mel we'd have a **hoedown** and BBQ out on the back forty.

[2] After a pause Lord Ashton summed it up. "Truth be told, Fauntleroy, <u>if it were</u> up to Mel we'd have a hoedown and BBQ out on the back forty."

Hoedown: a community folk or square dancing party
Back forty: a remote, uncultivated acreage on a large
    piece of land
Comma not needed after #2 SO of 4 words or fewer
Use quotation marks with direct quotations
Set off NDAs with commas
Subjunctive mood: "if it *were*" b/c it isn't (Appendix)
Dress-ups: adverb clause

Big Lord Fauntleroy wasn't sympathetic. Well he's got to buck up and learn **decorous** kingly behavior sometime. As my mother always says "There's no time like the present".

    Big Lord Fauntleroy wasn't sympathetic. [T] "Well, he's got to <u>buck up</u> and learn <u>decorous</u> kingly behavior sometime. [5] As my mother always says, 'There's no time like the present.'"

Decorous: w/ propriety in conduct, manners, etc.
Indent ¶ (new speaker)
Use quotation marks with direct quotations
Use commas after introductory interjections
Use commas after #5 Sentence Openers
Use single ' ' for quotations within quotations
Periods & commas go inside quotation marks
Dress-ups: strong verb; quality adjective

Lord Ashton was in charge of castle preparations while Big Lord Fauntleroy undertook the **intimidating** task of designing a web page advertising the kings better points

    Lord Ashton was in charge of castle preparations, <u>while</u> Big Lord Fauntleroy <u>undertook</u> the <u>intimidating</u> task of designing a web page advertising the king's better points.

Intimidating: frightening; inducing fear (here, because overwhelming)
Indent ¶ (new topic)
Use comma to set off contrasting adv. clause (*while*)
Use apostrophes to show possession
Use a period at end of statements
Dress-ups: adverb clause; strong verb; quality adj.

---

having previously worked in marketing for a used car dealership Big Lord Fauntleroy is **adept** at Product Promotion undoubtedly, he is going two need all those special skills now.

[4] Having <u>previously</u> worked in marketing for a used car dealership, Big Lord Fauntleroy was <u>adept</u> at product promotion. [3] Undoubtedly he was going to need all those special skills now.

Adept: skillful; expert; proficient
Capitalize first word of sentences
Use commas after #4 SO (-ing phrase)
Don't switch tenses
Use lc for common nouns
Fused: use a period to separate 2 main clauses
Comma optional after #3 Sentence Opener
Homophone: two/to
Dress-ups: -ly adverb; quality adjective

Week 8

Court calligraphers and poets composed invitations requesting the presents of all the **eminent** citizens of the surrounding realms especially the 57 local princess's.

    Court calligraphers and poets composed invitations requesting the presence of all the <u>eminent</u> citizens of the surrounding realms, especially the fifty-seven local princesses.

Eminent: high in rank; distinguished
Indent ¶ (new topic)
Homophone: presents/presence
Use commas to set off nonessential phrases
Spell out numbers written as one or two words
Princesses is plural, not possessive
Dress-ups: quality adjective

This would be the 1st such festive event sense the disastrous flood, scullery maids polished and scrubbed morning noon and night eager to bring **luster** to even the smallest knob.

This would be the first such <u>festive</u> event since the <u>disastrous</u> flood. Scullery maids <u>polished and scrubbed</u> morning, noon, and night, eager to bring luster to even the smallest knob.

Luster: gloss; sheen; a shine
Spell out ordinal numbers
Homophone: sense/since
Comma splice: needs period, not comma (2 MC)
Use commas with 3 or more items in a series
Use commas to set off nonessential phrases (eager...)
Dress-ups: quality adjectives; dual verbs

The royal gardeners mulched trimmed pruned and transplanted exotic, **botanical** species from hothouses too pleasingly adorn the castle inside and out.

The royal gardeners mulched, trimmed, pruned, and transplanted <u>exotic</u> botanical species from hothouses to adorn the castle <u>pleasingly</u> inside and out.

Botanical: pertaining to plants
Use commas with 3 or more items in a series
No commas with cumulative adjectives
Homophone: too/to
Discuss not splitting infinitives (see Appendix)
Dress-ups: quality adjectives; -ly adverb

The Cook searched www.allrecipes.com, and watched iron chef every night for 3 weeks to plan a admirable scrumptious and yet **novel** menu.

The cook searched www.allrecipes.com and watched Iron Chef every night for three weeks to plan an admirable, <u>scrumptious</u>, and yet <u>novel</u> menu.

Novel: new; never seen before
Use lc for common nouns, UC for proper
No comma before *and* to join 2 compound verbs
Spell out numbers written as one or two words
Use *an* before a vowel: "an admirable"
Use commas with 3 or more items in a series
Dress-ups: quality adjectives

Week 9

Stable hands ironed thier livery, and readied stalls for an **influx** of visiting noble horses while court musicians tuned there lutes tweaked there harps and rosined there bows

Stable hands ironed their livery and <u>readied</u> stalls for an influx of visiting noble horses, <u>while</u> court musicians tuned their lutes, <u>tweaked</u> their harps, and <u>rosined</u> their bows.

Influx: a mass arrival or incoming
Spelling: *their* and homophone: *there/their*
No comma before *and* to join 2 compound verbs
Use commas w/ contrasting adv. clauses (*while ...*)
Use commas with 3 or more items in a series
Use a period at end of statements
Dress-ups: strong verbs; adverb clause

With only three days remaining before the ball Lord Ashton wringed her hands. I'm **apprehensive** that we may not be adequately prepared he told Big Lord Fauntleroy.

[2] With only three days remaining before the ball, Lord Ashton <u>wrung</u> his hands. "I'm <u>apprehensive</u> that we may not be <u>adequately</u> prepared," he told Big Lord Fauntleroy.

Apprehensive: uneasy; fearful
Indent ¶ (time has passed)
Comma needed after #2 SO of 5 or more words
Spelling: *wrung* is the past of *wring*. Pronoun: *his*
Use " " w/ direct quotations + comma (speaking vb)
Decoration: noun clause w/ "that." See Appendix
Dress-ups: strong verb; quality adjective; -ly adverb

We **dispatched** 57 invitations Lord Ashton continued which means we estimate a total of about 570 people, what with the princess's there lady in waiting the ladys of there lady in waitings and the rest of thier retinue. [quotation continues]

"We <u>dispatched</u> fifty-seven invitations," Lord Ashton continued, "<u>which</u> means we estimate a total of about 570 people, what with the princesses, their ladies-in-waiting, the ladies of their ladies-in-waiting, and the rest of their retinue. *[quotation continues]*

Dispatched: sent promptly on specific business
Use quotation marks with direct quotations
Spell out numbers written as one or two words
Use commas w/ verb of speaking & direct quotation
"What with" = taking into consideration
Use commas with 3 or more items in a series
Spelling: *princesses*; *ladies-in-waiting* (& hyphens)
Homophone and spelling: there/their
No closing quotation marks b/c continuous quotation
Dress-ups: strong verb; which clause

If the martha stewart courtly ball manual is correct—and its never yet failed us we can expect at least 40% of those invited or 228 Guests to **punctually** attend. *[quotation continues]*

[5] If the *Martha Stewart Courtly Ball Manual* is correct—and it has never yet failed us—we can expect at least 40% of those invited, or 228 guests, to attend <u>punctually</u>. *[quotation continues]*

Punctually: on time; without being late (-ly adverb)
No quotation marks b/c continued quotation
Titles of long works: UC + italicize (or underline)
It's = *it is* and sometimes *it has; it has* works better
Em-dash needs completing after "us"
Don't spell out numbers used w/ symbols: 40%
Avoid split infinitives
Use commas to set off nonessential phrase

Week 10

I'm not certain we can comfortably **accommodate** so many important personages; in truth, Lord Ashton had earned in the palace the reputation of a worrywart.

I'm not certain we can <u>comfortably</u> <u>accommodate</u> so many important personages." [2] In truth, Lord Ashton had earned in the palace the reputation of a worrywart.

Accommodate: provide with room and board (food)
No opening quotation marks b/c continued quotation
Close quotations with quotation marks
Separate only closely-related MCs with semicolons
Comma optional after #2 SO of 4 words or fewer
Dress-ups: -ly adverb; strong verb

More hopeful Big Lord Fauntleroy spoke with **unassailable** conviction as wealthy as King Mel is—and with the impressive job Ive done promoting him on the net he'll be percieved as quite a catch. *[quotation continues]*

[4] More hopeful, Big Lord Fauntleroy spoke with unassailable conviction. [5] "As wealthy as King Mel is—and with the impressive job I've done promoting him on the net— he'll be perceived as quite a catch. *[quotation continues]*

Unassailable: not subject to dispute or attack
Indent ¶ (new speaker)
Disguised #4, needs comma: "Being more hopeful,"
Fused: use a period to separate 2 main clauses
Use quotation marks with direct quotations
Contraction: *I've;* spelling: *perceived*
Em-dash needs completing after "net"
No closing quotation marks b/c continued quotation
Dress-ups: quality adjectives; adverb clause

I'm sure we'll have more then forty %. It wouldn't astonish me if every one shows, and the king will have princesses **galore** to chose between. *[quotation continues]*

I'm sure we'll have more than 40%. It wouldn't astonish me if everyone shows. The king will have princesses galore to choose among. *[quotation continues]*

Galore: in abundance
No quotation marks b/c continued quotation
Usage: *then/than* and *between/among* confusion
Don't spell out numbers used w/ symbols: 40%
Spelling: *everyone; choose (chose* is past tense)
Avoid stringing together sentences with *and*
Dress-ups: strong verb; adverb clause; quality adj.

I don't see any problem though you'll just need to open up the East and West wings, and notify the ritz hotel in case we need to send **surplus** guests they're way.

I don't see any problem, though. You'll just need to open up the east and west wings and notify the Ritz Hotel in case we need to send surplus guests their way."

Surplus: amount greater than needed (quality adj.)
Cont. quotation: don't open, but close, with "
Use commas to set off transitional words
Fused: use a period to separate 2 main clauses
Use lc for directions (usually); UC for proper nouns
No comma before *and* to join 2 compound verbs
Homophone: they're/their

Week 11

To days before the splendid ball maids where airing mattresses and ironing crisp linen sheets, and with the plans to test 57 princess's additional **eiderdowns** were shipped in courtesy of L L Bean.

[2] Two days before the splendid ball, maids were airing mattresses and ironing crisp linen sheets. [2] With the plans to test fifty-seven princesses, additional eiderdowns were shipped in courtesy of L. L. Bean.

Eiderdowns: quilts stuffed with eider-duck down
Indent ¶ (time has passed)
Homophone: *to/two;* spelling: *were* (not *where*)
Commas needed after #2 SO's of 5+ words (twice)
Poor choice of *and* to join main clauses
Spell out numbers written as one or two words
Princesses is plural, not possessive
Use periods after initials
Dress-ups: quality adjectives

The day before guests where to arrive the cook had a nervous breakdown trying to **scavenge** 570 sea urchins which were scarce that year, Big Lord Fauntleroy had two summon the iron chef himself too come finish final arrangements for the meals.

[2] The day before guests were to arrive, the cook had a nervous breakdown trying to scavenge 570 sea urchins, which were scarce that year. Big Lord Fauntleroy had to summon the Iron Chef himself to come finish final arrangements for the meals.

Scavenge: search anywhere, esp. for food
Spelling: *were,* not *where*
Disguised #2 (*During, In, On, At* that time period)
Comma needed after #2 SO of 5 or more words
Use commas to set off nonessential which clauses
Comma splice: needs period, not comma (2 MC)
Homophone: too/two/to
Capitalize proper nouns
Dress-ups: strong verbs; which clause; quality adj.

During the weeks of preparation unfortunate Mel had been shuffled off to the hunting lodge with only the company of his faithful laptop, and while there Mel **concocted** a unique, but brilliant plan.

[2] During the weeks of preparation, <u>unfortunate</u> Mel had been <u>shuffled</u> off to the hunting lodge with only the company of his faithful laptop. [5] While there, Mel <u>concocted</u> a <u>unique but brilliant</u> plan.

Concocted: devised, using skill and intelligence
Indent ¶ (new scene)
Comma needed after #2 SO of 5 or more words
Avoid stringing together sentences with *and*
Can count as a disguised #5: "he was" is implied
Use commas after #5 Sentence Openers
No comma before cc (*but*) to join 2 items in a series
Dress-ups: single & dual adjectives; strong verbs

Undermining his adviser's every step of the way in February, 2007, he sent a secret e-mail to each of the 57 princesses in hopes of eliminating some potentially sore toes.

[4] Undermining his advisers every step of the way, in February 2007 he sent a secret e-mail to each of the fifty-seven princesses in hopes of eliminating some <u>potentially</u> sore toes.

Undermining: to subvert (ruin, overthrow) by stealth (fm siege: digging under castle wall to bring it down)
Advisers is plural, not possessive
Use commas after #4 SO (-ing phrase)
No commas in dates when part of the date is omitted
Spell out numbers written as one or two words
Dress-ups: -ly adverb

Week 12

He secretly hopped alot yet scarcely dared too believe that he might find an **unaffected** soul mate some one with which he could spend the remainder of his life in marital happiness.

He <u>secretly</u> hoped a lot—yet <u>scarcely</u> dared to believe—that he might find an <u>unaffected</u> soul mate, someone with <u>whom</u> he could spend the remainder of his life in <u>marital</u> happiness.

Unaffected: sincere; genuine
Spelling: *hoped; someone.* Homophone: *too/to*
Sp.: *a lot* (a phrase worth banning but incl. for sp.)
Use em-dashes (or commas) for break in thought
Decoration: noun clause w/ "that." See Appendix
Use commas to set off nonessential phrases
Use *who* for people; here, *whom* b/c objective case
Dress-ups: -ly adverbs; quality adj's; who clause

Regardless he needed too correct the **erroneous** PR of his well meaning but misguided advisers, it just wasn't write to decieve people that way

[T] Regardless, he needed to correct the <u>erroneous</u> PR of his <u>well-meaning</u> but <u>misguided</u> advisers. It just wasn't right to deceive people that way!

Erroneous: inaccurate; false; untrue
Use commas after introductory transitional words
Homophone: too/to; write/right
Hyphenate words used as a single adj.: *well-meaning*
Comma splice: needs period, not comma (2 MC)
Spelling: *deceive* ("i before e except after c")
Use exclamation mark after exclamatory statements
Dress-ups: single and dual adjectives

Ignoring popular conventions Mel penned and **formatted** a traditional letter to send via e-mail far and wide. Flovia Flovenia February 31 2007 dear princesses

[4] Ignoring popular conventions, Mel <u>penned and formatted</u> a traditional letter to send via e-mail far and wide.

Flovia, Flovenia

February 28, 2007

Dear Princesses,

Formatted: arranged in specified form (i.e., used
    proper form for a personal letter)
Use commas after #4 SO (-ing phrase)
Write out or format as personal letter
Use commas between city and country
Date: February has only 28 days in odd years
Place a comma between the day and year in dates
Capitalize the first word in a salutation
Capitalize titles when used as NDAs
Follow the salutation of a personal letter w/ a comma
Dress-ups: dual verbs

Not wishing to entice you under **pretense** let me set the record straight, since I seek a wife, who will be open and honest, I figure you'll want the same from I.

    [4] Not wishing to <u>entice</u> you under pretense, let me set the record straight. [5] Since I seek a wife <u>who</u> will be open and honest, I figure you'll want the same from me.

Pretense: a false claim
Indent ¶ (start of body of letter)
Use commas after #4 SO (-ing phrase)
Comma splice: needs period, not comma (2 MC)
No comma w/ essential who clause (not *any* wife)
Use objective pronoun: "from me" (object of prep.)
Dress-ups: strong verb; who clause

Week 13

I'm 5' four inches with no **resemblance** too Mel Gibson unlike what you may have read, the only thing we have in common is our 1st name.

    I'm 5' 4" with no resemblance to Mel Gibson, unlike what you may have read. The only thing we have in common is our first name.

Resemblance: likeness; physical similarity
Indent ¶ (new topic)
Use numerals when numbers are used with symbols, and be consistent with symbols
Homophone: *too/to*; spell out ordinal numbers *(first)*
Use commas to set off nonessential phrases
Comma splice: needs period, not comma (2 MC)

My blond hair is as dull as **dishwater** and I wear thick, black-framed glasses, not contacts as depicted in my website; when I tried them once they made my eyes water.

My blond hair is as dull as dishwater, and I wear thick black-framed glasses, not contacts as depicted in my website. [5] When I tried them once, they made my eyes water.

Dishwater: extremely dull
Simile: hair is *like* dishwater (also a cliché)
Compound sentence needs comma: MC, cc MC
No commas with cumulative adjectives
Separate only closely-related MCs with semicolons
Use commas after #5 Sentence Openers

Also contrary two information at www.meetaprince.com I do not own a Harley, or have any thing in common with any one from the **upbeat** band *NSYNC.

[T] Also contrary to information at www.meetaprince.com, I do not own a Harley or have anything in common with anyone from the <u>upbeat</u> band *NSYNC.

Upbeat: cheerful
Note: no comma after "Also": it goes w/ "contrary"
Homophone: two/to
Comma after multiple introductory phrases
No comma before *or* to join 2 compound verbs
Spelling: *anything; anyone*
Dress-ups: quality adjective

Neither do I **relish** rock climbing or any other, extreme sports, tho' canoeing is alright, my preferred sport is hiking heights make me dizzy and speed makes me nervous

Neither do I <u>relish</u> rock climbing or any other extreme sports, <u>though</u> canoeing is all right. [6] My preferred sport is hiking. Heights make me dizzy, and speed makes me nervous.

Relish: enjoy; take pleasure in
No commas with cumulative adjectives
Spelling: *though* (spell out); *all right*
Comma splice: needs period, not comma (2 MC)
Fused: use a period to separate 2 main clauses
Compound sentence needs comma: MC, cc MC
Dress-ups: strong verb; adverb clause

Week 14

At the flovenian country fair I'm known to **eschew** rides with names like whirlwind avalanche or wipeout. In favor of the ferris wheel, or the long hilly slide.

[2] At the Flovenian Country Fair, I'm known to <u>eschew</u> rides with names like Whirlwind, Avalanche, or Wipeout in favor of the Ferris wheel or the long hilly slide.

Eschew: shun; avoid
Capitalize proper nouns
Comma needed after #2 SO of 5 or more words
Use commas with 3 or more items in a series
Correct fragment by joining phrase to sentence
No comma before *or* to join 2 items in a series
Dress-ups: strong verb

I love **ingenious**, computer games, and logic games as chess and Sudoku, and give me a square dance over a waltz any day.

I love ingenious computer games and logic games like chess and Sudoku. Give me a square dance over a waltz any day.

Ingenious: clever, original in invention (quality adj.)
No commas with cumulative adjectives
No comma before *and* to join 2 items in a series
Usage: *like/as* confusion
Poor choice of *and* to join main clauses

I don't **savor** singing in public, and have never dated Brittany Spears, in fact I've never dated much of any body sense my advisers never let me chose for myself.

I don't savor singing in public and have never dated Brittany Spears. [T] In fact, I've never dated much of anybody since my advisers never let me choose for myself.

Savor: appreciate fully; enjoy
No comma before *and* to join 2 items in a series
Comma splice: needs period, not comma (2 MC)
Use commas after introductory transitional words
Spelling: *anybody; since; choose*
Dress-ups: strong verb; adverb clause

My idea of a romantic evening is attending a hoedown **sauntering** in sherwood forest under the stars or developing a new computer program your's truely king Mel

My idea of a romantic evening is attending a hoedown, sauntering in Sherwood Forest under the stars, or developing a new computer program.

Yours truly,

King Mel

Sauntering: strolling; walking at a leisurely pace
Use commas with 3 or more items in a series
Capitalize proper nouns
Use a period at end of statements
Skip two lines before the closing
Capitalize the first word of the closing
No apostrophe with possessive pronouns *(yours)*
Spelling: *truly*
Comma needed after the closing
Skip two lines before the signature
Capitalize titles used with names

Week 15

After reading over his letter Mel found nothing to fault its **frank** and straightforward he thought and tells the princesses exactly whom I am. Wondering then what would happen Mel pressed "send".

[2] After reading over his letter, Mel found nothing to fault. "It's frank and straightforward," he thought, "and tells the princesses exactly who I am." [4] Wondering then what would happen, Mel pressed "send."

Frank: sincere; truthful; open
Indent ¶ (new topic)
Comma needed after #2 SO of 5 or more words
Fused: use a period to separate 2 main clauses
Use " " w/ direct quotations + commas (speaking vb.)
It's = it is. Nominative case: "I am he," so "who"
Use commas after #4 SO (-ing phrase)
Periods go inside closing quotation marks
Dress-ups: dual adjectives; who clause

The morning of the courtly ball the sun broke forth over the mountains in anticipation of the days **gala** event's as if nature herself was smiling on Flovenia.

[2] The morning of the courtly ball, the sun broke forth over the mountains in anticipation of the day's gala events, as if nature herself were smiling on Flovenia.

Gala: festive; showy; marked by lavish celebration
Indent ¶ (time has passed)
Disguised #2 (*On* implied); long, so needs comma
Possessive: *day's*, not *events*
Use commas to set off nonessential clauses
Subjunctive: as if nature *were*, b/c it isn't (Appendix)
Dress-ups: strong verb; adverb clause

On the previous evening March 15 2007 Big Lord Fauntleroy and Lord Ashton were to **fatigued** to fetch king Mel from his mountain retreat.

[2] On the previous evening, March 15, 2007, Big Lord Fauntleroy and Lord Ashton had been too fatigued to fetch King Mel from his mountain retreat.

Fatigued: tired; wearied
Commas needed around nonessential phrase (date)
Use commas in dates after the day and year
Use past perfect for different time in the past
Homophone: to/too
Capitalize titles used with names
Dress-ups: quality adjective

Determinedly, they sent his **valet** Frank too retreive him in time for a refresher course in appropriate, courtly ball behavior, with last minute pointers he might not come across as to unpromising.

[3] Determinedly, they had sent his valet, Frank, to <u>retrieve</u> him in time for a refresher course in appropriate courtly ball behavior. [2] With <u>last-minute</u> pointers he might not come across as too <u>unpromising</u>.

Valet: manservant who attends to personal needs
Use past perfect for different times in the past
Use commas to set off nonessential appositives
Homophone: *too/to* (twice)
Spelling: *retrieve*
No commas with cumulative adjectives
Comma splice: needs period, not comma (2 MC)
Hyphenate words that function as a single adjective
Dress-ups: strong verb; quality adjectives

Week 16

Frank felt otherwise believing that the task of **polishing** Mel was hopeless he allowed the king to sleep in knowing hed face the frustration of Mels advisers later in the morning.

[6] Frank felt otherwise. [4] Believing that the task of polishing Mel was hopeless, he allowed the king to sleep in, knowing he'd face the frustration of Mel's advisers later in the morning.

Polishing: refining; removing flaws of
Indent ¶ (back to present)
Fused: use a period to separate 2 main clauses
Decoration: noun clause w/ "that." See Appendix
Use commas after #4 SO (-ing phrase)
Use commas w/ nonessential phrases ("knowing…")
Apostrophes: contraction *(he'd)*; possessive *(Mel's)*

When king Mel finally awoke it was too a tense **flustered** Big Lord Fauntleroy snapping his manicured fingers alot. Lord Ashton followed close behind, wringing his petite palms.

[5] When King Mel <u>finally</u> awoke, it was to a <u>tense</u>, flustered Big Lord Fauntleroy <u>snapping</u> his manicured fingers a lot. Lord Ashton followed close behind, <u>wringing</u> his <u>petite</u> palms.

Flustered: agitated; nervous; upset
Indent ¶ (time has passed)
Capitalize titles used with names
Use commas after #5 Sentence Openers
Homophone: *too/to.* Spelling: *a lot*
Use commas with coordinate adjectives
Close is correct (can function as adverb or adj.)
Dress-ups: -ly adverb; dual & single adjectives

You must arise at once, your majesty, we have no time to loose!, **implored** Big Lord Fauntleroy while urging Lord Ashton to hurriedly fling open the curtains.

"You must arise at once, Your Majesty! We have no time to lose!" <u>implored</u> Big Lord Fauntleroy <u>while</u> urging Lord Ashton to <u>fling</u> open the curtains <u>hurriedly</u>.

Implored: begged urgently
Indent ¶ (new speaker)
Use quotation marks with direct quotations
UC: Your Majesty. Sp. confusion: *loose* vs. *lose*
Comma splice: needs " **!** " not comma (2 MC)
Do not use comma with an end mark of punctuation
Discuss not splitting infinitives (see Appendix)
Dress-ups: strong verbs; adverb clause; -ly adverb

In the few hours we have left you're outfit must be **refurbished** and we need to squeeze in another session with the image consultant Vannah

[2] "In the few hours we have left, your outfit must be <u>refurbished</u>, and we need to <u>squeeze</u> in another session with the image consultant, Vannah."

Refurbished: made clean, bright, fresh again
Comma needed after #2 SO of 5 or more words
Homophone: you're/your
Compound sentence needs comma: MC, cc MC
Use commas to set off nonessential appositives
Use a period at end of statements
Dress-ups: strong verbs

Week 17

Where is that foolish Frank **queried** Lord Ashton? He's suppose to have got you up by now he has left you too your own devices for to long all will be lost

"Where is that <u>foolish</u> Frank?" **queried** Lord Ashton. "He's supposed to have gotten you up by now. He has left you to your own devices for too long. [6] All will be lost!"

Queried: inquired; asked
Indent ¶ (new speaker)
Use quotation marks with direct quotations
Use " ? " after question, not at end of statement
Spelling: *supposed; too/to;* past participle: *gotten*
Fused: use a period to separate 2 main clauses (twice)
Use exclamation mark after exclamatory statements
Dress-ups: quality adjective; strong verb

"Now fellas replied Mel calmly I'm sure you mean well, what with your bustling activity and all. But I'd just as soon have a **manicure** as meet with an image consultant"!

[T] "Now, fellas," replied Mel <u>calmly</u>, "I'm sure you mean well, what with your <u>bustling</u> activity and all, but I'd just as soon have a manicure as meet with an image consultant!"

Manicure: nail treatment (trimming, smoothing)
Indent ¶ (new speaker)
Use commas after intro. transitions & around NDA's
Stop and start " " w/ interruption and add commas
Avoid starting sentences with coord. conjunctions
Exclamation inside " " if part of quoted material
Note: Mel doesn't want either but is misunderstood
Dress-ups: -ly adverb; quality adjective

Excellent cried Big Lord Fauntleroy! Fortunately, we have a manicure scheduled for 10.15. Not wishing to trigger farther distress among them Mel **capitulated**.

"Excellent!" cried Big Lord Fauntleroy. [3] "Fortunately, we have a manicure scheduled for 10:15."
[4] Not wishing to <u>trigger</u> further distress between them, Mel <u>capitulated</u>.

Capitulated: gave up resistance; surrendered
Indent ¶ (new speaker; new topic)
Use quotation marks with direct quotations
Use " ! " after exclamation, not at end of statement
Comma optional after #3 Sentence Opener
Use a colon between the hour and minutes
Use commas after #4 SO (-ing phrase)
Usage: *farther/further* & *among/between* confusion
Dress-ups: strong verbs

Now remember sire its **imperative** you choose a bride whose a true princess this evening at the ball, urged Lord Ashton, all Flovenia eagerly anticipates the announcement of your selection.

[T] "Now remember, Sire, it's <u>imperative</u> you choose a bride this evening at the ball <u>who</u>'s a true princess," <u>urged</u> Lord Ashton. "All Flovenia <u>eagerly</u> <u>anticipates</u> the announcement of your selection."

Imperative: absolutely necessary
Indent ¶ (new speaker)
Use quotation marks with direct quotations
Set off NDAs with commas; UC titles used as NDAs
It's = it is; who's = who is
Misplaced prep. phrase (She needs to be a princess all the time, not just this evening at the ball!)
Comma splice: needs period, not comma (2 MC)
Dress-ups: quality adj. & verbs; who; -ly adverb

Week 18

Sighing **abjectly** Mel followed Big Lord Fauntleroy Lord Ashton and Frank down the hall to the Royal Spa and Beauty Bar. Located next to the palace whirlpool.

[4] Sighing <u>abjectly</u>, Mel followed Big Lord Fauntleroy, Lord Ashton, and Frank down the hall to the Royal Spa and Beauty <u>Bar, located</u> next to the palace whirlpool.

Abjectly: miserably; hopelessly
Indent ¶ (new topic)
Use commas after #4 SO (-ing phrase)
Use commas with 3 or more items in a series
Correct fragment by joining phrase to prior sentence
Invisible *which* needs comma: "Bar, which was …"
Dress-ups: -ly adverb; invisible which clause

Resigned to the annoying **ministrations**, his advisers seem to think necessary in order for a King to appear in public he submitted to Vannahs manicure and hairstyling.

[7] Resigned to the <u>annoying</u> ministrations his advisers seemed to think necessary in order for a king to appear in public, he <u>submitted</u> to Vannah's manicure and hairstyling.

Ministrations: the acts of serving or aiding
No commas with essential clauses ("his advisers …")
Don't switch tenses ("seemed")
Use lc for titles without a name
Use commas after #7 Sentence Openers (-ed)
Use apostrophes to show possession
Dress-ups: quality adjective; strong verb

At last, the time arrived when dignitaries princesses and there **entourages** where to arrive with due ceremony and formalitys, the courtyard clock struck four oclock.

[2] At last the time arrived <u>when</u> dignitaries, princesses, and their entourages were to arrive with <u>due</u> ceremony and formalities. The courtyard clock <u>struck</u> four o'clock.

Entourages: groups of attendants
Indent ¶ (new topic)
Comma not needed after #2 SO of 4 words or fewer
Use commas with 3 or more items in a series
Spelling: *their; were; formalities; o'clock*
Comma splice: needs period, not comma (2 MC)
Dress-ups: adverb clause; quality adj.; strong verb

While the dinning hall glistened with: Bavarian crystal silver candlesticks and 100s of tall **tapers** waiting to be lit waiters stood idle by awaiting the onset of diner.

[5] While the dining hall <u>glistened</u> with Bavarian crystal, silver candlesticks, and hundreds of tall tapers waiting to be lit, waiters stood <u>idly</u> by awaiting the onset of dinner.

Tapers: small, slender candles
Spelling: *dining; dinner*
Use colon *only after MC* to introduce a list
Spell out numbers written as one or two words
Use commas after #5 Sentence Openers
Diction: the adverb *idly*, not adjective *idle*
Dress-ups: strong verb; -ly adverb

Week 19

Dignified, Lord Ashton and Big Lord Fauntleroy took there places at the head of the entry **balustrade** the ladder brushing off microscopic specks of dust from his lapel.

[7] Dignified, Lord Ashton and Big Lord Fauntleroy took their places at the head of the entry balustrade, the latter brushing off <u>microscopic</u> specks of dust from his lapel.

Balustrade: the railing & supporting posts in front of a gallery (or railing at side of staircase or gallery)
Note different meaning w/o a comma after 1st word
Homophone: there/their
Use commas to set off nonessential phrases
Usage: *ladder/latter* confusion
Dress-ups: quality adjective

The lady in waitings who stood expectantly on either side of the redcarpeted stares were too assist the arriving Princesses with unpacking, and donning they're **raiment** for the ball.

The ladies-in-waiting, <u>who</u> stood <u>expectantly</u> on either side of the red-carpeted stairs, were to assist the arriving princesses with unpacking and donning their raiment for the ball.

Raiment: clothing; apparel; attire
Sp./hyphen: *ladies-in-waiting; red-carpeted stairs*
Use commas to set off nonessential *who* clauses
Homophones: too/to; they're/their
Use lc for titles without a name
No comma before *and* to join 2 items in a series
Dress-ups: who clause; -ly adverb

Pacing in the courtyard the footman practiced low bows, and sneaked occasional **surreptitious** glances at the upstairs windows.

[4] Pacing in the courtyard, the footmen practiced low bows and <u>sneaked</u> <u>occasional, surreptitious</u> glances at the upstairs windows.

Surreptitious: secret or unauthorized
Use commas after #4 SO (-ing phrase)
Footmen is plural, not singular
No comma before *and* to join 2 compound verbs
Sp.: *sneaked & snuck* are correct, *sneaked* preferred
Use commas with coordinate adjectives
Dress-ups: strong verb; dual adjectives

There housemaids and indoor staff flung open wide the mullioned windows hopping the botanical fragrances would **waft** upstairs into the waiting guestroom's.

[T] There, housemaids and indoor staff <u>flung</u> open wide the <u>mullioned</u> windows, hoping the <u>botanical</u> fragrances would <u>waft</u> upstairs into the waiting guestrooms.

Waft: floated or carried by air
Use comma after intro. transition *(Their* would not make sense: the staff don't belong to the footmen)
Use commas w/ nonessential phrases *("hoping ...")*
Spelling: *hoping*
Guestrooms is plural, not possessive
Dress-ups: strong verbs; quality adjectives

Week 20

Ahem—Lord Ashton cleared his throat **conspicuously**. What time is it now? Four 15 Big Lord Fauntleroy nervously replied, it'll be alright he added uncertainly.

"Ahem—," Lord Ashton cleared his throat <u>conspicuously</u>. "What time is it now?"
"Four fifteen," Big Lord Fauntleroy <u>nervously</u> replied. "It'll be all right," he added <u>uncertainly</u>.

Conspicuously: noticeably; attracting attention
Indent ¶ (new speakers)
Use quotation marks with direct quotations
Use comma w/ speaking vb. & quotation (& w/ dash)
Spell out #s at start of sentence
Comma splice: needs period, not comma (2 MC)
Spelling: *all right*
Dress-ups: -ly adverbs

Four 30—maybe its not alright, Big Lord Fauntleroy mopped the sweat from his **puckered** brow. Its now 4.45, he whispered in a controlled, but flustered tone.

"Four thirty—maybe it's not all right." Big Lord Fauntleroy <u>mopped</u> the sweat from his <u>puckered</u> brow.
"It's now 4:45," he <u>whispered</u> in a <u>controlled but flustered</u> tone.

Puckered: gathered in small wrinkles
Indent ¶ (new speaker; time has passed)
Use quotation marks with direct quotations
Spell out #s at start of sentence
It's = it is (twice). Spelling: *all right*
Comma splice: needs period, not comma (2 MC)
Use a colon between the hour and minutes
No comma before *but* to join 2 items in a series
Dress-ups: strong verbs; single & dual adjectives

"Where could they be" Lord Ashton snapped under his breath to Big Lord Fauntleroy. The king's **epistle** had done it's job.

"Where could they be?" Lord Ashton <u>snapped</u> under his breath to Big Lord Fauntleroy.
The king's epistle had done its job.

Epistle: letter, especially a formal one
Indent ¶ (new speaker; new topic)
Use " ? " inside " ", even though sentence continues
Note use of past perfect tense
Its = possessive of *it*
Dress-ups: strong verb

"It's April 6 2007 already and it has taken us 3 weeks to take down all the banners un-make the guest chambers and write checks for all the extra retainers which we *didn't* need" exclaimed a wan and **peevish** Big Lord Fauntleroy.

"It's April 6, 2007, already, and it has taken us three weeks to take down all the banners, un-make the guest chambers, and write checks for all the extra retainers, <u>whom</u> we *didn't* need!" exclaimed a <u>wan and peevish</u> Big Lord Fauntleroy.

Peevish: cross; irritable
Indent ¶ (time has passed)
Use commas in dates after the day and year
Compound sentence needs comma: MC, cc MC
Spell out numbers written as one or two words
Use commas with 3 or more items in a series
Use commas to set off nonessential who clauses
Usage: *who* for people, plus *whom* b/c objective case
Use exclamation mark after exclamatory statements
Dress-ups: who clause; strong verb; dual adjectives

Week 21

I for one am fed up with eating leftovers from the feast that never happened. Even the Iron Chefs dishes **pall** after being reheated for the 15th time

"I, for one, am fed up with eating leftovers from the feast <u>that</u> never happened. Even the Iron Chef's dishes <u>pall</u> after being reheated for the fifteenth time!"

Pall: become distasteful or tiresome
Use quotation marks with direct quotations
Use commas around nonessential phrases
Which clause using *that* (see Appendix)
Use apostrophes to show possession
Spell out ordinal numbers
Could use exclamation mark or period at end
Dress-ups: which clause (using *that*); strong verb

Stop your **querulous** grievances Fauntleroy and help me fasten all the shutters in the Royal Relaxation Room, before the big screen plasma TV gets wet from all the rain sighed Lord Ashton. Ive never seen such a dark and stormy night.

"Stop your <u>querulous</u> grievances, Fauntleroy, and help me fasten all the shutters in the Royal Relaxation Room <u>before</u> the big screen plasma TV gets wet from all the rain," <u>sighed</u> Lord Ashton. "I've never seen such a dark and stormy night."

Querulous: full of complaints
Indent ¶ (new speaker)
Use quotation marks with direct quotations
Set off NDAs with commas
No commas w/ mid-sentence adv. clauses ("before")
Use comma with verb of speaking & direct quotation
Use apostrophes in contractions
Note cliché ("dark and stormy night")
Dress-ups: quality adj.; adverb clause; strong verb

Suddenly threw the hall echoed a clanging that could only mean someone had boldly braved the **blusterous** weather, and was droping the heavy, carved, bronze knocker repeatedly against the knocker plate.

[3] Suddenly through the hall <u>echoed</u> a clanging <u>that</u> could only mean someone had <u>boldly</u> <u>braved</u> the <u>blusterous</u> weather and was dropping the heavy carved bronze knocker <u>repeatedly</u> against the knocker plate.

Blusterous: blowing in violent and abrupt bursts
Indent ¶ (new topic)
Homophone: threw/through
Which clause using *that* (see Appendix)
Alliteration: "boldly braved the blusterous"
No comma before *and* to join 2 compound verbs
Spelling: *dropping*
No commas with cumulative adjectives
Dress-ups: strong verbs; which; -ly adv's; quality adj

Turning from his task at the shutters Big Lord Fauntleroy **waddled** down the hall with Lord Ashton at his heels calling to the footmen who should be alert two any activity in the courtyard

[4] Turning from his task at the shutters, Big Lord Fauntleroy <u>waddled</u> down the hall with Lord Ashton at his heels, calling to the footmen, <u>who</u> should have been alert to any activity in the courtyard.

Waddled: walked w/ short, rocking steps, like a duck
Use commas after #4 SO (-ing phrase)
Use commas to set off nonessential phrases
Use commas to set off nonessential clauses
Tense: *should have been,* to indicate ongoing action
Homophone: two/to
Use a period at end of statements
Dress-ups: strong verb; who clause

Week 22

The whether is so appalling that even our most **formidable** enemies would not brave such a night, remarked Big Lord Fauntleroy. So, who could be at the door

"The weather is so <u>appalling</u> that even our most <u>formidable</u> enemies would not <u>brave</u> such a night," <u>remarked</u> Big Lord Fauntleroy, "so <u>who</u> could be at the door?"

Formidable: of great strength; powerful
Use quotation marks with direct quotations
Spelling confusion: *weather* vs. *whether*
Use lc to continue interrupted quotations
Commas before, not after, coordinating conjunctions
Needs question mark, inside closing quotation marks
Dress-ups: quality adj's; strong verbs; who clause

This question was answered as soon as the heavy doors were swung opened revealing a bedraggled, young woman with **disheveled** hair and a soaking wet but pearl encrusted gown.

This question was answered as soon <u>as</u> the heavy doors were swung open, revealing a <u>bedraggled</u> young woman with <u>disheveled</u> hair and a <u>soaking wet but pearl-encrusted</u> gown.

Disheveled: untidy; disarranged
Indent ¶ (new topic)
Diction: *open,* not *opened*
Use commas to set off nonessential phrases
No commas with cumulative adjectives
Hyphenate words that function as a single adjective
Dress-ups: adv. clause; single and dual adjectives

Greetings I'm princess sweetie pie from Florentia Parmigiana the young lady **heralded** herself. Well actually my name is Anastasia Aurora Ariel Arista but everybody just calls me princess sweetie pie.

"Greetings! I'm Princess Sweetie Pie from Florentia, Parmigiana," the young lady <u>heralded</u> herself. "Well, actually, my name is Anastasia Aurora Ariel Arista, but everybody just calls me Princess Sweetie Pie."

Heralded: announced (strong verb)
Indent ¶ (new speaker)
Use quotation marks with direct quotations
Exclamation marks can follow intro. interjections
Capitalize proper nouns and titles used with names
Use commas between city and country
Use comma with verb of speaking & direct quotation
Use commas to set off transitional words
Compound sentence needs comma: MC, cc MC

"Of course. Lord Ashton bent into a low sweeping bow over her extended, right hand. As he moved to kiss her knuckles. But where is your **retinue**, surely you are not out unaccompanied on such a night

"Of course." Lord Ashton bent into a low, <u>sweeping</u> bow over her <u>extended</u> right hand <u>as</u> he moved to kiss her knuckles. "But <u>where</u> is your retinue? [3] Surely you are not out <u>unaccompanied</u> on such a night?"

Retinue: retainers who attend someone important
Indent ¶ (new speaker)
Use quotation marks with direct quotations
Use commas with coordinate adjectives ("low, …")
No comma with cumulative adj's ("extended right")
Correct fragment by joining dependent clause to MC
Comma splice: needs question mark, not comma
Needs closing question mark, inside quotation marks
Dress-ups: quality adjectives; adverb clauses

Week 23

Well Anastasia Aurora Ariel Arista a.k.a. Sweetie Pie explained they were having alot of trouble **cajoling** the horses through all the mud, and decided to stop down the mountain at the flovenian inn limited. *[quotation continues]*

[T] "Well," Anastasia Aurora Ariel Arista, a.k.a. Sweetie Pie, explained, "they were having a lot of trouble cajoling the horses through all the mud and decided to stop down the mountain at the Flovenian Inn Limited. *[quotation continues]*

Cajoling: wheedle; persuade; coax
Indent ¶ (new speaker)
Use quotation marks with direct quotations
Use comma with verb of speaking & direct quotation
Use commas around nonessential phrases
Spelling: *a lot*
No comma before *and* w/ 2 verbs *(having, decided)*
Capitalize proper nouns (name of inn)
No closing quotation marks b/c continued quotation

Finally, I decided two come up on my own because my over-protective guardian Miss Pittypat was driving me crazy, with all her fussing about the **accommodations** *[quotation continues]*

[3] Finally, I decided to come up on my own <u>because</u> my <u>overprotective</u> guardian, Miss Pittypat, was driving me crazy with all her fussing about the accommodations. *[quotation continues]*

Accommodations: lodging
No quotation marks b/c continued quotation
Comma optional after #3 Sentence Opener
Homophone: two/to
Use commas around nonessential appositives
No commas with essential phrases ("with …")
Use a period at end of statements
Dress-ups: adverb clause; quality adjective

Among us, she did'nt think the carpets were clean, and was making me prance from the bed to the **armoire** with my shoes on. *[quotation continues]*

[2] Between us, she didn't think the carpets were clean and was making me <u>prance</u> from the bed to the armoire with my shoes on. *[quotation continues]*

Armoire: a large, movable wardrobe
No quotation marks b/c continued quotation
Use *between* with two (groups, in this case)
Spelling: *didn't*
No comma before *and* to join 2 compound verbs
Dress-ups: strong verb

As if that wasn't enough she also insisted on stripping the top coverlets from all the mattresses because as she put it "they might be unclean" she mimicked the governess voice in a convincing **nasal** manner.

[5] As if that wasn't enough, she also insisted on stripping the top coverlets from all the mattresses <u>because</u>, <u>as</u> she put it, 'They might be unclean.'" She <u>mimicked</u> the governess's voice in a <u>convincing</u> <u>nasal</u> manner.

Nasal: sounding as if the nose were pinched
No open " " b/c quotation continues, but close "
Use commas after #5 Sentence Openers
Use commas to set off interrupting clauses
Use single ' ' for quotations within quotations
Capitalize the first word of a quoted sentence
Fused: use a period to separate 2 main clauses
Add apostrophe + "s" to indicate possession
Dress-ups: adverb clauses; strong verb; quality adj's

Week 24

Well we certainly welcome you alright retinue or not, Big Lord Fauntleroy **ineptly** hastened toward her looking like the cat that first discovered cream. So you are a real princess, with a real king and queen for parents and thrones and everything"?

[T] "Well, we <u>certainly</u> welcome you, all right, retinue or not." Big Lord Fauntleroy <u>ineptly</u> <u>hastened</u> toward her, looking like the cat <u>that</u> first discovered cream. "So you are a real princess, with a real king and queen for parents and thrones and everything?"

Ineptly: with awkwardness; clumsily; foolishly
Indent ¶ (new speaker)
Use quotation marks with direct quotations
Use commas after introductory interjections
Spelling: *all right*
Use commas around nonessential phrases (twice)
Comma splice: needs period, not comma (2 MC)
Simile: he is *like* the cat that first discovered cream
Question mark inside " " b/c part of quoted material
Dress-ups: -ly adv's; strong verb; which (that) clause

Of course I am Sweetie Pie squealed! I just couldn't wait to get here, even though I know I missed the ball, and I wonder if I am too late for the **renowned** mattress test?

[T] "Of course, I am!" Sweetie Pie <u>squealed</u>. "I just couldn't wait to get here, <u>even though</u> I know I missed the ball. I wonder <u>if</u> I am too late for the <u>renowned</u> mattress test?"

Renowned: famous
Indent ¶ (new speaker)
Use quotation marks with direct quotations
Use commas after introductory transitional words
Use " ! " after exclamation, not at end of statement
Avoid stringing together sentences with *and*
Dress-ups: strong verb; adverb clauses; quality adj.

I thought you said that was an ancient family secret Lord Ashton **plaintively** mumbled to Big Lord Fauntleroy I thought it was he whispered back we can't do any thing about that now.

"I thought you said that was an ancient family secret," Lord Ashton <u>plaintively</u> <u>mumbled</u> to Big Lord Fauntleroy.
"I thought it was," he <u>whispered</u> back. "We can't do anything about that now."

Plaintively: sadly; sorrowfully
Indent ¶ (new speakers)
Use quotation marks with direct quotations
Use comma with verb of speaking & direct quotation
Fused (twice): use a period to separate 2 main clauses
Spelling: *anything* is one word
Dress-ups: -ly adverb; strong verbs

After all I have heard so much about the tall **comely** King Mel, and his fabulous wealth from www.meetaprince.com that I can not begin to tell you how excited I am. He sounds like just my type, he sounds just like me

    [2] "After all, I have heard so much about the tall, <u>comely</u> King Mel and his fabulous wealth from www.meetaprince.com that I cannot begin to tell you how excited I am! He sounds like just my type; he sounds just like me!"

Comely: attractive (quality adjective)
Indent ¶ (new speaker)
Use quotation marks with direct quotations
Comma needed to prevent confusion: "After all I
    have heard," or "After all, …"?
Use commas with coordinate adjectives
No comma before *and* to join 2 items in a series
Decoration: noun clause w/ "that." See Appendix
Spelling: *cannot*
Use exclamation marks after exclamatory statements
Comma splice, this one best fixed with a semicolon

Week 25

Um … certainly … the mattress test … right … yes well right this way Lord Ashton **stammered** he pulled himself together you must be worn out from your journey and hungry to.

    "Um … certainly … the mattress test … right … yes, well, right this way," Lord Ashton <u>stammered</u>. [6] He pulled himself together. "You must be worn out from your journey and hungry, too."

Stammered: spoke with pauses and repetitions
Indent ¶ (new speaker)
Use quotation marks with direct quotations
Use commas to set off interjections ("yes, well, …")
Use comma with verb of speaking & direct quotation
Fused (twice): use a period to separate 2 main clauses
Homophone: to/too + comma with transitional word
Dress-ups: strong verb

I could eat a horse Sweetie Pie agreed with evident pleasure, what does this palace usually dish up she queried? Well we weren't expecting you Lord Ashton **hedged** But I believe we have some appetizing leftovers.

    "I could eat a horse," Sweetie Pie agreed with <u>evident</u> pleasure. "What does this palace <u>usually</u> <u>dish up</u>?" she <u>queried</u>.
    [T] "Well, we weren't expecting you," Lord Ashton <u>hedged</u>, "but I believe we have some <u>appetizing</u> leftovers."

Hedged: evaded; stalled
Indent ¶ (new speakers)
Use quotation marks with direct quotations
Use comma with verb of speaking & direct quotation
Comma splice: needs period, not comma (2 MC)
Use " ? " after question, not at end of statement
Use commas after introductory interjection
Use lc for "but"—continues interrupted quotation
Dress-ups: quality adj's; -ly adverb; strong verbs

After bringing the princess a heated up urchin diner from the kitchen Lord Ashton **escorted** her to the lady in waitings to get her settled into her bedchamber

    [2] After bringing the princess a heated-up urchin dinner from the kitchen, Lord Ashton <u>escorted</u> her to the ladies-in-waiting to get her settled into her bedchamber.

Escorted: accompanied as a guide & showing honor
Indent ¶ (new topic)
Hyphenate words that function as a single word
Spelling: *dinner; ladies-in-waiting*
Comma needed after #2 SO of 5 or more words
Use a period at end of statements
Dress-ups: strong verb

With all the comforter's and mattress's pilled high on top of the small round pea Lord Ashton left the room to the ladies, and **rejoined** Big Lord Fauntleroy in the hall outside.

[2] With all the comforters and mattresses <u>piled</u> high on top of the small round pea, Lord Ashton left the room to the ladies and <u>rejoined</u> Big Lord Fauntleroy in the hall outside.

Rejoined: returned to the company of
Comforters and *mattresses* are plural, not possessive
Spelling: *piled*
"Small round " correct w/o comma (cumulative adj.)
Comma needed after #2 SO of 5 or more words
No comma before *and* to join 2 compound verbs
Dress-ups: strong verbs

Week 26

Among the 2 of them the advisers were uncertain of her **veracity** but with no other princess in sight she was they're best bet.

[2] Between the two of them, the advisers were <u>uncertain</u> of her veracity, but with no other princess in sight, she was their best bet.

Veracity: truthfulness
Use *between* with two people. Spell out "two"
Comma needed after #2 SO of 5 or more words
Compound sentence needs comma: MC, cc MC
Comma after "sight": "with … sight" is like a #2 SO
Homophone: they're/their
Dress-ups: quality adjective

Besides it was evident that she did not recieve the corrections Mel sent out, perhaps because her retinue had to travel so far, and his **missive** may have passed them on there journey.

[T] Besides, it was <u>evident</u> that she had not received the corrections Mel had sent out, perhaps <u>because</u> her retinue had had to travel so far and his missive may have passed them on their journey.

Missive: letter; written communication
Use commas after introductory transitional words
Decoration: noun clause w/ "that." See Appendix
Use past perfect for 2 different times in the past
Spelling: *received* ("*i* before *e* except after *c*")
No comma b/c two *because* clauses, 2nd understood
Homophone: there/their
Dress-ups: quality adjective; adverb clause

By the next morning however thier fears were **squashed** and thier hopes realized, and Princess Sweetie Pie passed the test effortlessly

[2] By the next morning, however, their fears were <u>squashed</u> and their hopes realized. Princess Sweetie Pie passed the test <u>effortlessly</u>!

Squashed: silenced; crushed
Indent ¶ (time has passed)
Use commas to set off transitional words
Spelling: *their*
Poor choice of *and* to join main clauses
Use exclamation mark after exclamatory statements
Dress-ups: strong verb; -ly adverb

Cutting off her complaints about the uncomfortable sleeping arrangements she was **conducted** by Lord Ashton and Big Lord Fauntleroy into king mels room.

[4] Cutting off her complaints about the uncomfortable sleeping arrangements, Lord Ashton and Big Lord Fauntleroy <u>conducted</u> her into King Mel's room.

Conducted: led; guided
Use commas after #4 SO (-ing phrase)
Illegal #4: word after " , " should do the *inging*
    (fixing this also rids sentence of passive voice)
Capitalize names and titles used with names
Use apostrophes to show possession
Dress-ups: strong verb

Week 27

Sire Big Lord Fauntleroy announced in his best royal adviser voice you have a new **fiancée** and here she is too meet you!

"Sire," Big Lord Fauntleroy announced in his best royal adviser voice, "you have a new fiancée, and here she is to meet you!"

Fiancée: a woman to whom a man is engaged (a man
    engaged is a fiancé). Indent ¶ (new speaker)
Use quotation marks with direct quotations
Use comma with verb of speaking & direct quotation
Compound sentence needs comma: MC, cc MC
Homophone: too/to

He led a beamming Sweetie Pie into the bedroom where Mel sat propped high on pillows; hopping that Sweetie Pie will not get to close a look at her **intended** Lord Ashton rushed around lowering the drapes, so only dim lighting fills the room.

He led a <u>beaming</u> Sweetie Pie into the bedroom, <u>where</u> Mel sat <u>propped</u> high on pillows. [4] Hoping that Sweetie Pie would not get too close a look at her intended, Lord Ashton <u>rushed</u> around lowering the drapes, so only dim lighting filled the room.

Intended: one's fiancée
Indent ¶ (new topic)
Spelling: *beaming; hoping*
Use commas w/ nonessential adj. clauses (where…)
Separate only closely-related MCs with semicolons
Decoration: noun clause w/ "that." See Appendix
Don't switch tenses *(would; filled)*
Homophone: to/too
Use commas after #4 SO (-ing phrase)
Dress-ups: quality adj's; adverb clause; strong verb

What a horrible night I had Sweetie Pie began. First my hovering overprotective governess drove me crazy, and then the mud and rain ruined my favorite pearl-**encrusted** gown, and my best pair of glass slippers she wailed.

"What a horrible night I had!" Sweetie Pie began. [T] "First, my hovering, overprotective governess drove me crazy, and then the mud and rain ruined my favorite pearl-encrusted gown and my best pair of glass slippers," she wailed.

Encrusted: coated as if with a crust
Indent ¶ (new speaker)
Use quotation marks with direct quotations
Use exclamation mark after exclamatory statements
Use commas after introductory transitional words
Use commas with coordinate adjectives
No comma before *and* to join 2 items in a series
Use comma with verb of speaking & direct quotation
Dress-ups: dual adjectives; strong verb

Next that **harridan** you call a lady in waiting insisted that the only bed this palace could offer was one piled 20 feet high with mattresses and comforters! *[quotation continues]*

[T] "Next, that harridan you call a lady-in-waiting insisted that the only bed this palace could offer was one piled twenty feet high with mattresses and comforters! *[quotation continues]*

Harridan: a scolding old woman
Use quotation marks with direct quotations
Use commas after introductory transitional words
Hyphenate words that function as a single noun
Decoration: noun clause w/ "that." See Appendix
Spell out numbers written as one or two words
No closing quotation marks b/c continued quotation

Week 28

It took a ladder for me to climb to the top and I felt **vertigo** when peeping over the edge of the highest mattress, your lucky I didn't loose my diner *[quotation continues]*

It took a ladder for me to climb to the top, and I felt vertigo when peeping over the edge of the highest mattress. You're lucky I didn't lose my dinner! *[quotation continues]*

Vertigo: sensation of dizziness
No quotation marks b/c continued quotation
Compound sentence needs comma: MC, cc MC
Comma splice: needs period, not comma (2 MC)
Your/you're, loose/lose, diner/dinner confusion
Exclamation (or period) at end of sentence
Dress-ups: adverb clause; strong verb

On top of every thing else that mattress felt like it had a boulder in the middle of it which means it'll be the first thing I'll **pitch** when I redecorate this dump. *[quotation continues]*

[2] "On top of everything else, that mattress felt as if it had a boulder in the middle of it, which means it'll be the first thing I'll pitch when I redecorate this dump. *[quotation continues]*

Pitch: toss; throw; hurl
Indent ¶ (new topic)
Start new par. in cont. quotation with " but no close "
Spelling: *everything* is one word
Comma needed after #2 SO of 5 or more words
Usage: *like/as if* confusion
Use commas to set off nonessential *which* clauses
Dress-ups: adverb & which clauses; strong verbs

It was so lumpy I'm black and blue all over this a.m., just climbing down the ladder my bones ached **intolerably**, I must look like a wreck.

It was so lumpy I'm black and blue all over this morning. [4] Just climbing down the ladder, I felt my bones ache intolerably. [6] I must look like a wreck."

Intolerably: unbearably; unendurably
No open " " b/c quotation continues, but close "
Usage: use words instead of casual abbreviations
Comma splices: need periods, not commas (2 MC)
Use commas after #4 SO (-ing phrase)
Illegal #4: word after " , " should do the *inging*
Simile: her appearance is *like* a wreck
Dress-ups: strong verb; -ly adverb

Mel sinked deeper into his pillows away from the screeching girl who didn't even seem **cognizant** he was in the room apparently she needed only a soap-box, and cared little about her audience.

Mel sank more <u>deeply</u> into his pillows, away from the <u>screeching</u> girl, <u>who</u> didn't even seem <u>cognizant</u> he was in the room. [3] Apparently she needed only a soap-box and cared little about her audience.

Cognizant: aware; conscious
Indent ¶ (new topic)
Spelling: *sank.* Comparative of adv.: "more deeply"
Use commas around nonessential phrases
Use commas to set off nonessential *who* clauses
Fused: use a period to separate 2 main clauses
Soap-box: a literal or figurative improvised platform
    from which to deliver a speech or harangue
No comma before *and* to join 2 compound verbs
Dress-ups: -ly adverb; quality adjectives; who clause

Week 29

The next thing to **jettison** will be the chef who's scrambled eggs and grits with their distinctive sea-urchin aftertaste are the worse I have ever tasted!

"The next thing to <u>jettison</u> will be the chef, <u>whose</u> scrambled eggs and grits with their <u>distinctive</u> sea-urchin aftertaste are the worst I have ever tasted!"

Jettison: discard; throw out
Indent ¶ (new speaker)
Use quotation marks with direct quotations
Use commas to set off nonessential w/w clauses
Whose = possessive form of *who*
Use superlatives for comparisons of 3 or more: *worst*
Dress-ups: strong verb; who clause; quality adjective

Will she never cease **jabbering** Mel thought, while vaguely listening to her droning, what have Ashton and Fauntleroy done to me now *[quotation continues]*

"Will she never cease jabbering?" Mel thought, <u>while</u> <u>vaguely</u> listening to her droning. "What have Ashton and Fauntleroy done to me now? *[quotation continues]*

Jabbering: talking rapidly and idly or unintelligibly
Indent ¶ (new speaker)
Use quotation marks with thoughts
Use question marks after questions (twice)
Comma splice: needs period, not comma (2 MC)
No closing quotation marks b/c continued quotation
Dress-ups: adverb clause; -ly adverb

If only she'd stop **haranguing** me I might be able to clearly think, faced with this awkward predicament he reasoned that there must be a way out.

[5] If only she'd stop haranguing me, I might be able to think <u>clearly</u>." [7] Faced with this <u>awkward</u> predicament, he <u>reasoned</u> that there must be a way out.

Haranguing: delivered a long, scolding attack
Continued quotation, so no opening " but closing "
Use commas after #5 Sentence Openers
Discuss not splitting infinitives (see Appendix)
Comma splice: needs period, not comma (2 MC)
Use commas after #7 Sentence Openers (-ed)
Decoration: noun clause w/ "that" (see Appendix)
Dress-ups: -ly adverb; quality adjective; strong verb

I've got it he suddenly shouted startling even Princess Sweetie Pie from her **tirade** and unsettling his well-intentioned advisers who had never scene such a look in Mels eyes before.

"I've got it!" he <u>suddenly</u> shouted, <u>startling</u> even Princess Sweetie Pie from her tirade and <u>unsettling</u> his <u>well-intentioned</u> advisers, <u>who</u> had never seen such a look in Mel's eyes before.

Tirade: a prolonged critical outburst
Indent ¶ (new topic)
Use quotation marks with direct quotations
Use exclamation mark after exclamatory statements
Use commas to set off nonessential phrases
Use commas to set off nonessential *who* clauses
Homophone: *scene/seen.* Apostrophe: *Mel's*
Dress-ups: -ly adverb; quality adjectives; who clause

Week 30

Dressed in his comfortable clothes, but ready for a **skirmish** Mel stormed into the cabinet meeting too hours later, and demanded a change in the law.

[7] Dressed in his comfortable clothes but ready for a skirmish, Mel <u>stormed</u> into the cabinet meeting two hours later and demanded a change in the law.

Skirmish: a brisk conflict or dispute
Indent ¶ (time has passed)
No comma before *but* to join 2 items *(dressed, ready)*
Use commas after #7 Sentence Openers (-ed)
Homophone: too/two
No comma before *and* to join 2 compound verbs
Dress-ups: strong verb

Princess or not he refused to marry some overly **fastidious** woman which couldn't rest comfortably on 20 mattresses, and who did she think she was taking over the palace this way?

Princess or not, he refused to marry some <u>overly</u> <u>fastidious</u> woman <u>who</u> couldn't rest <u>comfortably</u> on twenty mattresses. <u>Who</u> did she think she was, taking over the palace this way?

Fastidious: excessively delicate; hard to please
No " " b/c his thoughts are couched in third person
Use commas to set off nonessential phrases
Use *who* for people, *which* for things
Spell out numbers written as one or two words
Avoid stringing together sentences with *and*
Comma to avoid misreading: "did she think she was taking" or "who did she think she was"?
Dress-ups: -ly adverbs; quality adj.; who clauses

Its high time I took charge around here the king thundered no more balls no more princesses no more **matrimonial** snares I'll find my own wife

"It's high time I took charge around here!" the king <u>thundered</u>. "No more balls. No more princesses. No more <u>matrimonial</u> snares! I'll find my own wife."

Matrimonial: relating to marriage (snare: trap)
Indent ¶ (new speaker)
Use quotation marks with direct quotations and " ! "
It's = it is
Fused: use a period to separate 2 main clauses
Acceptable fragments need periods or exclamations
Dress-ups: strong verb; quality adjective

Knowing Mel would not **recant** his advisers decided it was not worth thier positions to force the issue, thus they made excuses to Princess Sweetie Pie, and sent her packing back too the flovenia inn limited.

[4] Knowing Mel would not <u>recant</u>, his advisers decided it was not worth their positions to force the issue. [T] Thus they made excuses to Princess Sweetie Pie and sent her packing back to the Flovenia Inn Limited.

Recant: a formal withdrawing of an opinion
Indent ¶ (new topic)
Use commas after #4 SO (-ing phrase)
Spelling: *their*
Comma splice: needs period, not comma (2 MC)
No comma before *and* to join 2 compound verbs
Homophone: too/to
Capitalize proper nouns
Dress-ups: strong verb

Week 31

Taking her exit with finer grace then she took her visit she mustered up enough royal dignity to graciously depart, without **rancor** toward those who attended to her needs

[4] Taking her exit with <u>finer</u> grace than she had taken her visit, she <u>mustered</u> up enough <u>royal</u> dignity to depart <u>graciously</u>, without rancor toward those <u>who</u> had <u>attended</u> to her needs.

Rancor: ill will; resentment
Usage: *then/than* confusion
Use past perfect for 2 different times in the past
Use commas after #4 SO (-ing phrase)
Discuss not splitting infinitives (see Appendix)
Use a period at end of statements
Dress-ups: quality adj's & vb's; -ly adv.; who clause

Meanwhile far, far away in the land of Topeka Kansas Princess Dorothy a rather ordinary princess was taking a brake from designing computer games too walk her **diminutive** dog.

[T] Meanwhile, far, far away in the land of Topeka, Kansas, Princess <u>Dorothy, a</u> rather ordinary princess, was taking a break from designing computer games to walk her <u>diminutive</u> dog.

Diminutive: small; tiny
Indent ¶ (new scene)
Use commas after introductory transitional words
Use commas between city & state, and after state
Invisible *who* clause: "Dorothy, who was a…"
Use commas around nonessential phrases
Homophones: brake/break; too/to
Dress-ups: invisible who; quality adjective

As she returned to her cozy computer room she spied a flashing icon on her computer screen indicating that her freind a down to earth **unpretentious** princess from the land of Nashville Tenessee was online and sending her an IM.

[5] As she returned to her <u>cozy</u> computer room, she <u>spied</u> a <u>flashing</u> icon on her computer screen indicating that her <u>friend, a down-to-earth, unpretentious</u> princess from the land of Nashville, Tennessee, was online and sending her an IM.

Unpretentious: plain; not showy or falsely fancy
Use commas after #5 Sentence Openers
Decoration: noun clause w/ "that." See Appendix
Spelling: *friend; Tennessee*
Invisible *who* ("friend, who was…") plus commas
Hyphenate words that function as a single adjective
Use commas with coordinate adjectives
Use commas between city & state, and after state
Dress-ups: quality & dual adjectives; strong verb

Hey Dot check out the ongoing conversation in the Princess Chat Room. I know you aren't interested in eHarmony.com but there's a biography passing that you need to **scrutinize**. *[quotation continues]*

"Hey, Dot, check out the <u>ongoing</u> conversation in the Princess Chat room. I know you aren't interested in eHarmony.com, but there's a biography passing <u>that</u> you need to <u>scrutinize</u>. *[quotation continues]*

Scrutinize: examine with careful attention
Indent ¶ (new speaker)
Use quotation marks with direct quotations
Use commas after introductory interjections
Set off NDAs with commas
Compound sentence needs comma: MC, cc MC
Essential *which* clause using *that*; no comma
No closing quotation marks b/c continued quotation
Dress-ups: quality adj. & verb; which *(that)* clause

Week 32

Those air-headed Princesses from Fresno California and Albany New York are sending this e-mail around mocking some **pathetic** guy from Flovenia named Mel. Thing is he sounds sort of like your type lol!

Those <u>air-headed</u> princesses from Fresno, California, and Albany, New York, are sending this e-mail around mocking some <u>pathetic</u> guy from Flovenia named Mel. Thing is, he sounds sort of like your type, lol!"

Pathetic: evoking pity; miserably inadequate
No open " " b/c quotation continues, but close "
Use lc for titles without a name
Use commas between city & state, and after state
Use commas after introductory transitions
Use commas to set off nonessential phrases ("lol")
LOL = laugh out loud (computer jargon)
Dress-ups: quality adjectives

Princess Dorothy pulled up the Princess Chat Room sight and sure enough there was the honest biography of King Mel accompanied by an uploaded digital photo. Hmm princess Dorothy **mused** to herself this guy does sound interesting!

Princess Dorothy pulled up the Princess Chat Room site, and sure enough, there was the honest biography of King Mel accompanied by an <u>uploaded</u> digital photo. "Hmm," Princess Dorothy <u>mused</u> to herself, "this guy does sound interesting!"

Mused: thought silently; contemplated
Indent ¶ (new topic)
Homophone: sight/site
Compound sentence needs comma: MC, cc MC
Use commas after introductory transitional words
Use quotation marks with direct quotations
Use comma with verb of speaking & direct quotation
Capitalize titles used with names
Dress-ups: quality adjective; strong verb

Epilogue: On April 6 2009 at the castle in Flovia Flovenia Flovenians had cause to rejoice in the nuptials of they're **eccentric** but loveable King Melvin, and his extraordinary though equally eccentric bride Princess Dorothy.

    Epilogue: [2] On April 6, 2009, at the castle in Flovia, Flovenia, Flovenians had cause to rejoice in the nuptials of their <u>eccentric but loveable</u> King Melvin and his <u>extraordinary</u> though <u>equally</u> eccentric bride, Princess Dorothy.

Eccentric: peculiar; unusual; odd
Indent ¶ (new topic)
Use commas in dates after the day and year
Use comma after 2+ intro. prepositional phrases
    (comma optional after "2007")
Use comma between city and country
Homophone: they're/their
No comma before *and* to join 2 items in a series
Use commas around nonessential appositives
Dress-ups: dual and quality adjectives; -ly adverb

Displaying fanfare and **felicity** the Flovenians fanned through the streets in eager celebration overjoyed that their king had at last found him a bride.

[4] Displaying fanfare and felicity, the Flovenians <u>fanned</u> through the streets in eager celebration, overjoyed that their king had at last found himself a bride.

Felicity: great happiness
Use commas after #4 SO (-ing phrase)
Alliteration: "fanfare & felicity, Flovenians fanned"
Use commas to set off nonessential phrases
Decoration: noun clause w/ "that." See Appendix
Pronoun: *himself*, not *him*
Dress-ups: strong verb

Week 33

In the castle, Big Lord Fauntleroy rolled his eyes **resignedly** when Princess Dot commented on her 1st night at the palace, contrary to all popular expectations she declared she, "slept like a log".

    [2] In the castle Big Lord Fauntleroy <u>rolled</u> his eyes <u>resignedly</u> <u>when</u> Princess Dot commented on her first night at the palace. [2] Contrary to all popular expectations, she declared she "slept like a log."

Resignedly: with submission and resignation
Indent ¶ (new scene)
Comma optional after short #2 SO, needed after long
Spell out ordinal numbers
Comma splice: needs period, not comma (2 MC)
Periods & commas go inside quotation marks
No comma before quotation b/c no verb of speaking
    introducing the quotation. Contrast: She declared,
    "I slept like a log."
Dress-ups: strong verb; -ly adverb; adverb clause

Fortunately however Mel had trashed that **discommodious** pea requirement long ago Princess Dot may not look like a bona fide princess was suppose to look but she was the only, true princess in his eyes.

[3] Fortunately, however, Mel had <u>trashed</u> that <u>discommodious</u> pea requirement long ago. Princess Dot may not look <u>as</u> a <u>bona fide</u> princess was supposed to look, but she was the only true princess in his eyes.

Discommodious: inconvenient; troublesome
Use commas to set off transitional words
Fused: use a period to separate 2 main clauses
Usage: *like/as* confusion
Spelling: *supposed*
Compound sentence needs comma: MC, cc MC
No commas with cumulative adjectives
Dress-ups: strong verb; quality adjectives;
    adverb clause

When the museum **curator** came begging for the famous pea to conspicuously display in the regal room of the museum of flovenia king mel confessed that the palace was devoid of those wretched legumes

    [5] When the museum curator came begging for the famous pea to display <u>conspicuously</u> in the Regal Room of the Museum of Flovenia, King Mel confessed that the palace was devoid of those <u>wretched</u> legumes.

Curator: person in charge of a museum
Indent ¶ (new scene)
Discuss not splitting infinitives (see Appendix)
Capitalize proper nouns
Use commas after #5 Sentence Openers
Decoration: noun clause w/ "that." See Appendix
Use a period at end of statements
Dress-ups: -ly adverb; quality adjective

Graciously he offerred to substitute in it's place a preserved sea urchin in **tribute** to the disastrous night that almost landed him a false princess, and should you drop by the museum you can view it their to this day.

[3] Graciously he offered to substitute in its place a <u>preserved</u> sea urchin in tribute to the <u>disastrous</u> night <u>that</u> almost <u>landed</u> him a false princess. [5] Should you drop by the museum, you can view it there to this day.

Tribute: a gift as an expression of gratitude or recognition (used humorously here)

Spelling: *offered*. Homophone: *their/there*

Its = possessive of *it*

Which clause using *that* (see Appendix)

Avoid stringing together sentences with *and*

Disguised #5: "*If* you should" is implied

Use commas after #5 Sentence Openers

Dress-ups: quality adj's; which (*that*); strong verb

Sir Gawain and the Green Knight

Introduction

Recommended for grades nine through twelve, "Sir Gawain and the Green Knight" is divided into thirty-three weeks, with four passages to rewrite and correct each week. See the Introduction under Teaching Procedure.

Starting with Week 4, I stop marking #1 Subject Openers, but continue discussing them if needed. I tell my students they should not expect to find all errors in the Fix-Its, since the stories both teach new concepts and reinforce old. In the Appendix you will find a fuller discussion of style and most grammar issues.

"Sir Gawain and the Green Knight" poses comprehension difficulties for some students since the story is set in an unfamiliar time, place, and culture. As you discuss the sentences each week, I recommend you check students' reading comprehension first, discussing the events leading up to and including that week's reading. I find it particularly helpful to guide students through the scenes with the lovely lady, who is reminiscent of Potiphar's wife, helping them understand why Gawain must remain courteous to her despite her abhorrent behavior.

Background to "Sir Gawain and the Green Knight"

Written near the end of the fourteenth-century, *Sir Gawain and the Green Knight* stands alongside Chaucer's *Canterbury Tales* as one of the greatest literary works of all times. Little is known of the author, who, based on the poem's difficult dialect, likely lived about 150 miles north of London (Chaucer's home). The Gawain poet used alliteration in nearly every line, so in my prose version I have tried to replicate some alliteration, making note of it occasionally, as well as the poem's unusual sentence patterns and medieval courtly language.

Because students may be interested in the original, I have included below a few lines that are found near the beginning of the poem. To the right of each line, I have provided a nearly literal translation. You may enjoy comparing the two and helping students discover how many words are similar.

The original poem employs two interesting characters that students probably do not know. The first is the Old English (and Middle English in the North, where this poet resided) character *þ*, which is our modern "th." "Þis kyng," for example, is pronounced something like "this king" and says the same. The other odd character, "ȝ," is our "gh," which people used to pronounce, making words like "knight" challenging to speak. Two of my favorite words are in the last two lines: "loveliest" used to be "love-lookest"; "comeliest" used to be "comely-lookest."

Þis kyng lay at Camylot vpon Kryst masse	This king lay at Camelot upon Christmas (Christ's mass)
With mony luflych lorde, ledez of þe best,	With many lovely lords, ladies of the best,
Rekenly of þe Rounde Table alle þo rich breþer,	Arrayed of the Round Table all those rich brothers
With rych reuel oryȝt and rechles merþes.	With rich revel aright and reckless mirth.
Þer tournayed tulkes by tymez ful mony,	There tourneyed true men by times full many,
Justed ful jolilé þise gentyle kniȝtes,	Jousted full jollily these gentle knights,
Syþen kayred to þe court caroles to make.	Since (after that) carried to the court, carols to make.
For þer þe fest watz ilyche ful fiften dayes,	For there the feast was in force full fifteen days,
With alle þe mete and þe mirþe þat men couþe avyse;	With all the meat and the mirth that men could devise;
Such glaum ande gle glorious to here,	Such gaiety and glee, glorious to hear,
Dere dyn vpon day, daunsyng on nyȝtes. ...	Brave din upon day, dancing on night. ...
Þe most kyd knyȝtez vnder Krystes seluen,	The most noble knights under Christ known,
And þe louelokkest ladies þat euer lif haden,	And the loveliest ladies that ever life had,
And he þe comlokest kyng þat þe court haldes.	And he the comeliest king that the court held.

My version of the poem is an abridged prose translation, so I encourage students to read the complete poem. An exciting adventure and morality tale, it has a little bit of something that both girls and boys enjoy, as well as deeper themes of temptation, self-preservation, honor, and truthfulness.

Sir Gawain and the Green Knight

Fix-Its and Corrections

Grammar, Skills, and Vocabulary

Week 1

Long ago in the days of King Arthur the most courteous of British Kings an adventure occured **unparalleled** by any other wonder of Arthurs Court at Camelot.

[2] Long ago in the days of King <u>Arthur, the</u> most courteous of British kings, an adventure occurred <u>unparalleled</u> by any other wonder of Arthur's court at Camelot.

Unparalleled: not equaled or matched
Indent ¶ (new topic)
Disguised #2 (*During, In, On, At* that time period)
Invisible *who* needs commas: "Arthur, who … kings"
Use lc for titles without a name and common nouns
Spelling: *occurred.* Use apostrophes for possession
Dress-ups: invisible who clause; quality adjective

One Christmastide, the king was enjoying a 15 day feast with the noblest knights in Christendom and their fair ladies, thronging the castle from faraway lands guests **vaingloriously** jousted during the day, and heartily feasted at night.

[2] One Christmastide the king was enjoying a fifteen-day feast with the noblest knights in Christendom and their fair ladies. [4] Thronging the castle from <u>faraway</u> lands, guests <u>vaingloriously</u> jousted during the day and <u>heartily</u> feasted at night.

Vaingloriously: vainly; boastfully
Christmastide: time fm. Christmas to after New Year
Christendom: the Christian world
Disguised #2; comma optional
Spell out numbers written as one or two words
Hyphenate words that function as a single adjective
Comma splice: needs period, not comma (2 MC)
Use commas after #4 SO (-ing phrase)
No comma before *and* to join 2 compound verbs
Dress-ups: quality adjective; -ly adverbs

After monks welcomed the coming year on New Years day with chants in the chapel the **convivial** company congregated in the great hall took their seats and waited for the meat to be served.

[5] After monks had <u>welcomed</u> the coming year on New Year's Day with chants in the chapel, the <u>convivial</u> company <u>congregated</u> in the great hall, took their seats, and waited for the meat to be served.

Convivial: friendly; agreeable; jovial
Use past perfect for 2 different times in the past
Use apostrophes to show possession and UC "Day"
Use commas after #5 Sentence Openers (note that
    "after" can start an adverb clause—see Appendix)
Alliteration: "chants … chapel"; "convivial company
    congregated"
Use commas with 3 or more items in a series
Dress-ups: strong verbs; quality adjective

King Arthur sat in the middle of the high dais with his Queen on one side and his favorite nephew the youthful Sir Gawain on his other. **Succulent** the fare

[1] King Arthur sat in the middle of the high dais with his queen on one side and his favorite nephew, the youthful Sir Gawain, on his other. [6] <u>Succulent</u> was the fare.

Succulent: highly enjoyable; delectable
Dais: a raised platform for seats of honor
Use lc for titles without a name
Use commas with "the youthful … G.": nonessential
Correct fragment by adding a verb
Use a period at end of statements
Dress-ups: quality adjective

Week 2

Accompanied by drums and pipes trumpets announced each course, **deftly**, rare dainties were served on platters of silver with a wide variety of meats on cloth. No bounty was spared by the King for his stalwart guests and their lovely ladies.

[7] Accompanied by drums and pipes, trumpets <u>announced</u> each course. [3] Deftly, rare dainties were served on platters of silver with a wide variety of meats on cloth. [1] The king had spared no bounty for his <u>stalwart</u> guests and their lovely ladies.

Deftly: skillfully (especially with using one's hands)
Use commas after #7 Sentence Openers (-ed)
Comma splice: needs period, not comma (2 MC)
1st passive acceptable b/c we don't care who served
Convert 2nd passive to active: "The king spared ..."
Use lc for titles without a name ("king")
Use past perfect for 2 different times in the past
Dress-ups: strong verb; quality adjective

Barely had the 1st course been served when a noise abruptly interrupted the joyful **din**, into the hall rode a stranger. A marvel to behold.

      [3] Barely had the first course been served <u>when</u> a noise <u>abruptly</u> interrupted the joyful din. [2] Into the hall rode a <u>stranger, a</u> marvel to behold.

Din: loud, confused noise; clamor
Indent ¶ (new topic)
Spell out ordinal numbers
Note: No comma needed to set off adv. clause (when)
Comma splice: needs period, not comma (2 MC)
Correct fragment by joining phrase to MC w/ comma
Dress-ups: adverb clause; -ly adverb; invisible who

In stature the knight was half-again larger then the tallest knight of his court, sitting atop his noble steed the guests of the hall felt he loomed **portentously** over them.

[2] In stature the knight was half-again larger than the tallest knight of the king's court. [4] Sitting atop his noble steed, he <u>loomed</u> <u>portentously</u> over the guests of the hall.

Portentously: ominously; threateningly
Usage: *then/than* confusion
Comma splice: needs period, not comma (2 MC)
Pronoun confusion: "his" should refer to Arthur
Use commas after #4 SO (-ing phrase)
Illegal #4: word after " , " should do the *inging*
(the guests aren't doing the sitting!)
Dress-ups: strong verb; -ly adverb

What struck silence into one and all however was his hue; man, and gear, and horse were as green as grass his noble **raiment** was dark green from his ermine trimmed hood to his tight hose and tall, riding boots.

[1] What <u>struck</u> silence into one and all, however, was his hue: man and gear and horse were as green as grass. [1] His noble raiment was dark green, from his ermine-trimmed hood to his tight hose and tall riding boots.

Raiment: clothing; attire
Use commas to set off transitional words
Use colon (not ";") after MC to give an explanation
No commas when *and*'s connect items in a series
Fused: use a period to separate 2 main clauses
Use commas to set off nonessential phrases
Hyphenate words that function as a single adjective
No commas with cumulative adjectives
Dress-ups: strong verb

Week 3

His thick beard and his steeds main and tale all were of the same green hue. Frightfully no other weapon was borne by this **audacious** knight not even a shield for defense accept an immense, green ax.

[1] His thick beard and his <u>steed's</u> mane and tail—all were of the same green hue. [3] Frightfully, this <u>audacious</u> knight <u>bore</u> no other weapon, not even a shield for defense, except an immense green ax.

Audacious: recklessly brave; bold and fearless
Use apostrophes to show possession
Homophones: *main/mane, tale/tail*
Spelling: *accept/except* confusion
Use em-dash for a break in thought and for emphasis
Comma optional after #3 S.O. (use the pause test)
Convert passive to active voice
Use commas around nonessential phrases
No commas with cumulative adjectives
Dress-ups: quality adjective; strong verb

Straight to the high dais stepped the horse while scanning the noble assembly. Where is the captain of this crowd?, he **bellowed**, as if doubting, who in the hall held rule.

[2] Straight to the high dais stepped the horse, <u>while</u> the strange knight <u>scanned</u> the noble assembly. "Where is the captain of this crowd?" he <u>bellowed</u>, <u>as if</u> doubting <u>who</u> in the hall held rule.

Bellowed: shouted in a deep voice
Indent ¶ (new topic)
Dangling modifier: the horse isn't doing the scanning
Use commas with adverb clauses of contrast
Use quotation marks with direct quotations
Do not use comma with an end mark of punctuation
No commas to set off essential *who* clauses
Dress-ups: adverb clauses; strong verbs; who clause

The stranger was hailed by Arthur. Fellow in faith, you have found the king, pray **tarry** awhile and join my guests on this joyous occasion.

[6] Arthur <u>hailed</u> the stranger. "Fellow, in faith, you have found the king. Pray <u>tarry</u> awhile and join my guests on this <u>joyous</u> occasion."

Tarry: remain; stay. Pray: elliptical for "I pray you"
Indent ¶ (new speaker)
Convert passive to active voice
Use quotation marks with direct quotations
Comma after "fellow": not fellow or brother in faith; "in faith" is an expression meaning "in truth"
Comma splice: needs period, not comma (2 MC)
Dress-ups: strong verbs; quality adjective

My errand is not to linger in gaiety. The **outlandish** knight replied. Since your praise King is puffed up so high, and since you're nights of the Round Table are reputed the best in both arms and courtesy I have seeked you out. *[quotation continues]*

"My errand is not to <u>linger</u> in gaiety," the <u>outlandish</u> knight replied. [5] "Since your praise, King, is <u>puffed up</u> so high and <u>since</u> your Knights of the Round Table are reputed the best in both arms and courtesy, I have <u>sought</u> you out. *[quotation continues]*

Outlandish: freakishly strange, as in appearance
Indent ¶ (new speaker)
Use quotation marks with direct quotations
Correct fragment by joining phrase to MC w/ comma
No comma before *and* to join 2 items in a series (here, two adv. clauses, each starting with "since")
Homophone: you're/your; nights/knights. Sp: *sought*
Use commas after #5 Sentence Openers
No close quotation marks b/c quotation continues
Dress-ups: strong verbs; quality adj.; adverb clause

Week 4

I challenge this court to a Christmas game, if anyone of the young knight's here is truely bold and **valiant** let him take up my ax, and strike a single blow against me. *[quotation continues]*

I challenge this court to a Christmas game. [5] If any one of the young knights here is truly bold and <u>valiant</u>, let him take up my ax and strike a single blow against me. *[quotation continues]*

Valiant: brave; heroic; worthy
No quotation marks because continued quotation
Comma splice: needs period, not comma (2 MC)
Usage: any one = any single member of a group
Knights is plural, not possessive.   Spelling: *truly*
Use commas after #5 Sentence Openers
No comma before *and* to join 2 compound verbs
Dress-ups: quality adjective
Continue numbering Subject Openers [#1] if needed

If I survive in a twelvemonth and a day I will stoutly return one blow for the other, and although murmurs arose among the astounded guests at that **provocative** challenge no man stepped forward.

[5] If I survive, in a twelvemonth and a day I will <u>stoutly</u> return one blow for the other."
[5] Although murmurs arose among the <u>astounded</u> guests at that <u>provocative</u> challenge, no man stepped forward.

Provocative: tending to provoke or irritate
Indent ¶, 2nd part (new topic)
Continue quotation where the last sentence left off
Use commas after #5 Sentence Openers (twice)
Note: the "If" clause ends w/ "survive"; "in a twelve-month …" goes with the 2nd part of the sentence
Close continued quotation with quotation marks
Poor choice of *and* to join sentences
Dress-ups: -ly adverb; quality adjectives

131

Is this truly Arthurs house the horseman demanded? Where now are your boastful words your grand deeds your daring and valor you all **cower** and quake, with no wound even felt!

"Is this truly Arthur's house?" the horseman demanded. "Where now are your boastful words, your grand deeds, your daring and valor? You all <u>cower and quake</u>, with no wound even felt!"

Cower: cringe, as in fear or shame
Indent ¶ (speaker)
Use quotation marks with direct quotations
Use apostrophes to show possession
Use " ? " after question, not at end of statement
Use commas with 3 or more items in a series
Fused: use a question to separate these main clauses
Dress-ups: dual verbs

The youngest of Arthur's knights Sir Gawain blushed to the roots at the **aspersions** cast on the company who were still stunned by the visitor shamefully, no one had yet taken action.

[4] The youngest of Arthur's knights, Sir Gawain <u>blushed</u> to the roots at the aspersions cast on the company, <u>who</u> were still <u>stunned</u> by the visitor. [3] Shamefully, no one had yet taken action.

Aspersions: unfavorable remarks
Indent ¶ (new topic)
Disguised #4 ("Being the youngest …") + comma
Alternative: treat "Sir Gawain" as an appositive with commas on both sides, making this a #1 opener
Use commas to set off nonessential who clauses
Fused (2 MCs): period placement shows whether "shamefully" goes with the words before or after
Dress-ups: strong verbs; who clause

Week 5

Stepping forward reluctantly he responded I know well that I am the weakest of these **illustrious** knights, truly the loss of my life would be the least of any, I accept your challenge Sir Knight.

[4] Stepping forward <u>reluctantly</u>, he responded, "I know well that I am the weakest of these <u>illustrious</u> knights. [3] Truly the loss of my life would be the least of any. I accept your challenge, Sir Knight."

Illustrious: renowned; famous; highly distinguished
Use commas after #4 SO (-ing phrase)
Comma placement shows whether "reluctantly" goes with the words before or after
Use comma with verb of speaking & direct quotation
Use quotation marks with direct quotations
Decoration: noun clause w/ "that" (see Appendix)
Comma splices: need periods, not commas (2 MC)
Set off NDAs with commas
Dress-ups: -ly adverb; quality adjective

If I ride out of this hall the horseman countered. You must assure me on oath that you will locate me in one year and one day for an identical stroke, seek me North from here at the Green Chapel where many **ken** me well as the Green Knight.

[5] "If I ride out of this hall," the horseman <u>countered</u>, "you must assure me on oath that you will locate me in one year and one day for an <u>identical</u> stroke. Seek me north from here at the Green Chapel, <u>where</u> many <u>ken</u> me well as the Green Knight."

Ken: know
Indent ¶ (new speaker)
Use quotation marks with direct quotations
Use commas after #5 Sentence Openers
Use comma with verb of speaking & direct quotation
Use lc to continue interrupted quotations
Comma splice: needs period, not comma (2 MC)
Use lc for directions
Use comma to set off nonessential adj. clause (where)
Dress-ups: strong verbs; quality adj.; adverb clause

Since I hold a seat at the Round Table Sir Gawain rejoined you may be assured that I will **scrupulously** honor my word, and at that, the hefty ax was handed to Sir Gawain by the Green Knight, and then he lowered his neck, baring it for the blow.

[5] "Since I hold a seat at the Round Table," Sir Gawain <u>rejoined</u>, "you may be <u>assured</u> that I will <u>scrupulously</u> honor my word." [2] At that, the Green Knight handed the <u>hefty</u> ax to Sir Gawain and then lowered his neck, <u>baring</u> it for the blow.

Scrupulously: with strict regard for what is right
Indent ¶ (new speaker; new topic)
Use quotation marks with direct quotations
Use commas after #5 Sentence Openers
Use comma with verb of speaking & direct quotation
Decoration: noun clause w/ "that" (see Appendix)
Poor choice of *and* to join main clauses
Convert passive to active voice, then drop comma and "he"
Dress-ups: strong verbs & adjectives; -ly adverb

Wielding the ax high above his head it was brought down sharply upon the bare neck by Gawain a blow so **redoubtable** that the head was hewn from the shoulders, and fell to the floor.

[4] Wielding the ax high above his head, Gawain brought down <u>sharply</u> upon the bare neck a blow so <u>redoubtable</u> that the head was <u>hewn</u> from the shoulders and fell to the floor.

Redoubtable: arousing fear or awe; formidable
Use commas after #4 SO (-ing phrase)
Illegal #4: word after " , " should do the *inging*
    (fixing this also rids sentence of passive voice)
Decoration: noun clause w/ "that" (see Appendix)
"Was hewn" acceptable passive: focus is on head
No comma before *and* to join 2 compound verbs
Dress-ups: -ly adverb; quality adjective; strong verb

Week 6

Unruffled and self-assured the Green Knight did not fall; leaping on his steed he stretched forth his hands grabbed his bloody head from the floor and heaving it up to the saddle rode thunderously to the door.

    [7] <u>Unruffled and self-assured</u>, the Green Knight did not fall. [4] Leaping on his steed, he stretched forth his hands, grabbed his bloody head from the floor, and, heaving it up to the saddle, rode <u>thunderously</u> to the door.

Unruffled: undisturbed; calm
Indent ¶ (new topic)
Use commas after #7 Sentence Openers (-ed)
Separate only closely-related MCs with semicolons
Use commas after #4 SO (-ing phrase)
Use commas with 3 or more items in a series
Use commas to set off nonessential phrases ("heaving
    it up to the saddle")
Dress-ups: dual adjectives; -ly adverb

Remember Sir Gawain came his parting words. Come to the Green Chapel a twelvemonth and a day or be counted a **recreant** knight".

"Remember, Sir Gawain," came his parting words, "come to the Green Chapel a twelvemonth and a day or be counted a <u>recreant</u> knight."

Recreant: cowardly
Use quotation marks with direct quotations
Set off NDAs with commas
Use comma with verb of speaking & direct quotation
Use lc to continue interrupted quotations
Periods go inside closing quotation marks
Dress-ups: quality adjective

When the following autumn arrived Sir Gawain set off in his finest armor from Camelot on his richly **caparisoned** horse Gringolet.

    [5] When the following autumn arrived, in his finest armor Sir Gawain set off from Camelot on his <u>richly caparisoned</u> horse, Gringolet.

Caparisoned: outfitted with ornamental covering
Indent ¶ (time has passed)
Use commas after #5 Sentence Openers
Misplaced prep. phrase (is the armor from Camelot,
    or did he wear it when he set off?)
Use commas to set off nonessential appositives
Dress-ups: -ly adverb; quality adjective

As I may be directed by God I am bound to unearth the grim man in green, and to bear a blow from his ax he told his **liege** lord at parting. With care in his heart King Arthur commended Sir Gawain to Christ.

[5] "As God may direct me, I am bound to <u>unearth</u> the <u>grim</u> man in green and to bear a blow from his ax," he told his <u>liege</u> lord at parting.
    [2] With care in his heart, King Arthur <u>commended</u> Sir Gawain to Christ.

Liege: entitled to the loyalty and service of subjects
Indent ¶, 2nd part (new topic)
Use quotation marks with direct quotations
Convert passive to active voice
Use commas after #5 Sentence Openers
Alliteration: "grim ... green"; "bear a blow"
No comma before *and* to join 2 items (infinitives)
Use comma with verb of speaking & direct quotation
Comma needed after #2 SO of 5 or more words
Dress-ups: strong verbs; quality adjectives

Week 7

Marked with a **pentangle** deep significance was conveyed by Gawain's shield, according to legend, the wise King Solomon had long ago devised the pentangle a 5 pointed star drawn without lifting the pencil as a symbol of truth.

[7] Marked with a pentangle, Gawain's shield <u>conveyed</u> deep significance. [2] According to legend, the wise King Solomon had long ago devised the <u>pentangle, a</u> five-pointed star drawn without lifting the pencil, as a symbol of truth.

Pentangle: a five-pointed, star-shaped figure
Indent ¶ (new topic)
Use commas after #7 Sentence Openers (-ed)
Illegal #7: noun after " , " should do the -*ed* action
   (fixing this also rids sentence of passive voice)
Comma splice: needs period, not comma (2 MC)
Use commas to set off nonessential phrases
Spell out "five" and hyphenate compound adj.
Dress-ups: strong verb; invisible which clause

Such an emblem was well deserved buy the **peerless** prince Gawain. True two his word and faultless in courteous speech worthy Sir Gawain exemplified the highest virtues of knighthood rooted in his allegiance too Christ.

The peerless prince Gawain well deserved such an emblem. [4] True to his word and <u>faultless</u> in courteous speech, worthy Sir Gawain <u>exemplified</u> the highest virtues of <u>knighthood, rooted</u> in his allegiance to Christ.

Peerless: having no equal; without rival; matchless
Convert passive to active voice
Homophones: buy/by; two/too/to (twice)
Keep lc for "prince" b/c it's not used as a title here
Disguised #4 ("Being true to his word …")
Use commas after #4 SO
Invisible *which* needs comma: "virtues of
  knighthood, which were rooted …"
Dress-ups: quality adj.; strong verb; invisible which

On his journey North, Gawain encountered few obstacles but of everyone he inquired, none knew **aught** of the Green Chapel, or of a knight solely green.

[2] On his journey north Gawain <u>encountered</u> few obstacles, but of everyone he inquired, none knew aught of the Green Chapel or of a knight <u>solely</u> green.

Aught: anything whatever
Indent ¶ (new scene)
Use lc for directions
Comma optional after #2 SO of 4 words or fewer
Compound sentence needs comma: MC, cc MC
No comma before *or* to join 2 items in a series
Dress-ups: strong verb; -ly adverb

Winter loomed, cold rains fell from the clouds, and froze before touching earth, and among rocks in a bleak barren wilderness Gawain slept **intermittently** in his armor.

[6] Winter loomed. Cold rains fell from the clouds and froze before touching earth. [2] Among rocks in a <u>bleak, barren</u> wilderness, Gawain slept <u>intermittently</u> in his armor.

Intermittently: alternately ceasing + beginning again
Comma splice: needs period, not comma (2 MC)
No comma before *and* to join 2 compound verbs
Poor choice of *and* to join main clauses
Use commas w/ coordinate adjectives (bleak, barren)
Use commas after 2+ intro prepositional phrases
Dress-ups: dual adjectives; -ly adverb

Week 8

By Christmas Eve, Gawain began to despair of ever finding his **implacable** foe, fearing lest his name be tarnished he spurred Gringolet forward.

[2] By Christmas Eve Gawain began to despair of ever finding his <u>implacable</u> foe. [4] Fearing lest his name be <u>tarnished</u>, he <u>spurred</u> Gringolet forward.

Implacable: unbending; merciless; unappeasable
Indent ¶ (time has passed)
Comma optional after #2 SO of 4 words or fewer
Comma splice: needs period, not comma (2 MC)
Use commas after #4 SO (-ing phrase)
Dress-ups: quality adjective; strong verbs

An hour past, preceeding through cheerless woods near the Aisle of Anglesey in North Wales, and mindful of the morrow Sir Gawain prayed for some **haven**, where he might attend services the next day.

[6] An hour passed. [4] Proceeding through <u>cheerless</u> woods near the Isle of Anglesey in North Wales and mindful of the morrow, Sir Gawain prayed for some haven <u>where</u> he might attend services the next day.

Haven: a place of shelter and safety
Homophone: past/passed; aisle/isle. Sp.: *proceeding*
Comma splice: needs period, not comma (2 MC)
No comma before *and* to join 2 items in a series
    (proceeding and mindful)
Use commas after #4 SO (ends w/ "morrow")
Morrow: the next day, i.e., Christmas
No commas with essential adj. clauses ("where …")
Dress-ups: quality adjective; adverb clause

No sooner had his prayer concluded then he was conscious of a wondrous dwelling, inside a moat, with fair and green grounds. As luxuriant a castle as he ever observed. With helmet in his hands he **proffered** his thanks to Jesus which listened to his prayer.

No sooner had his prayer concluded than he was conscious of a <u>wondrous</u> dwelling inside a moat with fair and green grounds, as <u>luxuriant</u> a castle <u>as</u> he had ever observed. [2] With helmet in his hands, he <u>proffered</u> his thanks to Jesus, <u>who</u> had listened to his prayer.

Proffered: offered for acceptance
Usage: *then/than* confusion
No commas w/ essential phrases ("inside a moat")
Correct fragment by joining phrase to MC w/ comma
Use past perfect for 2 different times in the past
    ("he had ever observed"; "Jesus had listened")
Comma needed after #2 SO of 5 or more words
Use commas to set off nonessential w/w clauses
Use *who* for people, *which* for things
Dress-ups: quality adjectives; adverb clause; strong
    verb; who clause

Crossing the drawbridge and riding through the **portcullis** the porter heard Sir Gawain's request for lodging; faithfully servants came forth to attend to his horse, and welcome the warrior.

    [4] Crossing the drawbridge and riding through the portcullis, Sir Gawain <u>requested</u> lodging from the porter. [3] Faithfully, servants came forth to attend to his horse and welcome the warrior.

Portcullis: an iron grating in the entry of a castle
Indent ¶ (new scene)
Use commas after #4 SO (-ing phrase)
Illegal #4: noun after " , " should do the *inging*
Separate only closely-related MCs with semicolons
Comma best after this #3 SO to prevent misreading
    as "faithful servants"
No comma before *and* to join 2 compound verbs
Dress-ups: strong verb

Week 9

Escorted into the castle Sir Gawain met with a lavish reception, and recieving him most **affably** in his home the Lord of the Castle invited him to restfully and merrily spend with them the Holy Days.

[7] Escorted into the castle, Sir Gawain met with a <u>lavish</u> reception. [4] Receiving him most <u>affably</u> in his home, the lord of the castle invited him to spend with them the holy days <u>restfully and merrily</u>.

Affably: pleasantly; warmly; in a friendly manner
Use commas after #7 Sentence Openers (-ed)
Poor choice of *and* to join main clauses
Spelling: *receiving*
Use commas after #4 SO (-ing phrase)
Use lc for common nouns
Avoid split infinitives (see Appendix)
Dress-ups: quality adjective; single and dual
    -ly adverbs

What is here is holy yours his host most **munificently** offered, strong of stature yet fair-spoken he seemed to Sir Gawain well suited to be the master of such a mighty stronghold.

    "What is here is <u>wholly</u> yours," his host most <u>munificently</u> offered. [4] Strong of stature yet fair-spoken, he seemed to Sir Gawain well suited to be the master of such a mighty stronghold.

Munificently: generously; bountifully
Indent ¶ (new speaker)
Use quotation marks with direct quotations
Homophone: holy/wholly
Use comma with verb of speaking & direct quotation
Comma splice: needs period, not comma (2 MC)
Disguised #4 ("Being strong …"); needs comma
Dress-ups: -ly adverbs

At that evenings banquet, Sir Gawain disclosed his identity. Admitting to be of the brotherhood of the high famed Knights of the Round Table. When he revealed his name to the lord of the castle his host laughed **lustily** and long.

[2] At that evening's banquet Sir Gawain <u>disclosed</u> his identity, admitting to be of the brotherhood of the <u>high-famed</u> Knights of the Round Table. [5] When he revealed his name to the lord of the castle, his host laughed <u>lustily</u> and long.

Lustily: enthusiastically; heartily; with great spirit
Indent ¶ (time has passed)
Use apostrophes to show possession
Comma optional after #2 SO of 4 words or fewer
Correct fragment by joining phrase to MC
Hyphenate words that function as a single adjective
Use commas after #5 Sentence Openers
Alliteration: "laughed lustily and long"
Dress-ups: strong verb; quality adjective; -ly adverb

Gawains renown had spread to this northern clime, of all knights on earth he was the most honored. So the nobles at the high table whispered to one another "now we shall witness dazzling **eloquence**, and gallant manners".

Gawain's renown had <u>spread</u> to this northern clime. [2] Of all knights on earth, he was the most honored. The nobles at the high table whispered to one another, "Now we shall witness <u>dazzling</u> eloquence and <u>gallant</u> manners."

Eloquence: powerful and effective language
Use apostrophes to show possession
Comma splice: needs period, not comma (2 MC)
Comma needed after #2 SO of 5 or more words
Avoid starting sentences w/ coord. conjunctions *(so)*
Use comma w/ vb. of speaking + direct quotation; UC
No comma before *and* to join 2 items in a series
Periods go inside closing quotation marks
Dress-ups: strong verb; quality adjectives

Week 10

In the evening, Gawain accompanied his host to the Christmas Eve service while the lords lady watched from a private room **adjacent**. Eager to meet the visiting knight. She appeared after the service.

[2] In the evening Gawain accompanied his host to the Christmas Eve service, <u>while</u> the lord's lady watched from a private room <u>adjacent</u>. [4] Eager to meet the visiting knight, she appeared after the service.

Adjacent: adjoining; lying nearby
Indent ¶ (time has passed)
Comma optional after #2 SO of 4 words or fewer
Use commas with adv. clauses of extreme contrast
Use apostrophes to show possession
Correct fragment by joining phrase to MC that
    follows (makes better sense that way)
Disguised #4 ("Being eager ..."); takes comma
Dress-ups: adverb clause; quality adjective

Dressed in bright red fair and elegant to behold, with her high headdress **festooned** with pearls. Secretly, Sir Gawain thought: "that in beauty she surpassed the queen herself."

[7] Dressed in bright red, she was fair and elegant to behold, with her high headdress <u>festooned</u> with pearls. [3] Secretly, Sir Gawain thought that in beauty she <u>surpassed</u> the queen herself.

Festooned: decorated with a string suspended in
    loops between points
Use commas after #7 Sentence Openers (-ed)
Correct fragment by adding a subject and verb
No punctuation needed to introduce indirect speech
No quotation marks around indirect speech
Dress-ups: quality adjective; strong verb

Both welcomed Gawain warmly bringing him to a cozy inviting fire in the castle where he provided entertainment and lighthearted **diversions**.

Both welcomed Gawain <u>warmly</u>, bringing him to a <u>cozy</u>, <u>inviting</u> fire in the castle, <u>where</u> the host provided entertainment and <u>lighthearted</u> diversions.

Diversions: entertainment that distracts the mind
Use commas to set off nonessential phrases
    ("warmly" goes with "welcomed," not "bringing")
Use commas with coordinate adjectives
Use commas with nonessential adj. clauses ("where")
Unclear antecedent: "he" could be the host or Gawain
Dress-ups: -ly adv.; dual & single adj's; adv. clause

For 3 days Sir Gawain, and visiting nobles and ladies enjoyed the hospitality of there host and his charming wife that wholly season; **prudently** however Gawain knew he must depart, when the other guests took there leave on the morrow.

[2] For three days Sir Gawain and visiting nobles and ladies enjoyed the hospitality of their host and his charming wife that holy season. [3] Prudently, however, Gawain knew he must depart <u>when</u> the other guests took their leave on the morrow.

Prudently: wisely; sensibly   Morrow: next day
Indent ¶ (new topic)
Spell out numbers written as one or two words
No comma before *and* to join 2 items (Gawain counts
    as one item, "nobles and ladies" as the other)
Homophone: there/their; wholly/holy
Separate only closely-related MCs with semicolons
Use commas to set off transitional words
No commas with mid-sentence adv. clauses (when…)
Dress-ups: adverb clause

Week 11

Politely his host inquired what dire state of affairs forced you to both voluntarily and courageously quit the gaiety of Camelot. An urgent errand Gawain replied **evasively**.

[3] Politely his host <u>inquired</u>, "What <u>dire</u> state of affairs forced you to quit the gaiety of Camelot both <u>voluntarily and courageously</u>?"
"An urgent errand," Gawain replied <u>evasively</u>.

Evasively: vaguely; avoiding the question
Indent ¶ (new speakers)
Use comma with verb of speaking & direct quotation
Use quotation marks with direct quotations
Capitalize the first word of a quoted sentence
Avoid split infinitives (see Appendix)
Use question mark after questions
Dress-ups: strong verb and adj.; dual & single -lys

By chance have you **intelligence** of the Green Chapel, or of the lone knight which lives there in comparable hue of green? *[quotation continues]*

[2] "By chance, have you intelligence of the Green Chapel or of the <u>lone</u> knight <u>who</u> lives there in comparable hue of green? *[quotation continues]*

Intelligence: information; news
Use quotation marks with direct quotations
Use commas after introductory transitional words
No comma before *or* to join 2 items in a series
Use *who* for people, *which* for things
No close quotation marks b/c quotation continues
Dress-ups: quality adjective; who clause

I settled with this knight to **rendezvous** at that spot on New Years day and I would more willingly keep my appointment then gain all the wealth in the world! With but 4 days remaining I dare not tarry here longer.

I <u>settled</u> with this knight to <u>rendezvous</u> at that spot on New Year's Day, and I would more <u>willingly</u> keep my appointment than gain all the wealth in the world! [2] With but four days remaining, I dare not <u>tarry</u> here longer."

Rendezvous: meet at a prearranged time and place
No open quotation marks b/c quotation continues
Apostrophe & UC: "New Year's Day"
Compound sentence needs comma: MC, cc MC
Usage: *then/than* confusion
Spell out numbers written as one or two words
Comma needed after #2 SO of 5 or more words
Close quotation with quotation marks
Dress-ups: strong verbs; -ly adverb

To Gawain's **unfeigned** surprise his host smiled deeply your search then has ended he asserted, linger here four more days and my servant shall escort you to that very spot by the prearranged time, the Green Chapel is but two miles distant.

[2] To Gawain's <u>unfeigned</u> surprise, his host smiled <u>deeply</u>. "Your search, then, has ended," he <u>asserted</u>. "<u>Linger</u> here four more days, and my servant shall <u>escort</u> you to that very spot by the <u>prearranged</u> time. The Green Chapel is but two miles distant."

Unfeigned: not pretended; sincere; genuine
Indent ¶ (new speaker)
Comma optional after #2 SO of 4 words or fewer
Fused: use a period to separate 2 main clauses
Use quotation marks with direct quotations
Use commas to set off transitional words
Use comma with verb of speaking & direct quotation
Comma splices: need periods, not commas (2 MC)
Compound sentence needs comma: MC, cc MC
Dress-ups: quality adj's; -ly adverb; strong verbs

Week 12

Guffawing gleefully at this unexpected news Sir Gawain promised to with pleasure abide with his host and his lovely lady until the new year. Any task that you might devise for me shall gladly be undertaken he vowed with a light heart.

[4] Guffawing <u>gleefully</u> at this unexpected news, Sir Gawain promised to <u>abide</u> with pleasure with his host and his lovely lady until the new year. "I shall <u>gladly</u> <u>undertake</u> any task <u>that</u> you might <u>devise</u> for me," he <u>vowed</u> with a light heart.

Guffawing: laughing heartily
Indent ¶ (new speaker)
Use commas after #4 SO (-ing phrase)
Avoid split infinitives (see Appendix)
Correct lc with "new year" since it refers to the event, the approaching new year, not New Year's Day
Use quotation marks with direct quotations
Convert passive to active voice
Use comma with verb of speaking & direct quotation
Dress-ups: -ly adv's; strong verbs; which (using *that*)

That evening, the host entertained the **doughty** knight with witty conversation and fine fellowship. At last he gazed at his gallant guest, and proposed a bargain will you do my bidding as you boasted?

[2] That evening, the host entertained the <u>doughty</u> knight with <u>witty</u> conversation and fine fellowship. [2] At last he <u>gazed</u> at his <u>gallant</u> guest and proposed a bargain. "Will you do my bidding <u>as</u> you boasted?"

Doughty: valiant; bold; fearless
Indent ¶ (time has passed)
Disguised #2 (*During, In, On, At* that time period)
Alliteration: "fine fellowship"; "gazed … gallant guest"
No comma before *and* to join 2 compound verbs
Fused: use a period to separate 2 main clauses
Use quotation marks with direct quotations
Dress-ups: quality adj's; strong verb; adverb clause

I shall do so indeed responded the valiant knight as long as I remain under your **commodious** roof I shall abide by your laws. Because you have endured many hardships you are lacking in rest, and nourishing fare his host replied.

"I shall do so, indeed," responded the <u>valiant</u> knight. [5] "As long as I remain under your <u>commodious</u> roof, I shall <u>abide</u> by your laws."
[5] "Because you have <u>endured</u> many hardships, you are lacking in rest and <u>nourishing</u> fare," his host replied.

Commodious: spacious and convenient
Indent ¶ (new speakers)
Use quotation marks with direct quotations
Use commas to set off transitional words
Fused: use a period to separate 2 main clauses
Use commas after #5 Sentence Openers (twice)
No comma before *and* to join 2 items in a series
Use comma with verb of speaking & direct quotation
Dress-ups: quality adjectives; strong verbs

Comfortably lay in bed in your chamber until late, then meet whenever you wish to dine with my wife which will sit by your side, and **desultorily** converse at table to cheer our guest, I will spend my time hunting while you lie late and rest.
[quotation continues]

[3] "Comfortably lie in bed in your chamber until late, then meet <u>whenever</u> you wish to dine with my wife, <u>who</u> will sit by your side and <u>desultorily</u> <u>converse</u> at table to cheer our guest. I will spend my time hunting <u>while</u> you lie late and rest.
[quotation continues]

Desultorily: randomly; without set plan
Use quotation marks with direct quotations
Usage: *lay/lie* confusion
Use *who* for people, *which* for things
Use commas to set off nonessential *who* clauses
No comma before *and* to join 2 compound verbs ("sit … and … converse")
Comma splice: needs period, not comma (2 MC)
No close quotation marks b/c quotation continues
Dress-ups: adverb clauses; who clause; -ly adverb; strong verb

---

Week 13

One more request. Agree now to this whatever I gain in the woods I will reward you in the evening while all that you have **indubitably** gained you must bestow on me, promise my friend to make this exchange, whether hands be empty or full.

      "One more request. Agree now to this: whatever I gain in the woods I will reward you in the evening, <u>while</u> all <u>that</u> you have <u>indubitably</u> gained you must <u>bestow</u> on me. Promise, my friend, to make this exchange, whether hands be empty or full."

Indubitably: in a manner that cannot be doubted
Indent ¶ (new topic)
Comprehension: make clear the bargain being made
Start new par. in continued quotation with "
"One more request" acceptable fragment in dialogue
    but not a #6 since it is not a sentence (no verb)
Use colon after MC to give an explanation
Use commas to set off adv. clause of contrast (while)
Comma splice: needs period, not comma (2 MC)
Set off NDAs with commas ("my friend")
Dress-ups: adv. clause; which (*that*); -ly adv.; verb

Though your request seems strange I shall **amiably** engage in such sport Sir Gawain agreed and the two men laughed together and continued their mirth.

      [5] "Though your request seems strange, I shall <u>amiably</u> engage in such sport," Sir Gawain agreed, and the two men laughed together and continued their mirth.

Amiably: agreeably; in a good-natured manner
Indent ¶ (new speaker)
Use quotation marks with direct quotations
Use commas after #5 Sentence Openers
Use comma with verb of speaking & direct quotation
Compound sentence needs comma: MC, cc MC
Dress-ups: -ly adverb

The next morning while the leige lord of the castle was out hunting Sir Gawain slumbered late in his bed under embroidered silk covers with **opulent** brocaded curtains drawn around the bed.

      [2] The next morning <u>while</u> the liege lord of the castle was out hunting, Sir Gawain <u>slumbered</u> late in his bed under <u>embroidered</u> silk covers with <u>opulent, brocaded</u> curtains drawn around the bed.

Opulent: luxurious; exhibiting great wealth
Indent ¶ (time has passed and new scene)
Disguised #2 (*During, In, On, At* that time period)
Spelling: *liege*
Use commas after 2 or more introductory elements
No comma before "silk" correct (cumulative adj's)
Use commas with coordinate adjectives
Dress-ups: adverb clause; strong verb; single and
    dual adjectives

After daylight began to gaily glimmer through the cracks in the shutters a noise stirred him, peering **surreptitiously** through the curtain that din made Gawain wonder what could have caused it.

[5] After daylight began to <u>glimmer</u> <u>gaily</u> through the cracks in the shutters, a noise <u>stirred</u> him. [4] Peering <u>surreptitiously</u> through the curtain, Gawain wondered what could have caused that din.

Surreptitiously: in a way marked by stealth, secrecy
Avoid split infinitives (see Appendix)
Use commas after #5 Sentence Openers (Tricky #5:
    after is a conjunction here, not preposition)
Comma splice: needs period, not comma (2 MC)
Use commas after #4 SO (-ing phrase)
Illegal #4: noun after " , " should do the *inging*
    (it's Gawain, not the din, who's peering)
Dress-ups: strong verbs; -ly adverbs

Week 14

Caught off guard he drew in his breath, and pretended to doze; it was the stunning lady of the castle! Softly, she stealed to his bedside drew the curtain aside and sat by his side leisurely watching the **intrepid** knight in his slumber.

[7] Caught off guard, he drew in his breath and pretended to <u>doze</u>. It was the <u>stunning</u> lady of the castle! [3] Softly she stole to his bedside, drew the curtain aside, and sat by his side, <u>leisurely</u> watching the <u>intrepid</u> knight in his slumber.

Intrepid: brave; courageous; bold
Use commas after #7 SO (w/ past participle *caught*)
No comma before *and* to join 2 compound verbs
Separate only closely-related MCs with semicolons
Comma optional after #3 Sentence Opener
Spelling: *stole* is the past of *steal*
Use commas with three or more items in a series
Use commas to set off nonessential phrases
Dress-ups: strong verb; quality adjectives; -ly adverb

Still she lingered, **disconcerted** Sir Gawain considered his best course of action in this embarrasing situation determining that discourse might work better then a pretense of sleep.

[6] Still she <u>lingered</u>. [7] Disconcerted, Sir Gawain considered his best course of action in this embarrassing situation, determining that discourse might work better than a pretense of sleep.

Disconcerted: confused; w/ his self-possession upset
Indent ¶ (a little time has passed)
Comma splice: needs period, not comma (2 MC)
Use commas after #7 Sentence Openers (-ed)
   (note: the meaning shifts without the comma)
Spelling: *embarrassing*. Usage: *then/than* confusion
Use commas to set off nonessential phrases
Dress-ups: strong verb

Stretching his limbs, and yawning noisy he pretended to be startled from slumber while he opened his eyes wide in **bafflement**.

[4] Stretching his limbs and yawning <u>noisily</u>, he pretended to be <u>startled</u> from slumber <u>while</u> he opened his eyes wide in bafflement.

Bafflement: confusion from not understanding
No comma before *and* to join 2 items in a series
Usage: needs adverb *noisily,* not adjective *noisy*
Use commas after #4 SO (after "noisily")
Note that *wide* can be an adverb as well as an adj.
Dress-ups: -ly adverb; strong verb; adverb clause

Good morning Sir Gawain exclaimed the gay lady! You are an **imprudent** sleeper to let someone slip in, now you are my captive, you who the world admires as the most chivalrous courteous and honorable of knights.

"Good morning, Sir Gawain!" exclaimed the gay lady. "You are an <u>imprudent</u> sleeper to let someone slip in. Now you are my captive, you <u>whom</u> the world admires as the most <u>chivalrous</u>, <u>courteous</u>, and <u>honorable</u> of knights."

Imprudent: unwise; not showing good sense
Indent ¶ (new speaker)
Use quotation marks with direct quotations
Set off NDAs with commas
Place " ! " after exclamation, not at end of statement
Alliteration: "sleeper … someone slip"
Comma splice: needs period, not comma (2 MC)
Use *whom* for objective case
Use commas with 3 or more items in a series
Dress-ups: quality adjectives; who clause

Week 15

Countering her light banter Gawain pondered how to politely **extricate** him from the ladies unseemly flattery and attentions without appearing ill-mannered.

[4] Countering her light banter, Gawain <u>pondered</u> how to <u>extricate</u> himself <u>politely</u> from the lady's <u>unseemly</u> flattery and attentions without appearing <u>ill-mannered</u>.

Extricate: disentangle; free or release
Indent ¶ (new topic)
Use commas after #4 SO (-ing phrase)
Avoid split infinitives (see Appendix)
Usage: needs reflexive *himself; lady's* is possessive
Dress-ups: strong verbs; -ly adverb; quality
   adjectives (*unseemly* = imposter -ly)

As a knight of the round table he had to honor the chivalric code which obligated him at all times to courtesy in speech as well as daring deeds and valor in **arms**.

[2] As a Knight of the Round Table, he had to honor the <u>chivalric</u> code, <u>which</u> <u>obligated</u> him at all times to courtesy in speech as well as daring deeds and valor in arms.

Arms: weapons (i.e., in using them); warfare
Note: "as" sometimes starts #2 sentences (see trick
   in Appendix for distinguishing #2s from #5s)
Capitalize proper nouns
Comma needed after #2 SO of 5 or more words
Use commas to set off nonessential which clauses
Dress-ups: quality adj.; which clause; strong verb

In good faith he replied I am not he of who you speak, as I am altogether unworthy of such lofty regard. Nay Sir Gawain your well-proven **prowess** attests to your renown, in this spot I have trapped the hearts desire of all lady's of the kingdom.

[2] "In good faith," he replied, "I am not he of <u>whom</u> you speak, <u>as</u> I am altogether <u>unworthy</u> of such <u>lofty</u> regard."

    "Nay, Sir Gawain, your <u>well-proven</u> prowess <u>attests</u> to your renown. [2] In this spot I have <u>trapped</u> the heart's desire of all ladies of the kingdom."

Prowess: exceptional bravery, skill, or strength
Indent ¶, 2nd part (new speaker)
Use quotation marks with direct quotations
Use comma with verb of speaking & direct quotation
Use *whom* for objective case
Set off NDAs with commas
Comma splice: needs period, not comma (2 MC)
Use apostrophes to show possession
Ladies is plural, not possessive
Dress-ups: who & adv. clauses; quality adj's & verbs

Madam your **beneficence** abounds but your praises reflect only your courtesy, they do not pertain to me! Not so Sir Knight. Unless reports lie you're incomparable repute extends far beyond Camelot. However my words do not draw from fame alone. *[quotation continues]*

    "Madam, your beneficence <u>abounds</u>, but your praises reflect only your courtesy. They do not <u>pertain</u> to me!"
    "Not so, Sir Knight. [5] Unless reports lie, your <u>incomparable</u> repute <u>extends</u> far beyond Camelot.
    [T] "However, my words do not <u>draw</u> from fame alone. *[quotation continues]*

Beneficence: the quality of being kind or charitable
Indent ¶ (new speakers; new topic)
Use quotation marks with direct quotations
Set off NDAs with commas (twice)
Compound sentence needs comma: MC, cc MC
Comma splice: needs period, not comma (2 MC)
Use commas after #5 Sentence Openers
Homophone: you're/your
Start new paragraph in continued quotation with "
Use commas to set off transitional words
No close quotation marks b/c quotation continues
Dress-ups: strong verbs; quality adjective

Week 16

These past few days, my own observations have confirmed to me, that if I were too hunt high and low for a husband of all men in the world none could surpass you in wit, and **comeliness**, courtesy, and courtly gaiety, none other on earth should take me for a wife.

[2] These past few days my own observations have <u>confirmed</u> to me, that <u>if</u> I were to hunt high and low for a husband, of all men in the world none could <u>surpass</u> you in wit and comeliness, courtesy and courtly gaiety. None other on earth should take me for a wife."

Comeliness: attractiveness; beauty
No open quotation marks b/c quotation continues
Comma optional after #2 SO of 4 words or fewer
Comma after "me" needed to avoid misreading
Subjunctive mood: "if I were" is correct (Appendix)
Homophone: too/to
Use commas after introductory adverb clauses
Variation for commas w/ four items: 1 and 2, 3 and 4
Comma splice: needs period, not comma (2 MC)
Close quotations with quotation marks
Dress-ups: strong verbs; adverb clause

You are **indissolubly** united two a superior man uttered Sir Gawain. Although I esteem the praise you have showered on me here, and consider myself your night in the name of Christ.

    "You are <u>indissolubly</u> <u>united</u> to a superior man," <u>uttered</u> Sir Gawain, "<u>although</u> I <u>esteem</u> the praise you have <u>showered</u> on me here and consider myself your knight in the name of Christ."

Indissolubly: in a permanent or binding manner
Indent ¶ (new speaker)
Use quotation marks with direct quotations
Homophones: two/to; night/knight
Use comma with verb of speaking & direct quotation
Correct fragment by joining dependent clause to MC
No comma before *and* to join 2 compound verbs
   (esteem and consider)
Dress-ups: -ly adverb; strong verbs; adverb clause

Thus they talked on in this light fashion until noon; when the graceful lady gaily took her leave with one parting **ploy**. Seeming stern she suggested our guest must not be, Sir Gawain.

[T] Thus they talked on in this light fashion until noon, <u>when</u> the graceful lady <u>gaily</u> took her leave with one parting ploy. [4] Seeming <u>stern</u>, she suggested, "Our guest must not be Sir Gawain."

Ploy: maneuver or stratagem to gain advantage
Indent ¶ (new topic)
Use commas, not semicolons, w/ nonessential clauses
Use commas after #4 SO (-ing phrase)
Use comma with verb of speaking & direct quotation
Use quotation marks with direct quotations
Capitalize the first word of a quoted sentence
No comma after "be" ("Sir Gawain" is not an NDA)
Dress-ups: adverb clause; -ly adverb; quality adj.

Concerned, **lest** he had been faulty in his courtly speech the knight asked why do you suggest that. Such a courteous knight as Gawain is reputed to be, had he remained so long in a fair ladies company, would at least have claimed a kiss.

[7] Concerned lest he had been <u>faulty</u> in his courtly speech, the knight asked, "Why do you suggest that?"
"Such a <u>courteous</u> knight <u>as</u> Gawain is <u>reputed</u> to be, had he remained so long in a fair lady's company, would at least have <u>claimed</u> a kiss."

Lest: for fear that
Indent ¶ (new speakers)
Comma comes after whole -ed phrase, not the word
Use comma with verb of speaking & direct quotation
Use quotation marks with direct quotations + UC
Use question mark after questions
Lady's is possessive, not plural
Dress-ups: quality adj's; adverb clause; strong verbs

Week 17

Gentle lady I grant it at once he exclaimed! With that she leaned down her charming head, and bestowed a kiss on his cheek, graciously they **commended** one another to Christ until at last she departed.

"Gentle lady, I grant it at once!" he exclaimed.
[2] With that she <u>leaned</u> down her charming head and <u>bestowed</u> a kiss on his cheek. [3] Graciously they <u>commended</u> one another to Christ, <u>until</u> at last she <u>departed</u>.

Commended: entrusted; committed to another's care
Indent ¶ (new speaker; new topic)
Use quotation marks with direct quotations
Set off NDAs with commas
Place " ! " after exclamation, not at end of statement
No comma before *and* to join 2 compound verbs
Comma splice: needs period, not comma (2 MC)
Use comma to set off contrasting adv. clause ("until")
Dress-ups: strong verbs; adverb clause

The moment she exited Sir Gawain much relieved to have escaped with but a kiss collected his wits, leaping from his bed he called his steward to assist him, and **donned** his handsome raiment in haste.

[2] The moment she exited, Sir Gawain, much relieved to have escaped with but a kiss, collected his wits. [4] Leaping from his bed, he called his steward to assist him and <u>donned</u> his handsome raiment in haste.

Donned: put on; dressed in
Indent ¶ (new topic)
Comma optional after #2 SO of 4 words or fewer
Use commas around nonessential phrases (much…)
Spelling: *relieved*
Comma splice: needs period, not comma (2 MC)
Use commas after #4 SO (-ing phrase)
No comma before *and* to join 2 compound verbs
Dress-ups: strong verb

He sped straightway to chapel where he restored his strength of heart and purpose knowing he must soon bear the bleak, and **austere** blow.

He <u>sped</u> straightway to chapel, <u>where</u> he <u>restored</u> his strength of heart and purpose, knowing he must soon bear the <u>bleak and austere</u> blow.

Austere: severe in appearance; uncompromising
Use commas around nonessential adj. clauses
  ("where…" and "knowing…")
Alliteration: "bear the bleak"
No comma before *and* to join 2 items in a series
Dress-ups: strong verbs; adverb clause; dual
  adjectives

When his **brawny** host returned from the hunt that evening as agreed the worthy Lord deposited at Gawains feet a deer the finest game he had seen in many a long winter.

[5] When his <u>brawny</u> host returned from the hunt that evening, as agreed the worthy lord <u>deposited</u> at Gawain's feet a <u>deer, the</u> finest game he had seen in many a long winter.

Brawny: muscular; strong
Indent ¶ (time has passed)
Use commas after #5 SO (note: "as agreed" makes
    more sense w/ what follows than what precedes)
Use lc for titles w/o a name. *Gawain's* is possessive
Invisible *which* needs comma: "deer, which was"
Dress-ups: quality adj.; strong verb; invisible which

Week 18

What do you think, the host asked his guest, have I won with my bow a worthy **guerdon**. In good faith replied Gawain I have gained the greatest by far.

"What do you think?" the host asked his guest. "Have I won with my bow a <u>worthy</u> guerdon?"
    [2] "In good faith," replied Gawain, "I have gained the greater by far."

Guerdon: a reward or payment
Indent ¶, 2nd part (new speaker)
Use quotation marks with direct quotations
Use question mark after questions (twice)
Comma splice: needs period, not comma (2 MC)
Use commas w/ verb of speaking & direct quotations
Use the comparative adjective when comparing two
Dress-ups: quality adjective

And he kissed his host on the cheek in a **seemly** manner. And laughing loud at his bargain the noble host inquired, where he had recieved such a prize. That was no part of our bargain, Sir Gawain smiled. Press me no farther for I have honored my vow.

He kissed his host on the cheek in a <u>seemly</u> manner.
    [4] Laughing loud at his bargain, the noble host inquired <u>where</u> he had received such a prize. "That was no part of our bargain," Sir Gawain smiled. "Press me no further, for I have <u>honored</u> my vow."

Seemly: decent; appropriate (adj.—imposter -ly)
Indent ¶, 2nd part (new topic)
Avoid starting sentences with coord. conjunctions
Usage: *loud* is correct; it can be an adverb or adj.
Use commas after #4 SO (-ing phrase)
No comma with mid-sentence adv. clause ("where")
Spelling: *received*   Usage: *farther/further* confusion
Use quotation marks with direct quotations
Compound sentence needs comma: MC, cc MC
Dress-ups: quality adj.; adverb clause; strong verb

The next morning, while his host was out hunting Gawain again recieved a visit in his Brocaded Bower from the **pulchritudinous** Lady.

    [2] The next morning <u>while</u> his host was out hunting, Gawain again received a visit in his <u>brocaded</u> bower from the <u>pulchritudinous</u> lady.

Pulchritudinous: physically beautiful; comely
Indent ¶ (time has passed)
Use comma at the end of 2 or more intro. elements
Spelling: *received*
Alliteration: "brocaded bower"
Use lc for common nouns
Dress-ups: adverb clause; quality adjectives

Coyly, she peeked inside the curtain where with more subtle arts then ever she tried to **irresistibly** attract the virtuous knight with her charms.

[3] Coyly she <u>peeked</u> inside the curtain, <u>where</u>, with more <u>subtle</u> arts than ever, she tried <u>irresistibly</u> to attract the <u>virtuous</u> knight with her charms.

Irresistibly: incapable of being resisted
Comma optional after #3 Sentence Opener
Use comma w/ nonessential adj. clause ("where...")
Use commas w/ nonessential phrase ("with...ever")
Usage: *then/than* confusion
Avoid split infinitives (see Appendix)
Dress-ups: strong verb; adverb clause; quality
    adjectives; -ly adverb

Week 19

Gallant Sir Gawain— she began if indeed you are that famed knight for you seem to have **disregarded** the lesson in courtesy, that I took such pains to teach you yesterday morn.

"Gallant Sir Gawain—," she began, "if indeed you are that famed knight, for you seem to have disregarded the lesson in courtesy that I took such pains to teach you yesterday morn."

Disregarded: ignored
Indent ¶ (speaker)
Use quotation marks with direct quotations
Note: em-dash used to indicate a break in thought
Use comma with verb of speaking & direct quotation
Compound sentence needs comma: MC, cc MC
No commas to set off essential *which (that)* clauses
Dress-ups: adv. clause; adj.; verb; which (using *that*)

Should your claim be true replied that determined hero I am indeed **culpable**, what lesson have I neglected to understand?

[5] "Should your claim be true," replied that determined hero, "I am indeed culpable. What lesson have I neglected to understand?"

Culpable: deserving blame
Indent ¶ (new speaker)
Use quotation marks with direct quotations
Disguised #5: "If" is implied
Use commas w/ verb of speaking & direct quotation
Comma splice: needs period, not comma (2 MC)
Dress-ups: quality adjectives; strong verb

My instruction in kissing answered the bold lady. When a **damsel** finds favor with a courtly knight it accords good for him to freely claim a kiss.

"My instruction in kissing," answered the bold lady. [5] "When a damsel finds favor with a courtly knight, it accords well for him to claim a kiss freely."

Damsel: a young woman or girl
Indent ¶ (new speaker)
Use quotation marks with direct quotations
Use comma with verb of speaking & direct quotation
Use commas after #5 Sentence Openers
Usage: use the adverb *well* to modify a verb (accords)
Avoid split infinitives (see Appendix)
Dress-ups: quality adj. (imposter -ly); -ly adverb

Squirming again at the predicament in which he was placed her **indecorous** advances were parried by Gawain as best he could granting her only the freedom of kisses as befitted a well mannered knight.

[4] Squirming again at the predicament in which he was placed, Gawain parried her indecorous advances as best he could, granting her only the freedom of kisses as befitted a well-mannered knight.

Indecorous: not proper; unseemly
Indent ¶ (new topic)
Use commas after #4 SO (-ing phrase)
Illegal #4: noun after " , " should do the *inging*
   (fixing this also rids sentence of passive voice)
Use commas with nonessential phrases ("granting")
Hyphenate words that function as a single adjective
Dress-ups: which clause; strong verbs; quality
   adjectives

Week 20

At that promise, the lady bent down, and awarded Gawain a kiss, she then tried to intently engage him in **rhapsodizing** about the trials and bliss of true love.

[2] At that promise the lady bent down and awarded Gawain a kiss. She then intently tried to engage him in rhapsodizing about the trials and bliss of true love.

Rhapsodizing: talking with extravagant enthusiasm
Comma optional after #2 SO of 4 words or fewer
No comma before *and* to join 2 compound verbs
Comma splice: needs period, not comma (2 MC)
Avoid split infinitives (see Appendix)
Dress-ups: -ly adverb

How is it she pressed him that such a daring, young warrior as yourself reputed to be quite a charmer of fair ladies has never yet uttered so much as a phrase of the **flowery** language of love *[quotation continues]*

    "How is it," she <u>pressed</u> him, "that such a daring young warrior as yourself, <u>reputed</u> to be quite a charmer of fair ladies, has never yet <u>uttered</u> so much as a phrase of the <u>flowery</u> language of love? *[quotation continues]*

Flowery: ornate or elaborate in rhetoric
Indent ¶ (new speaker)
Use quotation marks with direct quotations
Use comma with verb of speaking & direct quotation
No commas with cumulative adjectives
Use commas around nonessential phrases
Use question mark after questions
No close quotation marks b/c quotation continues
Dress-ups: strong verbs; quality adjectives

Are you which all praise so **ingenuous** or do you perceive me so dim-witted so featherbrained fie Teach me the parlance of perfect love.

Are you <u>whom</u> all praise so <u>ingenuous</u>? Or do you perceive me so <u>dim-witted</u>? So <u>featherbrained</u>? Fie! Teach me the parlance of perfect love."

Ingenuous: artless; naive; lacking in cunning
Fie: used to express humorously the pretense of being
   shocked. Parlance: idiom; speech
No open quotation marks b/c quotation continues
Use *who* for people, *whom* with the objective case
Use question marks; exclamation after interjection
Close quotations with quotation marks
Dress-ups: who clause; quality adjectives

"May the Almighty Lord who we both serve bless you gracious lady you who would **condescend** to converse with such an unworthy knight, however to rise to the challenge of telling of love is a task beyond my simple ability. *[quotation continues]*

    "May the Almighty Lord, <u>whom</u> we both serve, bless you, gracious lady, you <u>who</u> would <u>condescend</u> to <u>converse</u> with such an unworthy knight. [T] However, to rise to the challenge of telling of love is a task beyond my simple ability. *[quotation continues]*

Condescend: lower oneself
Indent ¶ (new speaker)
Use quotation marks with direct quotations
Use commas to set off nonessential *who* clauses
Use *whom* for objective case
Set off NDAs with commas
Alliteration: "condescend to converse"
Period before "however" (CS); comma after
No close quotation marks b/c quotation continues
Dress-ups: who clauses; strong verbs

Week 21

I would count it folly indeed to discuss the texts of love and treat it's themes to one, which visibly **wields** more power in that craft than a 100 such as me

I would count it folly, indeed, to discuss the texts of love and treat its themes to one <u>who</u> <u>visibly</u> <u>wields</u> more power in that craft than a hundred such as me!"

Wields: exercises effectively
Close, but don't open, w/ " " b/c quotation continues
Use commas to set off transitional words
Its = poss. of *it*. Spell out #s written in 1-2 words
Use *who* for people; no comma b/c clause is essential
Usage: "me" is correct; "such as" functions as a prep.
Statement is exclamatory, but period or **!** would work
Dress-ups: who clause; -ly adverb; strong verb

Thus with many a clever stratagem the lovely lady attempted to disgracefully entice him to declare his love for her while he resisted all her advances, and **evinced** not the slightest **taint** of dishonor.

    [T,2] Thus with many a clever stratagem, the lovely lady attempted to <u>entice</u> him <u>disgracefully</u> to declare his love for her, <u>while</u> he resisted all her advances and <u>evinced</u> not the slightest taint of dishonor.

Evinced ... taint: showed clearly no trace of
   anything dishonorable
Indent ¶ (new topic)
Comma needed after #2 SO of 5 or more words
Avoid split infinitives (see Appendix)
Use comma to set off contrasting adv. clause
No comma before *and* to join 2 compound verbs
Dress-ups: -ly adverb; strong verbs; adverb clause

At last, when the sun was at it's **zenith** in the sky she leaned down imparted another kiss on his cheek and then took her leave in the most charming manner

[2] At last, <u>when</u> the sun was at its zenith in the sky, she leaned down, <u>imparted</u> another kiss on his cheek, and then took her leave in the most charming manner.

Zenith: the highest point
Use comma at the end of 2 or more intro. elements
Its = possessive of *it*
Use commas with 3 or more items in a series
Use a period at end of statements
Dress-ups: adverb clause; strong verb

Hastily Sir Gawain raised once more from his bed and he attended service in the chapel giving thanks two Jesus for shielding him from the ladies **wiles**.

[3] Hastily Sir Gawain rose once more from his bed and attended service in the chapel, giving thanks to Jesus for shielding him from the lady's wiles.

Wiles: deceitful cunning; artful, beguiling behavior
Usage: *raised/rose* confusion
Compound sentence needs comma: MC, cc MC
   Better to drop the 2nd subject (*he*) than to add " , "
Use commas to set off nonessential phrases
Homophone: two/to
Lady's is possessive, not plural

Week 22

For a second time, his host returned **expeditiously** from a victorious hunt in the evening dumping a monstrous boar on the floor at Sir Gawains feet.

[2] For a second time, in the evening his host returned <u>expeditiously</u> from a <u>victorious</u> hunt, dumping a <u>monstrous</u> boar on the floor at Sir Gawain's feet.

Expeditiously: swiftly; promptly
Indent ¶ (time has passed)
Misplaced prep. phrase (the hunt spanned all day)
Use commas to set off nonessential phrases
Use apostrophes to show possession
Dress-ups: -ly adverb; quality adjectives

Again I am immeasurably the winner of this sport laughed his guest! With that Sir Gawain returned to his host 2 kisses in a courteous manner refusing once more to reveal the source of such **amiability**.

"Again, I am <u>immeasurably</u> the winner of this sport!" laughed his guest. [2] With that, Sir Gawain returned to his host two kisses in a <u>courteous</u> manner, refusing once more to reveal the source of such amiability.

Amiability: friendly, sociable behavior
Indent ¶ (new speaker)
Use quotation marks with direct quotations
Use commas to set off transitional words
Place " ! " after exclamation, not at end of statement
Comma optional after #2 SO of 4 words or fewer
Spell out numbers written as one or two words
Use commas to set off nonessential phrases
Dress-ups: -ly adverb; quality adjective

That evening at revelry and feasting Sir Gawain **entreated** his host for permission too leave early on the morrow. Knowing it was the Eve of his fateful appointment.

[2] That evening at revelry and feasting, Sir Gawain <u>entreated</u> his host for permission to leave early on the morrow, knowing it was the eve of his <u>fateful</u> appointment.

Entreated: requested earnestly
Indent ¶ (time has passed)
Use commas after 2+ intro prepositional phrases
Homophone: too/to
Correct fragment by joining phrase to MC w/ comma
Use lc for common noun (*eve*)
Dress-ups: strong verb; quality adjective

The host **parried** his request twice I have tested you twice found you true; let us continue the game one more day, I promise you shall arrive at the Green Chapel in time.

[6] The host <u>parried</u> his request. "Twice I have tested you, twice found you true. Let us continue the game one more day. I promise you shall arrive at the Green Chapel in time."

Parried: evaded or dodged (term from fencing)
Fused: use a period to separate 2 main clauses
Use quotation marks with direct quotations
Use commas to separate contrasting elements
Separate only closely-related MCs with semicolons
Comma splice: needs period, not comma (2 MC)
Dress-ups: strong verb

Week 23

Just as the Savior of all was thrice tempted in the wilderness so to was Gawain to be tempted a 3rd time. Dark dreams haunted the hero through the night while he dismally pondered his eminent appointment with the **dour** host at the green chapel.

[5] Just as the Savior of all was thrice tempted in the wilderness, so too was Gawain to be tempted a third time. Dark dreams <u>haunted</u> the hero through the night <u>while</u> he <u>dismally</u> <u>pondered</u> his <u>imminent</u> appointment with the <u>dour</u> host at the Green Chapel.

Dour: severe; stern; gloomy
Indent ¶ (new topic)
Use commas after #5 Sentence Openers
Homophone: to/too
Spell out ordinal numbers
Alliteration: "haunted the hero"
Comma before "while" clause not required
Usage: *imminent/eminent* confusion
Capitalize proper nouns
Dress-ups: strong verbs & adj's; adv. clause; -ly adv.

Eager for success this 3rd try the lovely lady wasted no time, boldly she stalked into Sir Gawains chamber, and **unbarred** the shutters.

[4] Eager for success this third try, the lovely lady wasted no time. [3] Boldly she <u>stalked</u> into Sir Gawain's chamber and <u>unbarred</u> the shutters.

Unbarred: removed bars from; opened
Indent ¶ (new topic)
Spell out ordinal numbers
Disguised #4 ("Being eager ..."); needs comma
Comma splice: needs period, not comma (2 MC)
Use apostrophes to show possession
No comma before *and* to join 2 compound verbs
Dress-ups: strong verbs

Summoning his wits for a **skirmish** Gawain noticed how glorious was her bright attire in striking contrast to his dismal dreams, again the lady greeted the night with a kiss on his cheek

[4] Summoning his wits for a skirmish, Gawain noticed how <u>glorious</u> was her bright attire, in <u>striking</u> contrast to his <u>dismal</u> dreams. Again the lady greeted the knight with a kiss on his cheek.

Skirmish: brisk conflict or encounter (military term)
Use commas after #4 SO (-ing phrase)
Use commas to set off nonessential phrases
Comma splice: needs period, not comma (2 MC)
Homophone: night/knight
Use a period at end of statements
Dress-ups: quality adjectives

Her advances were so **blatant** this time however that Sir Gawain must needs except her proffered love, or offensively refuse, he bethought himself of the harm to his soul should he break his own oaths, and his fealty to the lord of that house.

Her advances were so <u>blatant</u> this time, however, that Sir Gawain must needs accept her <u>proffered</u> love or <u>offensively</u> refuse. He <u>bethought</u> himself of the harm to his soul should he break his own oaths and his fealty to the lord of that house.

Blatant: brazenly obvious
Bethought: thought, considered (used reflexively)
Fealty: faithfulness or fidelity to a lord
Use commas to set off transitional words
Usage: *accept/except* confusion
No comma before *or* to join 2 compound verbs
Comma splice: needs period, not comma (2 MC)
No comma before *and* to join 2 items in a series
Dress-ups: quality adj's; -ly adverb; strong verb

Week 24

By my Savior, that shall not befall Sir Gawain vowed to himself, and to all her entices, he attempted to respond with light **banter**.

[2] "By my Savior, that shall not <u>befall</u>," Sir Gawain <u>vowed</u> to himself. [2] To all her entices he attempted to respond with light banter.

Banter: an exchange of playful, teasing remarks
Use quotation marks with direct quotations, treating thoughts like speech
Use comma with verb of speaking & direct quotation
Avoid stringing together sentences with *and*
Comma optional after #2 SO of 4 words or fewer
Dress-ups: strong verbs

"Alas Sir Knight you must have a beloved maiden waiting for you at Camelot to be so **vexatious** and indifferent to my entreaties; grant me one more kiss and I shall depart. *[quotation continues]*

[T] "Alas, Sir Knight, you must have a beloved maiden waiting for you at Camelot to be so <u>vexatious and indifferent</u> to my entreaties. <u>Grant</u> me one more kiss, and I shall <u>depart</u>. *[quotation continues]*

Vexatious: annoying; troublesome
Indent ¶ (new speaker)
Use quotation marks with direct quotations
Use commas after introductory interjections
Set off NDAs with commas
Separate only closely-related MCs with semicolons
Compound sentence needs comma: MC, cc MC
No close quotation marks b/c quotation continues
Dress-ups: dual adjectives; strong verbs

Wait. One other **boon** I ask please except this simple souvenir from me, curiously, she untied a belt that was wrapped around her robes a skillfully embroidered belt of green silk.

"Wait! One other boon I ask: please accept this simple souvenir from me." [3] Curiously, she untied a belt <u>that</u> was wrapped around her <u>robes, a skillfully</u> embroidered belt of green silk.

Boon: a favor sought
Indent ¶ (new topic)
Start new paragraph & end continuous quotation w/ "
Use exclamation mark after exclamations
Use colon after MC to give an explanation
Usage: *accept/except* confusion
Comma splice: needs period, not comma (2 MC)
Invisible which w/ comma: "robes, which was a …"
Dress-ups: which clause (using *that*); -ly adverb

Nay I can not accept any token for I have none to impart, having journeyed far with no **superfluous** baggage, it would not be an equal exchange.

[T] "Nay, I cannot accept any token, for I have none to <u>impart</u>, having <u>journeyed</u> far with no <u>superfluous</u> baggage. It would not be an equal exchange."

Superfluous: more than is sufficient or required
Indent ¶ (new speaker)
Use quotation marks with direct quotations
Use commas after introductory transitional words
Spelling: *cannot* is one word
Compound sentence needs comma: MC, cc MC
Comma splice: needs period, not comma (2 MC)
Dress-ups: strong verbs; quality adjective

Week 25

If my present displeases you as to unworthy a gift were you to know it's **intrinsic** value you might cherish it otherwise for the man which possesses this piece of silk wearing it about his waist can not be killed by any means on earth.

[5] "If my present <u>displeases</u> you as too <u>unworthy</u> a gift, were you to know its <u>intrinsic</u> value, you might <u>cherish</u> it otherwise, for the man <u>who</u> possesses this piece of silk, wearing it about his waist, cannot be killed by any means on earth."

Intrinsic: belonging to the thing by its very nature
Indent ¶ (new speaker)
Use quotation marks with direct quotations
Homophone: to/too. *Its* = possessive of *it*
Use commas after #5 SOs and adverb clauses
Compound sentence needs comma: MC, cc MC
Use *who* for people, *which* for things
Use commas w/ nonessential phrases ("wearing …")
Spelling: *cannot* is one word
Dress-ups: strong verbs; quality adj's; who clause

Truly tempting was the offer, although he had been able to resist the ladies exquisite charms this **singular** souvenir could protect him from the peril, that he faced the next morning.

[6] Truly <u>tempting</u> was the offer! [5] Although he had been able to resist the lady's <u>exquisite</u> charms, this <u>singular</u> souvenir could protect him from the peril <u>that</u> he faced the next morning.

Singular: unusual or strange; odd
Indent ¶ (new topic)
Alliteration: "truly tempting"; "singular souvenir"
Comma splice: needs exclamation mark, not comma
Lady's is possessive, not plural
Use commas after #5 Sentence Openers
No commas to set off essential *which (that)* clauses
Dress-ups: quality adj's; which clause (using *that*)

Sir Gawain refused no longer, agreeing to conceal it from her noble liege lord he accepted her gift; before they parted Sir Gawain also recieved 3 kisses from the **amenable** lady.

[6] Sir Gawain refused no longer. [4] Agreeing to <u>conceal</u> it from her noble liege lord, he accepted her gift. [5] Before they parted, Sir Gawain also received three kisses from the <u>amenable</u> lady.

Amenable: agreeable; willing to act, agree, or yield
Comma splice: needs period, not comma (2 MC)
Use commas after #4 SO (-ing phrase)
Separate only closely-related MCs with semicolons
Use commas after #5 SO (*Before* = conjunction here)
Spelling: *received*
Spell out numbers written as one or two words
Dress-ups: strong verb; quality adjective

That evening, Sir Gawain exchanged three kisses nothing more for a fine fox his noble hosts spoils in the hunt, knowing well the pledge he made. **Baldly** the courteous knight proclaimed all that I owe to you I've openly paid.

[2] That evening Sir Gawain <u>exchanged</u> three kisses— nothing more—for a fine fox, his noble host's spoils in the hunt, knowing well the pledge he had made. [3] Baldly the courteous knight <u>proclaimed</u>, "All <u>that</u> I owe to you I've <u>openly</u> paid."

Baldly: in an open, undisguised manner (ironic, here)
Indent ¶ (new topic)
Comma optional after #2 SO of 4 words or fewer
Use em-dashes for emphasis (commas work too)
Use commas to set off nonessential phrases
Use apostrophes to show possession
Use past perfect for 2 different past times (had made)
Use comma with verb of speaking & direct quotation
Use quotation marks & UC for quoted sentence
Dress-ups: strong verbs; which (using *that*); -ly adv.

Week 26

New Years day dawned a **tempestuous** gray day with gusts of snow bearing down from the North. With great thankfulness Sir Gawain took his leave from his host who's guide was too escort him to the Green Chapel.

New Year's Day <u>dawned</u>, a <u>tempestuous</u> gray day, with gusts of snow bearing down from the north. [2] With great thankfulness Sir Gawain took his leave from his host, <u>whose</u> guide was to <u>escort</u> him to the Green Chapel.

Tempestuous: violent and stormy
Indent ¶ (time has passed)
Apostrophe and UC: "New Year's Day"
Use commas to set off nonessential phrases
Use lc w/ directions ("north" UC only if it's a region)
Use commas to set off nonessential clauses
Whose = possessive form of *who*
Homophone: too/to
Dress-ups: strong verbs; quality adj.; who clause

Secured with a knot the lady's silk belt was wound twice around Gawain's waist; inwardly **bolstered** he wore it not for it's wealth and beauty but for protection his sole defense.

[7] Secured with a knot, the lady's silk belt was wound twice around Gawain's waist. [3,7] Inwardly bolstered, he wore it not for its wealth and beauty, but for <u>protection, his</u> <u>sole</u> defense.

Bolstered: heartened; buoyed up
Use commas after #7 Sentence Openers (-ed) (twice)
Separate only closely-related MCs with semicolons
Its = possessive of *it*
Use commas to separate contrasting elements
Use commas to set off nonessential phrases
Dress-ups: invisible which clause; quality adjective

Ere they reached the edge of the Green Knights land his guide departed in dread. Warning Sir Gawain about the heartless giant which dwelled therein, and which granted mercy to no man.

[5] Ere they reached the edge of the Green Knight's land, his guide <u>departed</u> in dread, warning Sir Gawain about the <u>heartless</u> giant <u>who</u> <u>dwelled</u> therein and <u>who</u> granted mercy to no man.

Ere: before
Indent ¶ (new topic)
Use apostrophes to show possession
Use commas after #5 Sentence Openers
Alliteration: "departed in dread"
Correct fragment by joining phrase to MC w/ comma
Use *who* for people, *which* for things
No comma before *and* to join 2 items (2 who clauses)
Dress-ups: strong verbs; quality adj.; who clauses

With a quick prayer commending himself to Gods keeping Gawain approached the Chapel with **trepidation** as he drew near he heard an alarming din the sound of a monstrous ax being whetted on a grind stone.

[2] With a quick prayer commending himself to God's keeping, Gawain approached the chapel with trepidation. [5] As he drew near, he heard an <u>alarming</u> <u>din, the</u> sound of a <u>monstrous</u> ax being <u>whetted</u> on a grindstone.

Trepidation: apprehension; a state of dread
Use apostrophes to show possession
Use commas after 2 or more introductory elements
Use lc for common nouns
Fused: use a period to separate 2 main clauses
Use commas after #5 Sentence Openers
Use commas to set off nonessential phrases
Spelling: *grindstone* is one word
Dress-ups: quality adj's; invisible which; strong verb

Week 27

Rounding the corner of a huge mound his fearsome foe of strange **hue** appeared. Well met Sir Gawain greeted the Green Knight. You have kept your pledge. *[quotation continues]*

[4] Rounding the corner of a huge mound, he found his <u>fearsome</u> foe of strange hue.
        "Well met, Sir Gawain," greeted the Green Knight. "You have kept your pledge. *[quotation continues]*

Hue: color; variety of a color; appearance or form
Indent ¶, 2nd part (new speaker)
Use commas after #4 SO (-ing phrase)
Illegal #4: Gawain, not the GG, is doing the *inging*
Alliteration: "fearsome foe"; "greeted the Green"
Use quotation marks with direct quotations
Set off NDAs with commas
Use comma with verb of speaking & direct quotation
Dress-ups: quality adjective

Twelve months ago, you rose my ax for your blow, today you must **yield** me the same flinching no more then I did myself when you whacked off my head.

[2] Twelve months ago you raised my ax for your blow. Today you must <u>yield</u> me the same, <u>flinching</u> no more than I did myself <u>when</u> you <u>whacked</u> off my head."

Yield: give as due or required
No open quotation marks b/c quotation continues
Comma optional after #2 SO of 4 words or fewer
Usage: *rose/raised* and *then/than* confusion
Comma splice: needs period, not comma (2 MC)
Use commas to set off nonessential phrases
Close quotations with quotation marks
Dress-ups: strong verbs; quality adj.; adverb clause

I grudge not the return whatever it prove responded noble Sir Gawain. He proffered his head to the blade with good grace, and feigned a cheerful **façade**, loathe to seem fearful.

        "I <u>grudge</u> not the return, whatever it prove," responded noble Sir Gawain. He <u>proffered</u> his head to the blade with good grace and <u>feigned</u> a cheerful façade, <u>loath</u> to seem fearful.

Façade: a superficial appearance or artificial front
Indent ¶ (new speaker)
Use " " w/ direct quotations + comma w/ speaking vb
Use commas to set off nonessential clauses
No comma before *and* to join 2 compound verbs
Usage: *loathe/loath* confusion *(loath=reluctant)*
Dress-ups: strong verbs; quality adjective

Lifting high the huge ax the grim man in green brought it down with all his force Gawain glanced up at the great ax as it descended and his shoulders shrank from the sharp blow. The stroke was abruptly broken off by the **burly** man.

        [4] Lifting high the huge ax, the <u>grim</u> man in green brought it down with all his force. Gawain <u>glanced up</u> at the great ax <u>as</u> it descended, and his shoulders <u>shrank</u> from the sharp blow. The <u>burly</u> man <u>abruptly</u> <u>broke off</u> the stroke.

Burly: strong and muscular; large in bodily size
Indent ¶ (new topic)
Alliteration: "high the huge"; "grim man in green";
    "shoulders shrank … sharp"
Use commas after #4 SO (-ing phrase)
Fused: use a period to separate 2 main clauses
Compound sentence needs comma: MC, cc MC
Convert passive to active voice
Dress-ups: strong adj's & verbs; adv. clause; -ly adv.

Week 28

Mockingly the Green Knight addressed him. What, is this the **stalwart** Gawain of King Arthur's house which never yet fell back in the face of a foe, now you flinch for fear although you have felt no harm!

    [3] Mockingly the Green Knight addressed him. "What? Is this the <u>stalwart</u> Gawain of King Arthur's house, <u>who</u> never yet fell back in the face of a foe? [T] Now you <u>flinch</u> for fear, <u>although</u> you have felt no harm!"

Stalwart: strong and brave
Indent ¶ (new speaker)
Use quotation marks with direct quotations
Use question mark after questions (twice)
Use *who* for people, w/ comma b/c nonessential
Alliteration: "fell … face of a foe"; "flinch for fear"
Comma splice: needs question mark, not comma
Use comma w/ contrasting adv. clause ("although")
Dress-ups: quality adj.; who clause; verb; adv. clause

Be done with it sir, I shall stand my ground and not flinch an inch, I **vehemently** promise this on my honor Gawain affirmed.

    "Be done with it, sir. I shall stand my ground and not <u>flinch</u> an inch. I <u>vehemently</u> promise this on my honor," Gawain <u>affirmed</u>.

Vehemently: earnestly; fervently
Indent ¶ (new speaker)
Use quotation marks with direct quotations
Set off NDAs with commas ("sir")
Comma splices: need periods, not commas (2 MC)
Use comma with verb of speaking & direct quotation
Dress-ups: strong verbs; -ly adverb

Again the fearsome night raised high the ax, again he lowered it for the blow, again he withdrew the ax, before it harmed Gawain. But this time however Gawain made no **discernible** movement.

    Again the <u>fearsome</u> knight raised high the ax; again he lowered it for the blow; again he withdrew the ax <u>before</u> it harmed Gawain. [2] This time, however, Gawain made no <u>discernible</u> movement.

Discernible: perceptible; noticeable
Indent ¶ (new topic)
Homophone: night/knight
Use semicolons to separate closely-related MCs
No comma with mid-sentence adv. clause ("before")
Avoid starting sentences with coord. conjunctions
Disguised #2 (*During, In, On, At* that time period)
Use commas to set off transitional words
Dress-ups: quality adjectives; adverb clause

Aha I see you have regained your nerve the Green Knight **jeered**, now I can strike, and may you uphold the honor of King Arthur's brotherhood of knights. Enraged Gawain challenged him to finish what he began.

    "Aha! I see you have <u>regained</u> your nerve," the Green Knight <u>jeered</u>. [6] "Now I can strike. May you uphold the honor of King Arthur's brotherhood of knights."
    [7] Enraged, Gawain challenged him to finish what he had begun.

Jeered: mocked; taunted
Indent ¶ (new speaker; new topic)
Use quotation marks with direct quotations
Exclamation marks can follow intro. interjections
Use comma with verb of speaking & direct quotation
Comma splice: needs period, not comma (2 MC)
Avoid stringing together sentences with *and*
Use commas after #7 Sentence Openers (-ed)
Use past perfect for 2 different times in the past
Dress-ups: strong verbs

Week 29

This time the Green Knight gathered up the green ax sternly holding it high above his head; with a swift stroke down it fell, cleanly the edge of the blade **nicked** Gawain's neck nothing more than a slight cut.

[2] This time the Green Knight <u>gathered</u> up the green ax, <u>sternly</u> holding it high above his head. [2] With a swift stroke, down it fell. [3] Cleanly the edge of the blade <u>nicked</u> Gawain's neck—nothing more than a slight cut.

Nicked: made a shallow cut; wounded slightly
Comma for clarity: gathered sternly? sternly holding?
Separate only closely-related MCs with semicolons
Comma for clarity: stroke down? down it fell?
Comma splice: needs period, not comma (2 MC)
Em-dash to draw attention
Alliteration: "Green Knight gathered … green";
    "holding it high"; "swift stroke"; "nicked…neck"
Dress-ups: strong verbs; -ly adverb

When Gawain beheld his blood on the snow he grabbed his arms, and **accosted** the Green Knight I have born as I promised one blow in this place, if you attempt another I shall meet it as readily.

[5] When Gawain beheld his blood on the snow, he grabbed his arms and <u>accosted</u> the Green Knight. "I have <u>borne</u> <u>as</u> I promised one blow in this place. [5] If you attempt another, I shall meet it as <u>readily</u>."

Accosted: approached and spoke boldly
Indent ¶ (new speaker)
Use commas after #5 Sentence Openers (twice)
No comma before *and* to join 2 compound verbs
Fused: use a period to separate 2 main clauses
Use quotation marks with direct quotations
Usage: *born/borne* confusion
Comma splice: needs period, not comma (2 MC)
Dress-ups: strong verbs; adverb clause; -ly adverb

Fear not Sir Gawain, I owed you one hit and you've taken it, I'll demand no more. The first attempt was a **feint** given for the kiss you received from my comely wife. *[quotation continues]*

"Fear not, Sir Gawain. I owed you one hit and you've taken it. [6] I'll demand no more. The first attempt was a feint given for the kiss you received from my <u>comely</u> wife. *[quotation continues]*

Feint: a feigned, sham, or pretended attack
Indent ¶ (new speaker)
Use quotation marks with direct quotations
Set off NDAs with commas
Comma splices: need periods, not commas (2 MC)
Compound sentence: comma optional w/ short MCs
No close quotation marks b/c quotation continues
Dress-ups: quality adjective

The second I assigned for the morning you recieved 2 kisses; in both cases I left you unharmed for you **compensated** me according to our agreement. *[quotation continues]*

The second I assigned for the morning you received two kisses. [2] In both cases I left you unharmed, for you <u>compensated</u> me according to our agreement. *[quotation continues]*

Compensated: recompensed, or paid, for something
No quotation marks b/c continued quotation
Spelling: *received*
Spell out numbers written as one or two words
Separate only closely-related MCs with semicolons
Compound sentence needs comma: MC, cc MC
Dress-ups: strong verb

Week 30

On the third morning however you failed me; that is my silken belt about you which my wife use to wear, and which you neglected to repay, all this was my scheme! We made trial of the man deemed most **unblemished** in the entire kingdom. *[quotation continues]*

[2] "On the third morning, however, you failed me. That is my silken belt about you <u>which</u> my wife used to wear and <u>which</u> you <u>neglected</u> to repay. [6] All this was my scheme! We made trial of the man deemed most <u>unblemished</u> in the entire kingdom. *[quotation continues]*

Unblemished: faultless
Indent ¶ (new topic, same speaker)
Start new paragraph in continued quotation with "
Use commas to set off transitional words
Separate only closely-related MCs with semicolons
Usage: "used to," not "use to"
No comma before *and* to join 2 items in a series (here, two *which* clauses)
Comma splice: needs period, not comma (2 MC)
No close quotation marks b/c quotation continues
Dress-ups: which clauses; strong verb; quality adj.

And thus you have proven yourself compared to other valiant knights certainly you demonstrated a little **deficiency** in loyalty but your failure had nothing to do with courtship and purity. Rather you loved you're own life to well—the less then too blame

[T] Thus you have proven yourself, compared to other <u>valiant</u> knights. [3] Certainly you demonstrated a little deficiency in loyalty, but your failure had nothing to do with courtship and purity. [T] Rather, you loved your own life too well—the less then to blame!"

Deficiency: inadequacy; lack
No open quotation marks b/c quotation continues
Avoid starting sentences with coord. conjunctions
Fused: use a period to separate 2 main clauses
Compound sentence needs comma: MC, cc MC
Use commas after introductory transitional words
Homophone: you're/your; to/too
Final sentence works with an exclamation or period
Close quotations with quotation marks
Dress-ups: quality adjective

Filled with shame no less than with rage Gawain felt the blood burn in his face, a cowardly heart is a **bane** and a curse he exclaimed! Tearing from his waist the green belt he hastily handed it to his host.

[7] Filled with shame no less than with rage, Gawain felt the blood <u>burn</u> in his face. "A <u>cowardly</u> heart is a bane and a curse!" he exclaimed. [4] Tearing from his waist the green belt, he <u>hastily</u> handed it to his host.

Bane: a cause of harm or ruin
Indent ¶ (new topic and speaker)
Use commas after #7 Sentence Openers (-ed)
Comma splice: needs period, not comma (2 MC)
Use quotation marks with direct quotations
Place " ! " after exclamation, not at end of statement
Use commas after #4 SO (-ing phrase)
Alliteration: "hastily handed it to his host"
Dress-ups: strong verb & adj. (imposter -ly); -ly adv.

Your strike taught me cowardice to great a concern for my life and covetousness came afterward—both ill-suited to the loyalty and **largesse** belonging two knights now I am faulty and false. *[quotation continues]*

"Your strike taught me cowardice, too great a concern for my life, and covetousness came afterward—both <u>ill-suited</u> to the loyalty and largesse belonging to knights. Now I am <u>faulty and false</u>. *[quotation continues]*

Largesse: generosity, especially in bestowing gifts
Use quotation marks with direct quotations
Use commas to set off nonessential phrases
Homophone: to/too/two
Em-dash appropriate to draw attention
Alliteration: "loyalty and largesse"; "faulty and false"
Fused: use a period to separate 2 main clauses
No close quotation marks b/c quotation continues
Dress-ups: single and dual adjectives

Week 31

After I pledged to return to you all I earned in the day I broke my word to you, I confess my fault, let me earn back your grace and ever afterward I shall be **vigilant**.

[5] After I pledged to return to you all I had earned in the day, I broke my word to you. [6] I confess my fault. Let me earn back your grace, and ever afterward I shall be <u>vigilant</u>."

Vigilant: keenly watchful to detect danger; alert
No open " " b/c quotation continues, but close "
Use past perfect for 2 different times in the past
Use commas after #5 Sentence Openers
Comma splices: need periods, not commas (2 MC)
Compound sentence needs comma: MC, cc MC
Dress-ups: quality adjective

Laughing long the doughty knight rejoined lightly I consider myself well repaid for the harm that I've had. You've fully confessed your faults, and suffered **penance** at the tip of my blade. *[quotation continues]*

[4] Laughing long, the <u>doughty</u> knight <u>rejoined</u> <u>lightly</u>, "I consider myself well repaid for the harm <u>that</u> I've had. You've <u>fully</u> confessed your faults and suffered penance at the tip of my blade. *[quotation continues]*

Penance: punishment in token of penitence for sin
Indent ¶ (new speaker)
Alliteration: "Laughing long"
Use commas after #4 SO (-ing phrase)
Use comma with verb of speaking & direct quotation
Use quotation marks with direct quotations
No comma before *and* to join 2 compound verbs
No close quotation marks b/c quotation continues
Dress-ups: adj. & verb; -ly adv's; which (using *that*)

Satisfied I hold you freely forgiven as pure and honorable as when you were born. I return to you this green belt, may it serve as a **palpable** token, when you mingle with renowned nobles, of how you fared at the Green Chapel.

[7] Satisfied, I hold you freely forgiven, as pure and honorable as <u>when</u> you were born. I return to you this green belt. May it serve as a <u>palpable</u> token <u>when</u> you mingle with <u>renowned</u> nobles of how you <u>fared</u> at the Green Chapel."

Palpable: plainly seen; capable of being touched
No open quotation marks b/c quotation continues
Use commas after #7 Sentence Openers (-ed)
Alliteration: "freely forgiven"
Use commas to set off nonessential phrases (as pure)
Comma splice: needs period, not comma (2 MC)
No commas w/ mid-sentence adv. clauses ("when")
Close quotations with quotation marks
Dress-ups: adverb clauses; quality adj's; strong verb

God love you for this Sir Gawain gladly replied, I value it not for it's wealth or fine workmanship, but as a sign of excess when I ride into battle, or **consort** with courtly nobles. *[quotation continues]*

"God love you for this," Sir Gawain <u>gladly</u> replied. "I value it not for its wealth or fine workmanship, but as a sign of excess <u>when</u> I ride into battle or <u>consort</u> with courtly nobles. *[quotation continues]*

Consort: associate or keep company
Indent ¶ (new speaker)
Use quotation marks with direct quotations
Use comma with verb of speaking & direct quotation
Comma splice: needs period, not comma (2 MC)
Its = possessive of *it*
No comma before *or* to join 2 compound verbs
No close quotation marks b/c quotation continues
Dress-ups: -ly adverb; adverb clause; strong verb

Week 32

I shall never forget my **frailty**, when praise and prowess have flattered my heart a glance at this love-gift shall pierce my pride. *[quotation continues]*

I shall never forget my frailty. [5] When praise and prowess have <u>flattered</u> my heart, a glance at this love-gift shall <u>pierce</u> my pride. *[quotation continues]*

Frailty: moral weakness
No quotation marks b/c continued quotation
Alliteration: "forget my frailty"; "praise ... prowess"; "pierce my pride"
Comma splice: needs period, not comma (2 MC)
Use commas after #5 Sentence Openers
Dress-ups: strong verbs

Pray tell me one thing if you are not loathe since I lingered long in your house and enjoyed your fair **munificence**, what is your actual name

"Pray tell me one thing <u>if</u> you are not <u>loath</u> <u>since</u> I <u>lingered</u> long in your house and enjoyed your fair munificence: what is your actual name?"

Munificence: liberality in bestowing gifts
Indent ¶ (new topic, same speaker)
Start new paragraph in continued quotation with "
Usage: *loathe/loath* confusion
CS: use colon (to give explanation) instead of comma
Close with question mark and close quotation marks
Dress-ups: adverb clauses; quality adj.; strong verb

I am Bercilak de Hautdesert and I hold this barony through the power of Morgan le Faye who dwells at my castle cleverly she fashioned this disguise in order to test the courage fearlessness and nobility of Arthurs illustrious and **legendary** knights.

"I am Bercilak de Hautdesert, and I hold this barony through the power of Morgan le Faye, <u>who</u> dwells at my castle. [3] Cleverly, she <u>fashioned</u> this disguise in order to test the courage, fearlessness, and nobility of Arthur's <u>illustrious and legendary</u> knights."

Legendary: celebrated or described in legend
Indent ¶ (new speaker)
Use quotation marks with direct quotations
Compound sentence needs comma: MC, cc MC
Use commas to set off nonessential clauses
Fused: use a period to separate 2 main clauses
Comma optional after #3 Sentence Opener
Use commas with three or more items in a series
Use apostrophes to show possession
Dress-ups: who clause; strong verb; dual adjectives

After parting on cordial terms Gawain returned swiftly to Camelot, mortified he recounted his adventures to king Arthur wearing the green belt as a **baldric** slung over one shoulder.

[2] After parting on <u>cordial</u> terms, Gawain returned <u>swiftly</u> to Camelot. [7] Mortified, he <u>recounted</u> his adventures to King Arthur, wearing the green belt as a baldric <u>slung</u> over one shoulder.

Baldric: a belt worn diagonally from shoulder to hip
Indent ¶ (new scene)
Comma needed after #2 SO of 5 or more words
Comma splice: needs period, not comma (2 MC)
Use commas after #7 Sentence Openers (-ed)
Capitalize titles used with names
Use commas to set off nonessential phrases
Dress-ups: quality adjectives; -ly adverb; strong verb

Week 33

Behold sire Gawain confessed. This is the token of my shame my cowardice and my **covetousness** a sign of breaking my vow which I must wear to my grave. The king reassured Gawain.

      "Behold, Sire," Gawain confessed. "This is the token of my shame, my cowardice, and my <u>covetousness, a</u> sign of breaking my vow, <u>which</u> I must wear to my grave."
      [6] The king reassured Gawain.

Covetousness: greed; extreme desire for a possession
Indent ¶ (new speaker; new topic)
Use quotation marks with direct quotations
Set off NDAs with commas
Capitalize titles when used as NDAs
Use commas with three or more items in a series
Use commas to set off nonessential elements (twice)
Dress-ups: invisible which clause; which clause

Jointly, the King and Court agreed that a baldric of that same hue of green should **henceforth** be borne by each of the lords and the ladies of the Round Table.

[3] Jointly the king and court agreed that each of the lords and the ladies of the Round Table should henceforth <u>bear</u> a baldric of that same hue of green.

Henceforth: from now on; from this point forward
Comma optional after #3 Sentence Opener
Use lc for titles w/o a name and for common nouns
Decoration: noun clause w/ "that" (see Appendix)
Convert passive to active voice
Dress-ups: strong verb

In recognition of the courage and honor of that worthy knight Sir Gawain Arthur and his noble Knights each wore this sash **oblique** across the shoulder.

[2] In recognition of the courage and honor of that worthy knight Sir Gawain, Arthur and his noble knights each wore this sash <u>oblique</u> across the shoulder.

Oblique: slanting in direction, course, or position
Comma needed after #2 SO of 5 or more words
"Sir G" is a nonrestrictive appositive (takes commas), but omit 1st to avoid misreading as items in series
Use lc for common nouns
Dress-ups: quality adjective

And for evermore afterward the green banner became a token of the most **lauded** chivalry, and valor, ever glimpsed on this earth.

[2] For evermore afterward, the green banner became a token of the most <u>lauded</u> chivalry and valor ever glimpsed on this earth.

Lauded: praised; glorified
Avoid starting sentences with coord. conjunctions
Comma optional after #2 SO of 4 words or fewer
No comma before *and* to join 2 items in a series
No commas with essential phrases ("ever glimpsed on this earth")
Dress-ups: quality adjective

Appendix

For your student's convenience this appendix is reprinted in the student e-book. This appendix covers both style and grammar. On page A-19 you will find an Index, which should help you locate concepts easily.

Excellence in Writing Stylistic Techniques

To reinforce your students' efforts to add sentence variety and write in an interesting style, have them underline strong dress-ups and number sentence openers in the Fix-Its. If you are using the system promoted by the Institute for Excellence in Writing, these style tools will already be familiar to you. If not, the list below explains the most common of these. Included are pointers about how certain dress-ups and sentence openers help teach grammar.

Teach that dress-ups should include strong vocabulary and add flavor to the writer's style. If you teach more than one of these stories, you will see a shift in the types of words I mark as dress-ups, holding older students to a more rigorous standard than I hold younger students. A fourth grader working on "Tom Sawyer," for example, might legitimately count *obeyed* as a strong verb or *mighty* as a quality adjective, whereas a high school student would (or should!) more likely deem those words ordinary and mark *parried* or *ingenuous* instead.

Dress-ups: mark by underlining

For dress-ups in their own writing, encourage students to use at least one of each in every paragraph. In the Fix-Its, encourage students to locate examples of quality dress-ups.

"-ly" Adverb

Found anywhere except the first word in a sentence, this dress-up enriches by adding color and detail.

Example: Snow melted <u>rapidly</u> from the mountains each spring, which caused torrential floods.

Grammar: Count only -ly words that are adverbs, not imposter -ly's, which are adjectives like *princely, lonely, comely,* or *ghastly*.

Direct older students to distinguish true -ly adverbs from adjectives by understanding how those parts of speech work. Adjectives always modify, or describe, nouns; -ly adverbs modify verbs or adjectives (occasionally other adverbs). **Adverbs** answer questions like "when?" "where?" "why?" "how?" "in what way?" "how much?" and "to what extent?"

Strong Verb

The most powerful part of speech, the verb can make or break a sentence. Challenge students to distinguish truly strong verbs from ordinary ones.

Example: Compare   ordinary: "It'll be the first thing I'll throw away when I make changes."
       vs. strong: "It'll be the first thing I'll <u>pitch</u> when I <u>redecorate</u>."

Grammar: Teach younger students to recognize **verbs** by filling in these blanks with a form of the word in question. Yesterday he _____; today he _____; tomorrow he will _____.
(Yesterday he pitched; today he pitches; tomorrow he will pitch.)

Quality Adjective

Adding a quality adjective to writing adds zest to an otherwise dull sentence.

Example: The Flovenian advisors realized they had a <u>daunting</u> task.

Grammar: **Adjectives** describe nouns. Teach how to locate adjectives with this simple test: The _____ person or object. (the daunting task → the <u>daunting</u> object)

Who/Which Clause

A who/which clause is a dependent clause that begins with *who* or *which*. (Advanced students may also mark *whose*, *whom*, or *that* if the latter can replace *which*.) Underline **only** the *who* or the *which*, not the whole clause. Who/which clauses deepen content by adding new information to the sentence or help eliminate choppiness by combining two shorter sentences.

Example: The ladies-in-waiting, <u>who</u> stood expectantly on either side of the red-carpeted stairs, were to assist the arriving princesses.

Grammar: To keep the *who* or *which* from stealing the main verb, remove the who/which clause from the sentence and confirm that a complete thought (a sentence) remains. If not, the *who* or *which* may have stolen the main verb. Example: A bedraggled young woman stood at the door. → A bedraggled young woman who stood at the door. If I remove my *who* clause, I am left with only "A bedraggled young woman," which is not a complete thought. Instead, I need something more: A bedraggled young woman who stood at the door dripped water down her hair and into her shoes.

Also, use *who* for people, *which* for things or institutions. Animals are a tricky category. If they are just animals, use *which*. If they are beloved pets or if they take on human characteristics, like the frog in "The Frog Prince" or animals in Aesop's fables, use *who*.

Advanced Grammar: Who/which clauses function as adjectives and are set off with commas if they are nonessential (a.k.a. nonrestrictive) but take no commas if they are essential (restrictive). See the Appendix under Grammar: Commas: Rule 11 for further information about this important concept. If you teach who/which's as a dependent clause, it may help to understand that *who* or *which* is actually the subject of the clause.

Also advanced: Use *whom* instead of *who* when the *who* clause is the object of something (**objective case**), such as the object of a preposition or a direct object. Use *who* when it is in the **nominative case**, functioning as the subject of the sentence or, rarely, as a predicate nominative.

Trick: *he/him* substitution. If you can substitute *he* or *they*, use *who*; if *him* or *them*, use *whom*.
Who/whom saw Potter near the graveyard? *He* saw Potter, so *who* is correct.
He tells about lepers *who/whom* Jesus healed. Jesus healed *them*, so *whom* is correct. (direct object)
He bellowed his challenge, as if doubting *who/whom* in the hall held rule. *He* held rule, so *who* is correct.
I am not he of *who/whom* you speak. You speak of *him*, so *whom*. (object of preposition)

Invisible who/which (advanced): Who/which clauses followed by a "to be" verb can be invisible but implied. Example: "Through the trapdoor emerged a <u>cat, suspended</u> around its haunches by a string" (...emerged a cat, which was suspended).

Adverb Clause

Teach that adverb clauses may begin with one of these eight words: *when, while, where, as, since, if, although, because* (easy to learn by memorizing *www.asia.b*). Underline only the first word in the clause. Dress-ups are distinguished from sentence openers by not appearing at the beginning of a sentence.

Example: Lord Ashton was in charge of castle preparations, <u>while</u> Big Lord Fauntleroy undertook the intimidating task of designing a web page.

Grammar: An adverb clause is a **dependent clause**, which cannot stand on its own as a sentence. Other words, such as *until, whereas, wherever, whenever, as if,* and *unless,* can start adverb clauses, but younger students may find these challenging. See also under Sentence Openers, #5 Adverb Clause.

Grammar handbooks generally advise against using commas to set off adverb clauses in the middle of sentences. However, introductory adverb clauses—those that begin a sentence—are always followed by a comma (see Sentence Opener #5).

Advanced: Despite the general rule against commas, sometimes they make the sentence easier to follow, especially with examples of extreme contrast. Example: Mary was laughing, although tears streamed down her face. Commas can also prevent misreading, as with a *because* clause following a negative statement. Example: "He did not win the election, because he ran a negative ad campaign" implies that he lost the election, and this is the reason he lost it. "He did not win the election because he ran a negative ad campaign" implies that he won the election, but not for that reason.

Advanced: The *www* words "where" and "when" occasionally start adjective clauses instead of adverb clauses. When they do, they could be essential (no commas) or nonessential (commas). See Comma Rule #11. As with *who/which* clauses, using or not using commas may alter your meaning. Example: "He went to the store where pistachios were available" implies that other stores did not carry pistachios; he went to the one that did. "He went to the store, where pistachios were available" implies that he happened to find pistachios at the store he visited.

Sentence Openers: mark with numbers in brackets

For sentence variety in students' own writing, encourage them to use no more than two of the same kind of sentence opener in a row and to use at least one of each in every paragraph they write. With the Fix-Its, encourage students to identify the sentence patterns. After a few weeks, they can stop marking #1 Subject Openers and number only #2 through #7, unless #1 sentences still give them difficulty.

A few sentences will not easily fit any of these patterns. In IEW's writing instruction, Andrew Pudewa teaches how to identify many of these unusual patterns, and in this book I have included explanations for some of the disguised openers. You may prefer, however, to leave these unusual patterns unmarked.

#1 Subject

Subject openers essentially begin with the subject of the sentence, although articles and/or adjectives may precede them.

Examples: He became livid on the subject of modern gadgets—just so much folderol, in his opinion.
The convivial company congregated in the great hall. (The subject is *company*, but it is still a subject opener because *The* is an article and *convivial* an adjective.)

#2 Prepositional Opener

Examples: [2] During these reflections, King Morton shook his head in abject despair.
[2] After a pause Lord Ashton summed it up.

Grammar: Teach that **prepositions** are anything a squirrel can do with a tree: scamper *under* its limbs; climb *up* the trunk; sit *on* a branch. This does not work well with unusual prepositions like "during" or "concerning," but it covers most of them. A comma is required after long prepositional openers (usually five or more words) but optional with fewer than five.

Also teach that prepositions always work in phrases that follow this pattern: **preposition + noun (no verb).** That is, the phrase starts with a preposition and ends with a noun, with no verb inside. See under #5 Adverb Clause the trick to distinguish between #2s and #5s.

Advanced: Some sentences begin with what is effectively a **disguised #2**, in which a preposition is implied but not stated, as in "One morning…," where "In," "On," or "During one morning" is implied. The sentence sounds better without the preposition, but the opener functions as if it were there. You find this in sentences beginning with some kind of time frame: Wednesday; Two weeks ago; The evening of the ball.

#3 "-ly" Adverb Opener

Example: [3] Sadly, his amiable wife, Queen Mary, was traveling with him at the time.

Grammar: See under Dress-ups, "-ly" Adverb. The main difference between an -ly dress-up and -ly sentence opener is the flow of the sentence. Beginning the sentence with the -ly adverb gives a different kind of rhythm than placing it later in the sentence does. Usually "-ly" openers do not need a comma, as in this sentence. Let the pause rule be your guide: use a comma if you want a pause, no comma if you do not.

#4 "-ing" Opener

Example: [4] Throwing up their hands in exasperation, Lord Ashton and Big Lord Fauntleroy exited in a huff.

Teach this pattern for #4's: **-ing word/phrase + comma + person/thing doing the -inging + main verb.**

Check that #4 openers have these four elements. Although you do not have to use the grammatical terms, this is a present participial phrase that functions as an adjective describing the person or thing after the comma.

Advanced: If the sentence does not have all four elements in that order, it might be a #1 subject opener instead (an imposter #4) or it might be ungrammatical (an illegal #4).

Examples: [#1, a.k.a. imposter #4] Peering through the curtain left Gawain in wonder.
[legal #4] Sitting atop his noble steed, the Green Knight loomed portentously over the guests of the hall.
[illegal #4] Scanning the noble assembly, the horse rode straight to the high dais. (Should be: Scanning the noble assembly, the Green Knight rode straight to the high dais. The horse is not doing the scanning!)

If it is an imposter #4, the -ing word is actually a gerund, which functions as a noun. If it is an illegal #4, we call it a **dangling modifier.** The person or thing following the comma must be doing the action of the -ing word. I tease my high school students that I love dangling modifiers because they give me a good chuckle, albeit I have to take off a half point.

Advanced: Sentences beginning with adjective phrases followed by a comma followed by the subject could be viewed as **Disguised #4 Openers**, with the word *being* implied at the beginning of the sentence. Example: The boldest of them all, she swam up a broad river. Implied: *Being* the boldest of them all, she swam….

#5 Adverb Clause

Beginning a sentence with an adverb clause adds sentence variety and sometimes functions more logically than working the clause into a later part of the sentence. For example, moving the "when" clause in the following sentence to the end changes the meaning of the sentence (she could not locate it when he demanded it back, not at another time).

Example: [5] When he demanded it back, Dorinda mumbled something about not being able to locate it.

Grammar: #5 Sentence Openers (introductory adverb clauses) are dependent clauses that must be followed by a comma. See also under Dress-ups, Adverb Clause.

Prepositions like *after, before, since, as,* and *as if* can also function as subordinating conjunctions and begin adverb clauses. Trick to distinguish between #2s and #5s: Looking only at that opening phrase or clause, drop the first word—the preposition or conjunction in question. If you are left with a sentence, it is a #5 adverb clause; if not, it is a #2. Alternately, teach that it is probably a #5 if the group of words contains a verb, a #2 if it does not.

Example: (a) After supper, King Morton ordered Dorinda to set up Arthur in the Golden Guestroom. (b) After supper was finished, King Morton ordered Dorinda to set up Arthur in the Golden Guestroom. Sentence "a" starts with a #2 Prepositional Opener because "supper" is not a complete sentence; sentence "b" starts with a #5 Clausal Opener because "supper was finished" is a complete sentence. Also, sentence "b" starts with a #5 Clausal Opener because "After supper was finished" contains a verb.

#6 V.S.S., or Very Short Sentence

An occasional short sentence can pack a punch in paragraphs that otherwise have intricate and lengthy sentences.

Example: [6] King Morton esteemed values.

Grammar: The trick to #6s is that they must be short (2–4 words, or 5 if the words are all short) and they must be sentences (subject + verb). They should also be strong: a VSSS = Very Short *Strong* Sentence!

#7 (Advanced) "-ed" Opener

More difficult to form, the -ed opener begins with a word ending in -ed.

Example: [7] Groomed in courtly speech, Dorinda could talk like a princess when convenient.

Grammar: Like the #4 -ing opener, the -ed opener is a participle, this time a past participle, which functions as an adjective modifying the noun that follows. Also like the -ing opener, it must follow this pattern:
-ed word or phrase + comma + person or thing doing the -ed action + main verb.

Not all past participles work. Try forming a sentence that begins with *walked,* for example. The easiest to form are -ed words expressing feelings or emotions, often followed by the word *by*: surprised; defeated; energized.

"T," or Transitional Opener

An optional category, "T" works for sentences beginning with interjections, interrupters, or transitional words and expressions.

Common words and phrases in this class include the following: *however, therefore, thus, later, now, otherwise, indeed, first, next, finally, also, moreover, hence, furthermore, henceforth, likewise, similarly, in addition, on the other hand, in fact, for example.* Also included are a host of interjections, which can be followed by a comma *or* an exclamation mark, such as *ouch, wow, boom, whoosh.*

Note that when you add one of these words or phrases to an independent clause, the clause remains independent. See also under semicolons in "Grammar and Mechanics" in the Appendix.

Examples:
[T] "Moreover, didn't they realize cell phones were intended for emergencies only?" (transition)
[T] Oh, how gladly she would have shaken off all this pomp and laid aside the heavy wreath! (interjection)

Advanced Style

Used sparingly, as an artist might add a splash of bright color to a nature painting, these advanced stylistic techniques daringly or delicately decorate one's prose.

Alliteration

The repetition of the same initial consonant sounds in two or more words in close proximity, **alliteration** adds flavor to writing when used judiciously.

Example: Arthur was seeking some shady relief from the sweltering sun.

Similes and Metaphors

A simile is a comparison between two unlike things using the words *like* or *as*. A metaphor, harder to create, is a similar comparison but without the *like* or *as*.

Examples:
The ship dived like a swan between them. (simile)
The waves rose mountains high. (metaphor)

Duals

Deliberate use of dual adverbs, adjectives, or verbs, especially when the second word adds a different nuance to the meaning, enriches prose and challenges students to be precise with words chosen. Classic writers of the past like Charles Dickens have often employed the use of duals or even triples to convey their meaning.

Examples:
All who beheld her wondered at her graceful, swaying movements.
The ship glided away smoothly and lightly over the tranquil sea.

"That" as Noun Clause (advanced)

A noun clause is a dependent clause used as a noun. It can function in any of the ways that nouns function, as subject, direct or indirect object, or object of a preposition. Although noun clauses may begin with many words, in the last two stories students are encouraged to locate noun clauses starting with "that" only. Help them distinguish between an **adjective clause** beginning with "that" and substituting for a "which" clause, on the one hand, and a **noun clause** beginning with "that," on the other.

To tell the difference: If "that" begins an adjective clause, you can substitute "which" and it will still make sense. If "that" begins a noun clause, "which" does not work in its place.

Example:
"I know well that I am the weakest of these illustrious knights." (direct object) Can you say, "I know well which I am the weakest of knights"? No, so it is not an adjective clause but a noun clause.

Grammar and Mechanics

The rules in this Appendix are not intended to be exhaustive but to help parents and teachers with the punctuation and other concepts covered in *Fix-It!* They explain more fully the brief rules written beside the stories when further explanation might be helpful. Additional grammar concepts are covered in the Appendix under Excellence in Writing Style Techniques.

Definitions   Being able to identify correctly subjects, verbs, and clauses will help with punctuation.

Phrase: a group of related words without both a subject and a verb.

Dependent Clause (a.k.a. subordinate or weak clause): a group of related words with both a subject and a verb that cannot stand alone as a sentence.

Independent or **Main Clause** (a.k.a. strong clause): a group of related words with both a subject and a verb that can also stand alone as a sentence.

Sentence: a group of words with at least one independent clause. It could also have one or more dependent clauses and any number of phrases.

Indentation

Discuss whether you need to start new paragraphs in every Fix-It. In nonfiction, body paragraphs are organized by topic ideas. In fiction, especially with dialogue, the rules are more ambiguous, with different authorities citing different rules. Most, however, accept these basic guidelines. If the paragraphs are very short, you might not need a new paragraph for Rule 2 but should start one for a new speaker (Rule 1).

Rule 1. Begin a new paragraph each time a new person speaks.

> Aunt Polly seized her mischievous nephew by his collar. "I might 'a' guessed your foolery, Tom!"
> In a shrill tone Tom yelled, "My! Look behind you, Aunt Polly!" Aunt Polly reeled around, and Tom fled.

Rule 2. Begin a new paragraph to indicate a change of topic, a change of place, or a lapse of time.

If a character's speech continues into the next Fix-It, the passage will end with *"quotation continues."* Tell students they should not close the first passage with quotation marks and the next day should continue writing where they left off, using close quotation marks only at the end of the character's speech.

Capitalization

Rule 1. Capitalize the first word of a quoted sentence, even when it does not begin the full sentence.

> In her best courtly speech, she inquired, "Pray tell, who has tendered such a thoughtful offer?"

Rule 2. Use lowercase to continue interrupted quotations.

> "Princess," he began, "you have a visitor at the door."

Rule 3. Capitalize titles followed by names, but use lowercase for titles without a name.

> Just as the doctor knocked Potter out cold, Injun Joe stabbed Doc Robinson in the chest.

Rule 4. Capitalize titles when used alone as a **noun of direct address** (NDA), except for "sir" or "madam."

> "Oh, Judge, Injun Joe's in the cave!"

Rule 5. Capitalize calendar names (days of the week and months) but not seasons.

> During the summer the sleepy town was vigorously stirred by Muff Potter's trial.
> That distressing Tuesday night Tom and Huck watched helplessly.

Rule 6. Capitalize compass directions only when they refer to specific geographic regions, such as the South.

> On his journey north Gawain encountered few obstacles. (He is heading in a northward direction but not traveling to a region known as the North.)

Rule 7. Capitalize the first and last words of titles and all other words except articles *(a, an, the),* short conjunctions, and prepositions. (Some grammarians capitalize long prepositions.)

> A shy, small girl who lisped recited "Mary Had a Little Lamb."

Quotations

Rule 1. Use quotation marks with direct quotations but not with indirect speech, which usually begins with *that.*

> "It's no wonder that child has turned out so blemished," clucked Lady Constance.
> What Arthur failed to disclose was that only one demonstrated any gratitude for the kindness.

Rule 2. Commas and periods always go inside closing quotations (unless they are followed by parentheses, in which case they go after the parentheses).

> "It's gold, you know."

Rule 3. Exclamation marks and question marks go inside closing quotations when they are part of the material quoted; otherwise, they go outside. Also, use only one ending mark of punctuation—the stronger—with quotation marks, em-dashes excepted.

> "If only I could have my ball back, I would bestow a handsome reward on my benefactor!"
> "Dorinda, who was at the door?" King Morton inquired. (No comma in addition to the question mark.)

Rule 4. Use single quotation marks only for quotations within quotations.

> "She also insisted on stripping the top coverlets from all the mattresses because, as she put it, 'They might be unclean.'"

Rule 5. When a quotation is interrupted, close the first part and begin the second with quotation marks. Do not capitalize the first letter of the continuation.

> "At about midnight," he continued confidingly, "you take your cat to the graveyard."

Rule 6. Use italics or place quotation marks around words referred to as words. Trick: Insert "the word(s)" before the word in question to tell if this rule applies.

He would have none of this recent drivel of dropping "Sir" and "Madam" when addressing one's elders. (dropping the words "Sir" and "Madam")

Commas

Rule 1. Usually use commas to separate two or more adjectives before a noun.

Advanced: Use commas with **coordinate adjectives**, in which each adjective separately modifies the noun. Do not use commas with **cumulative adjectives**, in which the first adjective modifies the next adjective plus noun. The adjectives are cumulative if the last one deals with time, age, or color *or* if it forms a noun phrase with the noun. Trick to tell the difference: If you can insert the word *and* between the adjectives or if you can switch their order, they are probably coordinate adjectives and need a comma.

Huck followed him to the old haunted house just outside St. Petersburg. ("haunted house" → noun phrase)
"I have dishwater blond hair and wear thick, black-framed glasses." ("blond" → color; "thick and black-framed" and "black-framed, thick glasses" both work, so comma)

Rule 2. Use commas with three or more items in a series, which can involve any part of speech except conjunctions. Some grammar handbooks consider the comma before the final *and* optional, but since it can cause confusion to omit it, it is easier to include it always.

Muff Potter, Injun Joe, and young Doc Robinson tramped right up to the grave with a lantern, shovels, and a wheelbarrow.

Rule 3. Use commas after introductory prepositional phrases (#2 Sentence Openers) of five or more words. The comma is usually optional with fewer than five words. Let the pause test be your guide.

During the weeks of preparation, Mel had been shuffled off to the hunting lodge.
On his journey north(,) Gawain encountered few obstacles. (comma optional)

Rule 4. Use a comma after introductory transitional expressions and interjections. Also use commas on both sides of transitional or interrupting words or phrases that appear elsewhere in a sentence.

Moreover, didn't they realize cell phones were intended for emergencies only?
As grown-up girls, however, they could go when they pleased.
"Fellow, in faith, you have found the king." (Here, "in faith" means "indeed" or "in truth.")

Rule 5. Use commas after introductory adverb clauses (#5 Sentence Openers), even if they are short.

If any one of the young knights here is truly valiant, let him take up my ax.

Rule 6. Use commas after introductory –ing phrases (#4 sentence openers), even if they are short.

Excusing herself from the table, Dorinda hastened away.

Rule 7. Use a comma with a verb of speaking that introduces a direct quotation, whether the verb comes before or after the quotation.

"King Mel loathes courtly balls," Lord Ashton protested.
Lord Ashton protested, "King Mel loathes courtly balls."

Rule 8. Set off **nouns of direct address** (NDAs) with commas.

"We dunked our heads under the pump, Auntie."

Rule 9. Use a comma before a coordinating conjunction that joins two main clauses. Pattern: **MC, cc MC**

"He is of diminished princely stature, and he doesn't care for polo."

Coordinating conjunctions: *for, and, nor, but, or, yet, so* (FANBOYS). Note: In academic writing, do not begin a sentence with a coordinating conjunction since these words are supposed to join or connect two things, not begin a thought. In fiction, however, it is acceptable to start a sentence with a coordinating conjunction, especially in dialogue, because it gives the impression of the story hurrying along, though the practice should not be abused. In nonfiction, students should seek alternate ways to suggest *and, but, or so.*

Rule 10. Do not use a comma before a coordinating conjunction that joins two verbs (a compound verb) with the same subject. Note that in the example, there is not a second subject after the coordinating conjunction. It may help to think of this as joining only two items (two verbs) in a series. Pattern: **MC cc 2nd verb**

Johnny Miller <u>came</u> along <u>and</u> willingly <u>traded</u> his dead rat.

Rule 11. Set off who/which clauses and other non-introductory clauses and phrases with commas if they are **nonessential** (a.k.a. **nonrestrictive**). Do not put commas around them if they are **essential** (a.k.a. **restrictive**).

How to tell which one: Remove the clause or phrase in question to see if it alters the information in the main clause of the sentence. If the clause or phrase is necessary to the meaning of the main clause or if it specifies which one of something is being discussed, it is essential (restrictive) and should not be enclosed in commas. If it does not alter the meaning of the main clause or if the person or thing is adequately identified, it is nonessential and needs commas, even though it may be adding important information. "Nonessential" should not be taken to mean "unimportant."

Trick to distinguish: Put mental parentheses around the clause or phrase. If the sentence still seems to work, the clause or phrase is probably nonessential.

Note also: the word *that* can replace *which* only in essential clauses.

Some grammar books have dropped the first comma in nonessential clauses and phrases, but this book does not follow that practice.

Essential (a.k.a. restrictive, because it restricts the information to that particular one)

Lady Constance recalled a time in Dorinda's childhood when she had seemed lovable. (Presumably there were also times in her childhood when she did not seem lovable, so the *when* clause is essential to the meaning of the main clause and takes no comma. See advanced comment under Adverb Clause Dress-ups.)

"Huck, have you ever told anybody that secret which we been keepin' 'bout Injun Joe?" (The *which* clause specifies which secret "that" refers to—the one they had been keeping about Injun Joe—so is essential to the meaning of the main clause. Note that the word *which* would sound equally correct as *that* here, except you do not want the repetition of *that*.)

"Sire, it's imperative you choose a bride who's a true princess." (Would the sentence seem correct if you put parentheses around "who's a true princess"? No, so the clause is essential.)

Nonessential (nonrestrictive)

Lady Constance, her elder companion since childhood, had virtually given up on training her young charge. (The phrase inside the commas, while adding information, can be removed from the sentence without altering the fact that Lady Constance had given up on training her charge.)

She had confessed the truth to Lady Constance, who now played her trump card. (Nonessential, though important, because "who now played her trump card" can be removed from the sentence without changing the fact that she had confessed the truth to Lady Constance.)

Summer vacation, which the students eagerly anticipated, was approaching. (Summer vacation is approaching, regardless whether or not the students anticipate it. These sentences also work with parentheses around the clause instead of commas.)

Semicolons

Rule 1. Use semicolons to join main clauses when they are so intricately linked they belong in the same sentence.

"He sounds like just my type; he sounds just like me!"

Note: **Conjunctive adverbs** (words like *therefore, however, nevertheless, moreover, furthermore*) do not turn an independent clause into a dependent one; therefore, use a semicolon before the conjunctive adverb if it joins two independent clauses. Do not, however, precede all conjunctive adverbs with semicolons!

Note: A **comma splice** is the error caused by joining two independent clauses with only a comma when they need to be joined by something stronger, such as a semicolon, a period, or a comma plus a coordinating conjunction. A **fused sentence** is the error of joining two main clauses with no punctuation or coordinating conjunction. Both comma splices and fused sentences create **run-on** sentences.

Comma splice: Murmurs arose among the astounded guests at the provocative challenge, no man stepped forward.
Could be: Murmurs arose among the astounded guests at the provocative challenge; no man stepped forward.
Better: Murmurs arose among the astounded guests at the provocative challenge, but no man stepped forward.
Or: Murmurs arose among the astounded guests at the provocative challenge. No man stepped forward.

Rule 2. Use semicolons to separate items in a series when the items contain internal commas. (Rare)

Colons

Rule 1. Use a colon after a complete sentence to introduce an explanation or a list when phrases like *for example* or *that is* are not included.

"Yet one other boon I ask: please accept this simple souvenir from me."

Rule 2. Use a colon to separate the hour and minutes when specifying time of day. Also use a colon between chapter and verse(s) in Bible citations.

"We have a manicure scheduled for 10:15."
"Find Luke17:12."

Apostrophes

Rule 1. Use an apostrophe with contractions, placing it where the letter(s) have been removed. Note that in formal writing contractions should be avoided, but they are acceptable in fiction, especially in dialogue.

"The ferryboat won't get back till late. You'd better stay overnight."

Rule 2. Use an apostrophe to show possession. To form plural possessives, make the noun plural first, then add an apostrophe. An exception is irregular plural possessives like *children's* or *women's*.

The village's young folks gathered at the Thatchers' house.

Rule 3. Never use an apostrophe with **possessive pronouns** (*his, hers, its, theirs, ours, yours*) since they already show possession. Teach students the differences in these tricky pairs:

Possessive Pronoun	Contraction
its	it's (it is)
whose	who's (who is)
theirs	there's (there is)

Ellipsis Points

Rule 1. Use the ellipsis mark to signal hesitation or a reflective pause, especially in dialogue in fiction.

"Ahem ..." Lord Ashton cleared his throat conspicuously.
"Um ... certainly ... the mattress test."

Rule 2. In composition or academic writing, use three spaced periods (the ellipsis mark) to indicate an omission in a quotation. It is not necessary to use the ellipsis mark at the beginning or end of a quoted passage, even if the quotation does not start or end at the beginning or end of a sentence.

Rule 3. Advanced: In quoting another source, if the part you leave out spans more than one sentence, use four ellipsis points. The fourth one is actually a period.

Em-Dashes and Parentheses

Although em-dashes and parentheses should be used sparingly, especially in academic writing, they can both be effective tools when used properly. Make sure your students understand the difference between the **hyphen** (-), which joins things like compound words, and the em-dash (—).

Rule 1. Use **em-dashes** in place of commas when you want to emphasize or draw attention to something. Use **parentheses** in place of commas to minimize the importance of something or to offer an aside. Em-dashes are loud, parentheses quiet.

Worse, she was texting for amusement to her own sister, Maribella—in the same palace!
(Notice that in fairy tales, characters don't have great curiosity about such oddities as talking frogs.)

Rule 2. Use em-dashes to indicate an interruption in speech or a sudden break in thought.

"Injun Joe rushed at him with the knife and—" Crash!

Writing Numbers

Rule 1. Usage varies, but most editors favor spelling out numbers that can be expressed in one or two words and using figures for other numbers (unless there is a mixed list, in which case use figures).

The younger of his two daughters had racked up one thousand text messages on her cell phone in a single month!

Rule 2. Spell out ordinal numbers.

In another year the second sister was permitted to rise to the surface.

Rule 3. Advanced: When numbers are mixed with symbols, use figures.

"We can expect at least 40% of those invited to attend, or 238 guests."

Sentence Fragments

Rule 1. A **sentence fragment** is an error in which a sentence has phrases and/or dependent clauses but no independent clause.

Servants came forth, attending to his horse. Welcoming the warrior. (second part unacceptable fragment)

Rule 2. In fiction, and even in academic writing for some teachers, fragments that do not leave the reader hanging and that fit the flow of the paragraph are dramatic and effective. The Fix-Its permit such fragments, especially in dialogue when complete sentences would sound unnatural. The key is whether or not the fragment leaves the reader feeling as if something more is needed.

"Would you like me to rescue your ball?"
"Oh, yes!" (acceptable fragment—a phrase)

Because students often struggle with using fragments effectively in formal writing, many teachers forbid the use of any fragment. You might wish to discuss which fragments in the Fix-Its work well and which ones do not in order to arm students with the practice of recognizing sentence fragments. This will also help them distinguish phrases and dependent clauses from independent clauses.

Past Perfect Tense

Use the **past perfect** (*had* + past participle form of the verb) when relating two events that occurred in the past. The more recent event is couched in past tense, the earlier event in past perfect.

> One such frightful deluge swept away *[past tense]* worthy King William, who had reigned *[past perfect]* in Flovenia for fourteen peaceful years.

Subjunctive Mood (advanced)

Used infrequently, the **subjunctive mood** expresses contrary-to-fact conditions, especially with *wish* or *if* statements followed by a *be* verb. For present tense, all subjects take *be*; for past, *were*. To test: ask if the statement is literally true. If not, use subjunctive.

> Kissing his hand, the little mermaid felt as if her heart were already broken. (Her heart is *not* already broken, so the subjunctive is correct: "as if her heart were" rather than "her heart was.")

Active and Passive Voice (advanced)

Active voice is usually more interesting, more direct, and less wordy than passive voice. Use **active voice** unless the person or thing doing the main verb action is not known or not important. In **passive voice**, the person or thing being acted upon becomes the subject of the sentence, and the one doing the action is omitted or put in a "by someone/something" phrase.

To test, see if the sentence contains these four items in order: **a subject that is being acted upon + "to be" verb + action verb + ["by someone/something"]**. I place the fourth item in brackets because it may be implied rather than stated.

> Poor use of passive: The stranger was hailed by Arthur. (Fits the passive voice test: Somebody, Arthur, is hailing the stranger, so the subject is being acted upon + "to be" verb *was* + action verb *hailed* + "by someone," Arthur.)
> Active voice is less wordy and more direct: Arthur hailed the stranger.

> Worthwhile use of passive: Huck was thrown out of the assembly. (Here, the fourth item is implied. We do not care who threw him out; the action and person acted upon are more important than the actor.)

> Poor use of passive: Wielding the ax high above his head, it was brought down sharply. ("By Gawain" is understood. Note that this is also an instance of a dangling modifier: "it" is not doing the wielding. See under #4 Sentence Openers.)
> Active is clearer: Wielding the ax high above his head, Gawain brought it down sharply.

Split Infinitive (advanced)

A concern more of the past than the present, **split infinitives** are still worth teaching advanced writers since some high school and college-level English teachers will continue to mark them as incorrect. An infinitive is written as "to + the verb." To split one's infinitive is *to gracefully or inelegantly insert* one or more adverbs between "to" and its verb. The farther the distance between "to" and its verb, the more infelicitous the sound. Usually the adverb works just as stylishly elsewhere in the sentence, since adverbs have that distinctive advantage of shifting location without altering meaning. However, sometimes sentences sound awkward with the infinitive *not* split. I recommend teaching this concept for awareness and discouraging more capable writers from splitting their infinitives.

> Example: Her grandmother ordered eight great oysters to attach themselves to the tail of the princess to properly betoken her high rank.
> Better: Her grandmother ordered eight great oysters to attach themselves to the tail of the princess to betoken her high rank properly.

Abbreviations

These are abbreviations and acronyms used in the Fix-It notes.

adj.	adjective
adv.	adverb
b/t	between
b/c	because
cc	coordinating conjunction
coord.	coordinating
cont.	continued or continuous
CS	comma splice
D.O.	direct object
incl.	including
intro	introductory or introduction
lc	lowercase
MC	main clause
n.	noun
NDA	noun of direct address
par.	paragraph
prep.	preposition(al)
pron.	pronoun
S.	subject
SO	Sentence Opener
sp	spelling
UC	uppercase
vb.	verb
w/	with
w/o	without
w/w	who/which (dress-up)

Proofreading Symbols

¶   indent; start a new paragraph

⫪   do not indent; no new paragraph

◯   insert whatever punctuation is in the circle

⊥   Capitalize (3 underline marks)

⧸   use a lowercase letter (slanted line through the letter)

∧   insert word(s) or letter(s) here

℮   take out; delete

∼   reverse the order

add a space

‿   close the space

You may wish to copy these symbols onto card stock or make a large poster to display them for your students.

[!] = a symbol for the teacher
In the notes beside some of the Fix-Its, exclamations in brackets will alert you to advanced concepts you may wish to introduce to your students, depending on their ability. Sometimes the exclamation explains an error, although the students are not necessarily expected to catch it since it is advanced; sometimes it simply teaches a concept without a corresponding error in the Fix-It. In "Tom Sawyer," [!] concepts will sometimes recur later in the story as part of the teaching for that chapter.

Sample: Student Work

Original:

the glad **tidings** in st petersburg were that judge thatchers family was back in town. Beckys mother announced that theyd postponed the longed-for picnic long enough When Becky met Tom she confided weve been hearing how brave you were at the trial tom

Sample Student Work (usually handwritten):

Note that students will catch some of the errors but rarely all.

The glad tidings in St. Petersburg were that Judge

Thatcher's family was back in town. Becky's mother

announced that they'd postponed the longed-for picnic

long enough. When Becky met Tom, she confided, "We've

been hearing how brave you were at the trial Tom."

Tidings = information

Sample: In-class Teacher Correction

the glad tidings in st petersburg were that judge thatcher's family was back in town. Becky's mother announced that they'd postponed the longed-for picnic long enough When Becky met Tom she confided we've been hearing how brave you were at the trial tom

Appendix Index

For ease of locating certain grammatical terms, below is an index to such terms as explained in this Appendix. All page numbers refer to Appendix (A) pages. You will find these terms bolded in the previous pages.

About the Author

Pamela White received her Masters in English and ABD from Vanderbilt University, where she taught freshman composition courses as a graduate student. She has taught high school English at private schools and worked as a freelance copy editor for several publishers, including Thomas Nelson. Currently a home school parent/teacher, Pamela teaches weekly co-op and tutorial classes to home schooled students of all grades through high school, using the methods of the Institute for Excellence in Writing and her own Fix-It stories.

The author welcomes questions and comments. You can reach her at pamela@excellenceinwriting.com.